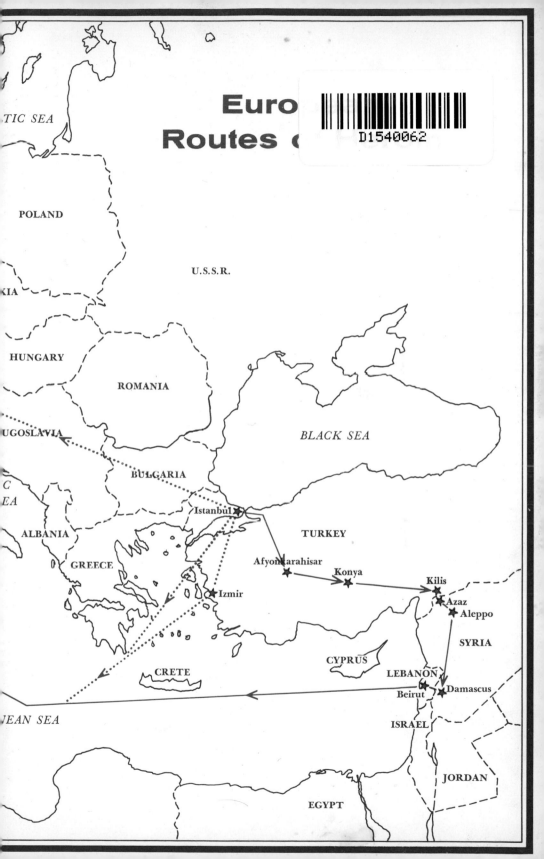

To Mike + Paula —

struggle on
for bigger + better books

your friend

Al Moscow

July. 68

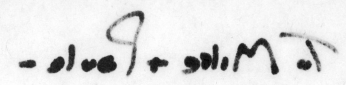

**BOOKS BY ALVIN MOSCOW**

*Collision Course: The Andrea Doria*
*and the Stockholm*

*Tiger on a Leash*

*A City in Fear*

*Merchants of Heroin*

# MERCHANTS OF HEROIN

## An In-Depth Portrayal
## of Business in the Underworld

## BY ALVIN MOSCOW

THE DIAL PRESS, INC.     1968     NEW YORK

*Library of Congress Catalog Card Number: 68-18637*
*Design by La Liberté*
*Drawing by Paul Bacon Studio*
*First printing 1968*
*Printed in the United States of America*

*To Sylvia Moscow*
*and*
*Henry and Warren Moscow*

# Acknowledgments

The secret, complex and ever-shifting world of organized crime and narcotics trafficking is closed to outsiders for the most obvious reasons. How this particular section of the underworld lives and operates at the present time was explained to me, an outsider, in great detail and with great patience by those law-enforcement officers who know the subject firsthand. They know that world intimately because they live in it daily, or, to be more precise, nightly, at considerable nerve-racking risk. For their cooperation, trust and patience in sharing their knowledge with me, I shall always be grateful.

First and foremost, I am happy to express here not only my appreciation of but also my respect and admiration for the officers and agents of the Federal Bureau of Narcotics I have met in the course of the almost four years I have spent on this book. Commissioner Henry L. Giordano and Deputy Commissioner George H. Gaffney made available to me thousands of pages of files, records and agents' reports pertinent to my inquiry. They also gave me the "green light" of complete access to all information which could be supplied on the man I called Levon Levonian and on all his cohorts.

Among the supervisors, agents and former agents of the Bureau of Narcotics who were of incalculable help to me were Andrew Tartaglino and Martin Pera in Washington, D.C.; Fred T. Dick, Larry Katz, Irving Lipschutz, Ben Thiesen and Howard

Chappell on the West Coast; Charles (Pat) Ward in Chicago; George M. Belk, Leonard Schrier, John Dolce and many others in New York. The Bureau's men working abroad—in Italy, France, Lebanon and Turkey—extended to me their hospitality and friendship along with information and I am indebted to them: Michael G. Picini, Albert Garofalo, Joseph Arpaio, Nicholas Panella, Victor Maria and Dennis Dayle.

I wish also to thank Deputy Chief Inspector Ira Bluth, commanding officer of the New York City Police Department Narcotics Squad for his cooperation.

I shall always remember the gracious reception I received in Turkey and the fullest cooperation extended to me by everyone I approached there, particularly that of Halit Elver, chief of the Turkish National Interpol Bureau in Ankara, and Gübrüz Atabeck, chief of the Treasury and Narcotics Section of the Istanbul Police. My appreciation is also due to General Ahmet Demir, then Director General of the Turkish National Police; Colonel Sadi Eninanç, chief of the Smuggling and Intelligence Section of the National Gendarmerie; General Ihsan Aras, Governor General of Afyon Province; Colonel Hüsnü Bezmez, commanding officer of the Gendarmerie of Afyon Province; and Selman R. Açba, director of the Opium Office of Toprak, the government's supervising agency on opium production. A special word of appreciation is due, I think, to the thirty-odd farmers of a small village on the outskirts of Afyon who feasted me one afternoon with a meal prepared in opium cooking oil (nontoxic), discussed opium farming with me in very practical terms and then showed me their small farms.

In France, I received hours of instruction, pertinent information and frank opinions on narcotics smugglers and smuggling over a good number of days from men who were exceedingly busy and I appreciated it then as I do now. My thanks go especially to Michael Hacq, national director of the Police Judiciaire; Charles Gillard, then chief of the Narcotics Section of the Police Judiciaire in Paris; and to Louis Lavalette, chief of the Police Judiciaire in Marseilles; Maurice Hug, chief of the Narcotics Section of the Police Judiciaire in Marseilles and Narcotics Squad Detective Robert Pasquier.

I am grateful for the cooperation of Colonel Nassib Daoud

Abou-Chacra, commandant of the Police Judiciaire in Beirut; Captain Wahib Abdel-Samad, Deputy Interpol Representative of Lebanon, and Captain Asad Fawaz, Director General of Customs, for much of the information I gathered about the Near East.

Interpol Headquarters in Paris, with its cross-reference files, helped me considerably in cross-checking information I received from other sources as well as in researching the past activities and associations of some of the smugglers portrayed in this book.

I wish to acknowledge with a special sense of appreciation the research and editorial support of the *Reader's Digest,* both of which helped make this a better book than it would have been otherwise. From the *Digest*'s European editorial office in Paris, Associate Editor John D. Panitza prepared the way for my own research through the continent and Francis Schell accompanied me from interview to interview, putting his marvelous command of five languages to excellent use. From Pleasantville, New York, I received heartening and useful words of advice from Maurice T. Ragsdale and Fulton Oursler, Jr.

Lest anyone miss what hardly needs to be said, it was Richard Baron, President of Dial Press, and E. L. Doctorow, Editor in Chief, who were instrumental in producing this book. Yet I must acknowledge with appreciation what I took to be their patience and confidence in the outcome of this project, which took more than twice the time originally planned. In the same sense, I am indebted to my literary agent, Phyllis Jackson, for making me the beneficiary of her experience and wisdom in all phases of turning an idea into a book between hard covers.

In the writing of this book, more than any I have done in the past, my whole family played a part, the most important probably being in helping me maintain my mental equilibrium while struggling to put words on blank paper. But, more than that, my wife, Deirdre, read the book in the rough chapter by chapter, serving as my chief critic; my son, Andy, transposed my editing from original to carbon copy, and my daughter Nina was a constant inspiration with the query every writer should be asked daily, "How many pages did you write today, Daddy?"

# Contents

# Prologue

Round the clock for every minute of the day and night, somewhere in these United States a man or a woman, most probably between the age of sixteen and forty, is injecting a solution of adulterated heroin, diluted with water, into his or her bloodstream and slipping off into a temporary reverie which gives total and absolute surcease from all the pains and problems of living. It is an escape from the here and now to a nebulous there and beyond, called euphoria. Some say it is a living death, a form of suicide.

For the individual who is unhappy for whatever reason, in physical pain or mental distress, heroin is a great temptation. Marijuana and cocaine provide a mere "high" and LSD takes you on a "trip" which may or may not be pleasurable, but heroin gives you complete relief, although temporary, from whatever ails you. The price one pays, however, is not merely five dollars a grain. Heroin demands the user's whole living life. It changes his body chemistry so that he must continue to take more and more and more to get the original degree of euphoria. It makes an addict out of the user, regardless of race, social status, education or level of intelligence.

For the United States, heroin addiction is becoming a social plague affecting the rich and the poor, the black and the white, the doctor as well as his patient, the college educated and the high school dropout; and most recently, the plague has spread from the ghettos of the big cities to the youth and the commuters of the middle-class suburbs. It is highly contagious. Addicts induce others to become addicts because, as with liquor, man is a social animal and he does not like to imbibe alone.

For every day of the year, at least one junkie dies in New York, a suicide, accident or homicide, due to either an overdose or a scarcity of heroin. They are almost all young people, these junkies dying before their time, in their teens and twenties, some in their thirties, very few past the age of forty, and yet their individual deaths evoke little sympathy. Death comes to the addict as the ultimate narcotic.

Short of death, however, heroin provides the most complete relief from the pain and suffering of life for those who cannot, or choose not to, cope with the physical or mental strains which beset them. More than anything else, it is the availability of heroin, as with the other narcotics, that determines which man and which woman will become a user. Almost all of America's heroin addicts live in this nation's largest cities, New York, Chicago, Detroit, Los Angeles, San Francisco, because that is where the heroin is. Almost half of all these addicts are Negro, not because of the color of their skins or any racial inheritance, but rather because Harlem and the other urban ghettos is where the heroin is. As the availability of the product spreads out from the cities, so in recent years has the incidence of drug addiction become increasingly familiar in the affluent suburbs.

Plain temptation, curiosity, a dare, boredom, frustration, the ineffable urge to let go and surrender are the reasons for taking that first fix. The invitation comes not from any pusher slinking around the corner; he does not give his product away free. That first shot is offered almost always by a friend, lover or spouse who seeks company as much as any social drinker. Heroin addiction is a contagious disease. It could conceivably reach epidemic proportions, spreading throughout the nation were it not for legislation and police enforcement stemming the flow and availability of heroin.

Prior to the enactment of the first narcotics law, the Harrison Act of 1914, one out of every four hundred Americans was addicted to morphine or other opium derivative; today, the official estimate is one out of every four thousand. But no one knows exactly how many heroin addicts or users there are in these United States. Those who run afoul of the law are counted and registered. But such bookkeeping in police stations throughout the land is always open to error, and those who escape the law are not counted at all. Addicts take their heroin in secrecy, in the privacy of their locked bathrooms, behind the closed doors of their tenement hovels, in the deep recesses of alleyways or up on empty rooftops, anywhere out of sight. There may be sixty thousand in all, as police authorities officially estimate, or there may be twice that number, as some experts believe, or there may even be twice that latter number, as many suspect. No one knows.

Heroin is king of the narcotics. It beguiles its subjects, wins their loyalty and then enslaves them. For heroin, they will sell everything they possess, steal anything within their reach, break every other loyalty, commit whatever crime may be necessary. Heroin is their religion, their measure of happiness, their material wealth, their reason for living.

However temporary, it is the state of euphoria which makes heroin the choice drug of narcotics users, no matter what their station in life. Actually, it disperses sense perception so that the user loses touch with reality, falling into a nodding semi-sleep, dreaming of paradise while in the midst of hell.

Heroin is derived chemically, like morphine, from opium, the elixir of a particular strain of poppy plant called *papaver somniferum,* the flower of sleep. Ten to twenty times more powerful than opium, stronger even than morphine, which is used medically to relieve the most terrible bodily pains, heroin is the most powerful of all pain-killing drugs. It is also a poison, as lethal as arsenic or strychnine: A strong enough potion will shock the central nervous system, coma ensues, and death follows in a matter of minutes.

But when heroin is introduced gradually in small amounts, the body's natural chemical balance adjusts itself remarkably to this foreign substance and a new balance is established. The process is known as tolerance. The body's tolerance for heroin builds up as time goes on so that the addict, in order to gain his original euphoria, is obliged to take more and more heroin. Nor does there seem to be any practical limit to the body's ability to adjust; only the addict's financial resources and ability to buy heroin set the limit of his daily dosage. Most addicts shoot one, two or perhaps three grains of heroin into their veins three, four or five times a day; some take stronger doses even more often. Twenty grains, for example, would be a hundred-dollar-a-day habit, which many junkies brag of but few attain. But even this amount does not approach the possible limits of physical tolerance.

The body's chemical tolerance for heroin, seemingly unlimited, is the primary reason for the failure of all attempts to date in this country, England, Israel and elsewhere to solve the addiction problem by doling out free or minimum cost so-called maintenance doses to addicts. Every addict uses heroin for his or her escape into euphoria, not for mere sustenance, and to reach that nodding paradise as time goes on, every addict needs more and more heroin, certainly more than any government is willing to dole out.

Some call it a living death. The addict's obsession for heroin is so all-consuming that it leaves the victim no time, no interest in anything other than heroin. Those who are truly addicted need to keep heroin in their bloodstream at all times, and the usual dosage wears off in four to six hours, disturbing the body's new chemical balance, bringing the pain and agony caused by withdrawal from the drug. Unable to hold a steady job, uninterested in food, family, shelter, clothing, the addict sinks gradually into the quicksand of dereliction. Yet, to buy his needed heroin, he must resort to whatever means he can: shoplifting; burglary; snatching; jostling; robbing cars, mailboxes and luggage; conning; forging; pimping; hustling; and pushing—all for a fraction of a teaspoonful of heroin a day. The need is steady and the price is high. It is fair to assume that more and more people would use heroin if the drug itself were more readily available. But society, recognizing the nature of the contagion, keeps the plague in check by its laws and the policemen who enforce those laws.

How many grains of heroin are consumed each year in America? No one knows for certain. The best estimate is given as one to one and a half tons! How much property America's addicts must rob and steal to buy that much heroin each year is computed to be upwards of one billion dollars!

The profits go to the merchants of heroin. For them, the

illicit traffic in narcotics is big business, the most lucrative single enterprise of all underworld ventures, requiring organization, planning, financial investments and risk of capital. Only the shrewdest and most intelligent rise to the top in the competition for the underworld market in narcotics. Not one of them uses the stuff himself, because it is well known that no one can ever trust a junkie.

The craft of the merchant is bringing a product from where it abounds and is cheap to where it is scarce and costly. It is strictly business.

Because no one yet has found a "cure" for the heroin addict, there is today, as in years past, a battle being waged daily between the "merchants" who seek to supply a lucrative market and the policemen society pays to curb the illicit traffic in narcotics and to prevent the drugs from reaching addicts and potential addicts.

This book is about that battle of wits between the best of our policemen and the very top criminals in the most lucrative racket of the underworld. With the cooperation of the Federal Bureau of Narcotics and the police forces of Turkey, Lebanon, France and England, and with the help of the editors of the *Reader's Digest,* I have tried to follow the techniques and activities of one outstanding heroin "merchant" and to trace one of his shipments from its source to its destination. What I found was a whole picture of organized crime—an exposure of life in the underworld.

Because it was manifestly impossible to attend and reproduce the actual clandestine meetings and conspiratorial conferences involved, it became necessary to change the names of the true participants and to reconstruct those meetings according to what was specifically known of them and the normal course taken at such conferences. Nevertheless, the characters and events portrayed in this book are true, or as true as it is possible to discern from men who knew of them.

# Part One

# 1

# Meeting in Istanbul

The crime was still in his mind and in the purpose of the trip, not to be found among his clothing or in his baggage. So, quite truthfully, he swore to the customs official at the Istanbul Airport that he had nothing to declare.

In the Beyoglu section of the city, down the street from the American Consulate, he was welcomed with oriental pleasure and courtesy by the staff of the Pera Palas Hotel, which catered to affluent diplomats, bankers, tourists and criminals alike. Later, on the night of his second day in the city, he presented himself at the famous Kervan Seray, near the Istanbul Hilton, and the maître d'hôtel genuflected, shiny black hair, pencil mustache, tailored dinner jacket, and led the visitor, Levon Levonian, into the most elegant nightclub in all of Turkey.

Levon Levonian was enjoying his trip, every minute of it. He was an Armenian, born and raised in southern France, but this was the land of his dead father and his father's father and his father before him. Levon's parents had fled Turkey after the First World War when the Turks had systematically gone about slaughtering Armenians, a half million of them or a million or more; but now the Armenians lived in peace in Istanbul alongside those Greeks, Jews, Chinese and other minorities who had survived the pogroms and had chosen to remain. Now Levon

Levonian was welcomed without suspicion, for Armenians once again were accepted as part of the life in Istanbul, where the East and the West and the new and the old blended to make this one of the great cities of the world. In his varied travels, Levonian discovered he could blend in with any local populace: Armenians were a minority without a homeland but they were everywhere. He could even find relatives in the major capitals of the world and in his business he counted this as an asset.

He was in the prime of life, just over thirty years, five feet eight inches tall, perhaps on the chubby side, with a large barrel chest and short legs. But his face was round and open, ingenuous and cheerful, with a straight long nose and large brown eyes beneath thick black symmetrical eyebrows. He thought himself quite handsome. To him, his girth signified affluence. Back home in Marseilles he used the name Léon, rather than the Armenian version. His friends referred to him as Little Léon, for he had the insouciant qualities of a small boy enjoying the sport of life. He relished the night life of the Place de l'Opéra, the girls, the sports cars, the good food, the adventure of living by one's wits. Unlike most all of the others, he had joined the underworld of Marseilles, which is the Chicago of France, not from want or necessity or poverty, but out of pure personal preference. He preferred a life of crime to working the long hours of his family's middle-class business of selling wholesale groceries. From the start, years before, he had that supreme vanity and amoral ego of master criminals around the world: He was convinced he was smarter than anyone else.

He walked with an aura of confidence. His tailored, expensive clothes earned for him the deference he sought from men, like headwaiters in nightclubs, who were paid to serve him. He could have been taken for a successful merchant, for it has been said that the entire craft of the merchant is the bringing of a thing from where it abounds and is cheap to where it is scarce and costly.

Léon Levonian was a merchant of heroin. New York was the Golden Market, where a pound of heroin, so small and so easily concealed, could be sold for ten thousand dollars or more wholesale and resold to those "stupid Americans" who paid five dollars for a tiny grain. The craft was in the bringing of the opium from

Turkey, where it was plentiful and cheap, to Marseilles where it could be converted, and shipping it to the United States where the profits were so enormous. The difficulty, of course, was that it was illegal. Every police force in every nation between the point of origin and the Golden Market sought to intercept the traffic and to put the merchants in jail. Consequently, the craft demanded skill of the highest order. For each new restriction or law imposed by a government, for each new trap or ploy devised by the police, the merchant had to find a new route of delivery, a safer method of operating, a new wrinkle in doing business. That was the game and, over the years, it had become very sophisticated indeed.

Levonian feasted his eyes upon the elegance of the Kervan Seray. A subterranean establishment on Republic Street, the Fifth Avenue of Istanbul, just in front of the gleaming Istanbul Hilton, its main room was oval, painted slate black with glowing golden-hued columns and draped alcoves. Tiny lights twinkled like stars from a high ceiling. Single candles flickered on the tables. Only the center dance floor was bathed in light. The semi-dark room suited Levonian's taste. Here, among more than a hundred people in a public place, a man could find privacy.

He followed the maître d' along the edge of the large black room to the American Bar, off to one side. It was a small, more intimate room, paneled in wood, with a handsome bar and brass foot rail running the length of the room. The customers were outnumbered by the hostesses, pretty, multi-lingual girls there to please lonely men and men alone, short of leaving the place with them.

Levonian eyed the girls as he ambled along the bar. Halfway across the room, he spied the man he had come to meet, standing at the far end of the bar, his back to the wall so that he could see everyone ahead of him, talking and laughing with two young hostesses. Yet, he did not miss the approach of Levonian. Their glances met at the same time.

He was short and fat, not much older than Levonian. His high round forehead and large tortoiseshell glasses gave him, in contrast to the rugged features of most Turks, the appearance of an intellectual. This was Ahmet Baykal, exporter-importer, one of the richest well-known men of Istanbul.

"Ah, my good friend, Levon-bey," the Turk cried out, extending his hand. "How good to see you again."

They shook hands and Ahmet made the introductions, using only first names, as is the custom in Turkey, and Levonian joined in the pleasantries. He accepted the drink Ahmet offered and he matched *double entendres* with the girls until Ahmet commented that it was almost midnight. "We must go in and watch the show now," he said. "They've got a new dancer who is spectacular."

In the large black room of the nightclub, the two men were escorted to a ringside table. To the casual observer, they appeared to be affluent, innocuous men in the prime of life, not much different from anyone else in the room, except perhaps that they were younger than most of the others who could afford this nightclub's prices. Ahmet Baykal, popular and respected throughout the considerable night life of Istanbul for the generous tips he bestowed, rejected the headwaiter's first choice of a table. Instead, he himself pointed to another table on the side of the center dance floor. Levonian admired his caution. It was hardly likely that the police were permitted to bug a table here with a listening device, but precaution was always essential. Nefarious and secret criminal schemes, whether they involve diamonds, narcotics or murder, are best negotiated in public places. No matter where, conspirators are wary of police listening in from behind the walls of offices, hideaways or homes.

At their table in the Kervan Seray, they were two men talking, and if they were under surveillance, the police might perhaps see the movement of their lips, but they could not know what they were saying.

The Istanbul police were well aware of Ahmet. They knew he was a smuggler. In fact, they counted him as the number-one smuggler of all of Turkey. Of course, Baykal knew the police knew, and, in turn, the police knew that Baykal knew. But knowledge is not enough. Police need substantive evidence or witnesses who will testify in court in order to make an arrest sustained by a conviction. But the more powerful a criminal grows and the more money at his disposal, the more difficult it becomes to catch and convict him. The wealthier Baykal became, the more money he had to protect the security of his illegal operations. He hired others to take the major risks and he paid where he had to pay for protection.

Neither the circumstances of his birth, his lack of education, nor his prior prison record impeded his progress. He had been born poor in 1928 in Kilis, a small town on the Syrian border, and that in itself was enough in Turkey to brand him a smuggler. He had been arrested only once, when he was a young man in 1951, for selling heroin in Istanbul. Having served his one year in jail and two years' banishment from Istanbul, he returned as a free man, older, wiser and more experienced. Setting himself and his brother up in a small office as importers-exporters, he had prospered fabulously.

Levonian admired and respected the success of Ahmet Baykal, for the Turk had gained what every smuggler desires: a round robin of smuggling. He smuggled opium out of Turkey and he smuggled all sorts of scarce commodities into Turkey. The scope of his operation and the size of his profits multiplied in geometric progression. As a rich man, he had gained the respect of the tradespeople of the city who sought to deal with him. Taxi drivers, shoe-shine boys, waiters, bar hostesses vied to serve him, for he was known as a generous man with his money. He lived in a sumptuous villa in Kadikoy, the "millionaire's row" of residences on the Asian side of the Bosporus. He drove a big American car. He owned real estate, two large office buildings in downtown Istanbul and a movie house under construction. He had important contacts, too, in the political and economic affairs of Istanbul, for he made *ad hoc* partnerships when and where he needed them—an Istanbul city councilman, a wealthy ship owner and others equally useful.

Opium was the kernel of his business. The demand of the market always outstripped the supply available in the underworld. No outsider, not even an Armenian like Léon Levonian, could venture successfully into the remote highlands of Anatolia, that part of Turkey which lay in Asia Minor, where the opium poppy fields flourished. They would be immediately suspect and reported to the police. Outsiders had to come to brokers in Istanbul like Baykal, who knew how to buy opium in Turkey, where sales were closely controlled by a government monopoly, and to deliver it beyond the borders. With the profits from opium, Baykal purchased abroad all sorts of things wanted by the people of Turkey and denied them by the high tariffs and taxes that their government imposed, to protect the nation's budding industries and to stem the flow of Turkish money out of country. Baykal smuggled everything from razor blades to automobiles, cosmetics to jewelry and gold, household goods to gourmet delicacies into Turkey. The severity of the government tariffs, as high as 100 percent on some items, was the margin of profit for the smuggler. The black market in almost all consumer goods flourished beyond control in Turkey. It was a way of life. Everyone who could, did smuggle. But Ahmet Baykal operated on the scale of an industry. Levonian had heard of some of his ventures and the police knew of others, but no one except Baykal himself knew the whole story. Each of his ventures was separate and distinct. The police could estimate the scope of his business only by his failures. His successes escaped detection. But between 1960 and 1962 alone, the police intercepted three of Baykal's illegal shipments of contraband into Turkey: forty thousand decks of playing cards from Beirut, a premium commodity in Turkey where card playing is a national pastime; a shipload of scarce coffee from Yemen totaling 150,000 tons; and more than two thousand gold watches from Switzerland. The contraband was seized and confiscated, but not once were the police able to make a case against the elusive Baykal. As word got around, his reputation spread beyond the immediate circle of his confederates. Only later, several years ahead of this story, were the police able to amass enough evidence to obtain a search warrant and to invade Baykal's luxurious villa. There they found his ready cash, above and beyond his investments, which he kept in his home as an escape-and-flee fund. Then even the police were surprised at the evidence of Baykal's smuggling acumen. The cash on hand added up to fifteen million Turkish liras, or the equivalent of fifteen thousand dollars.

"Let's talk first of pistachio nuts," said Baykal with a smile when they had been served their first drink at the table. "You will find the price too high to make it worth your while, but certainly you should be thinking it over. You can write or phone me your decision later." Baykal went on to quote prices on Gaziantep pistachio nuts, delivered by ship to Marseilles. Levonian easily committed the prices to memory. He had a quick mind and a vivid imagination. Just as he often amused himself with fantasies of his future life as a wealthy, comfortable and respected businessman, he could now visualize with pleasure, if the occasion arose, how he would answer questions of the police. "But, of course, I came to Istanbul for two reasons, business and pleasure. My aunt and uncle live here and I want to see them and, of course, I heard of Ahmet Baykal, he is a well-known man in the import-export business, and we talked of pistachio nuts. They are very popular in France where I have a grocery business, a very large business. No, I have not decided yet, so I placed no order, but once I find out what I could sell the nuts for in Marseilles, then I will be in a position to give an order to Ahmet-bey. It will be good for Turkey, will it not, to export hundreds of kilos of pistachio nuts each month." He would laugh if the police actually mentioned opium. Oh, he could put on a grand display of indignation. "I know nothing of opium. That is illegal. I deal in groceries, not in filthy narcotics. What do you take me for? Why don't you phone the Sûreté in Marseilles? They will tell you I have no police record; I am a respected businessman, not a crook!"

No matter what the Istanbul police knew or suspected or had been told, what could they prove? He had no police record in France and he did have that grocery business, a cover for this venture, which gave him an advantage in narcotics dealings over his colleagues in Marseilles. Of course, there was no particular reason to think the police here in Istanbul or back in Marseilles would know of his meeting with Baykal, but if they did, why then he had his story prepared.

Levonian's imaginary scene was interrupted by a question from Baykal. "Everything went well the last time, yes?"

"Yes, there was no trouble," replied Levonian with a smile.

"You see, there is truly nothing to worry about," said Baykal, "I have been in this business for many years, longer than you, and I know every step of the way, and I pay, I pay my people who work for me very well. We have a trust, too, that goes beyond money."

"That is most important," agreed Levonian, "and that is what we must have, you and I, a trust of one another so that never will anything go wrong, never will one betray the trust of others."

"And do your people, the ones you work with in Marseilles, do they understand this, too?"

"Of course."

"I ask you this because I have heard of someone, a friend, so to speak, who sold and delivered morphine base to someone in Marseilles, and he was not paid, he has not been paid to this day."

Levonian considered his reply. "That is always possible, as you know, as it is possible for someone to pay someone here for merchandise and then it is not delivered. It is a matter of trust, as you yourself said. Your friend must have been an amateur dealing with another amateur, someone new in the business. These things are handled in Marseilles by organizations and, as I told you, I work for the most powerful group in all of France. Your friend, I can tell you, made a mistake going to France. My people don't want anyone bringing stuff into Marseilles and trying to sell it themselves. We have our own chemists whom we have trained. That is why I buy only opium from you. For with our own chemists we can be sure we can make the finest merchandise which they want in America.

"What I have done," Levonian explained, "is to convince this group, this powerful group of which you do not know, that I can buy direct from you so that they would not have to rely on the Beirut people in the middle raising the price. And, so far, it has worked well. You should be satisfied. I have come to Istanbul now with a big order, twice the size of last time."

Baykal glowed with pleasurable anticipation.

"Five hundred kilos!" Levonian announced.

Baykal rubbed his hands together. "Good, I can handle that, but it will take a bit longer to gather that amount, you know."

Without comment, Levonian waited for him to go on.

"Three weeks from tomorrow, that would be the soonest," said Baykal.

"Three weeks from tomorrow, the same place, Azaz. Yes? The same coffee shop in the square, the table in the right corner?"

"Yes, the same as before," Baykal agreed, adding plaintively, "but the price . . . that will have to go up. It is getting more and more difficult to operate now and the farmers, they are not growing as much as they used to because of all the government restrictions."

"No, no, no," exclaimed Levonian in a whisper, interrupting the explanation. "I have increased the order and you will make more money this way, but I cannot increase the price. I have told my people what I will pay and that cannot be changed. We all must make a profit for this to be worthwhile."

The two men bargained on the price, in the tradition of businessmen everywhere. It was to be expected that the seller would try to get, if he could, a higher price, while the purchaser sought the best buy possible. Both men understood the form. In the end, in this instance as in most others, the customer held the strongest bargaining hand, for if he did not buy, the seller could not sell. The man from Marseilles controlled the situation.

They agreed upon the price Levonian had paid upon his previous business trip to Istanbul: 350 Turkish liras per kilo of opium. The total price was 175,000 T.L., paid half in advance and half following delivery.

By anyone's standards, even those of the affluent Ahmet Baykal, this was an outstanding order: Five hundred kilos was half a ton of opium, 1,100 pounds. And 175,000 T.L. was the equivalent of about $17,500 in American money, a fortune in his own country for three weeks of work, enough for Baykal to finance a shipload of contraband for his Turkish black market.

As the two men talked, up on the polished center stage a lithe and comely girl shed her veils and belly-danced in a brief costume of aquamarine sequins and tassels. The men sipped their drinks, pleased, talking in snatches, as the girl, with her dark hair flowing loosely over her smooth shoulders, gyrated and flexed. It was a suggestive dance designed to make every man in the nightclub imagine that he was a sultan in a Turkish harem of old.

"So, three weeks from tomorrow, Thursday, you must have your man at the corner table on the right side farthest from the door in the Blue Coffee Shop in the main square of Azaz," said Baykal. "Will it be the same man as the last time?"

"Yes, I hope so, the same man," replied Levonian.

"He should be there from, say, eight to ten o'clock and I will have the same man as before meet him, three weeks from tomorrow night. Right? Of course, if either man is not there on that night for any reason, the other must come back again to the coffee shop the next night and the next until they meet."

Levonian nodded. "Yes, I understand."

"For one week, seven nights," Baykal continued, "and then, if they have not met, we must talk on the telephone."

"Don't worry, my man will be there," Levonian assured him. He reached into his breast pocket and withdrew a fine, new alligator billfold from which he extracted a single Turkish lira note. "Allow me to provide the receipt on this occasion," Levonian said with a smile. Beneath the level of the table top, he carefully tore the lira bill on a diagonal halfway across its width and then on the opposite diagonal the remainder of the way. The half with the V torn out of one side he slipped back into a pocket of his billfold. The other half Levonian handed to the businessman across the table.

Baykal inspected the paper money briefly before tucking it away. "Very good," he announced with a smack of his thick lips. "They cannot miss knowing each other now."

"You know," Levonian said suddenly, "if for any reason one man or the other doesn't remember the other one, they should have a sign of recognition. Each man could scratch the tip of his nose, eh?"

Baykal laughed. "That is good, I will tell him. Mustafa will like that. I will tell him to scratch his nose instead of what he usually scratches, and then he can talk of pistachio nuts, five hundred kilos of pistachio nuts. There will be no mistake. Each will have his half of the lira note."

The two men sipped their drinks and watched the young belly dancer drape herself over one customer and then another as the nightclub photographer snapped flash shots for the tourists. Baykal, with a slight nod of his head, sent the girl past his own table. He arranged with Levonian to meet the following day for the payment of the advance money, half the price of the opium. They set also a date and place in Geneva, Switzerland, for the second payment, at which time, Levonian promised, he would place still another order.

For reasons he had not disclosed Léon Levonian was particularly pleased. This deal was far more important personally than the previous trip had been. That had been in the nature of a trial run. This would launch Léon Levonian as an entrepreneur in the underworld of narcotics. He was immensely satisfied with the deal he had negotiated and immensely pleased with himself. He also was looking forward to the traditional remainder of this evening. He knew he could expect from Ahmet Baykal, his host, a full round of pleasurable entertainment, and Istanbul was one of the great cities of the world for good food, whiskey and women.

# 2

# The Golden Crop

Two men, one hugging the other, rode grimly down a dirt road on a bouncing motorcycle, en route to the farm of Hasan Gokmen, one of the "rich" farmers of the district some twenty kilometers from Afyon. The jagged peaks and barren humps of the Great Sultan Mountains, which covered 20 percent of Afyon Province, loomed in the distance like a boundary wall. The November winds whipped through their thick turtleneck sweaters and woolen mufflers. It was gray and cold but not yet freezing. On either side of the road, the farmlands were empty and brown. The harvest was in, the seeds for next year's opium crops already planted, the pace of living slowed to winter hibernation. The farmers, ever so busy in the spring and fall, now had time for talking. And the paramount question throughout the farmlands concerned the winter: Would it snow before the first deep frost?

The old motorcycle labored under its double burden and the men bore their discomfort stoically. A motorcycle in the back highlands country of Turkey was vastly superior to the more prevalent mode of transportation, a mule or a horse. The men were intent upon buying five hundred kilos of opium, illegally, risking possible long prison terms, to fulfill an order placed by a man neither of them knew. Levon Levonian already had left the country, traveling beyond the reach of the Turkish police or gendarmes. But for the driver of the motorcycle, who was called Emin Deli (Crazy Emin), these five hundred kilos of raw opium would mean a profit of five hundred Turkish liras, and that would bring him closer to his heart's ambition. He had wanted for ever so long to buy a jeep, a secondhand jeep. With a jeep, he himself could buy black-market opium and sell it and become rich and powerful like the man behind him on the motorcycle.

Protected considerably from the wind by the expanse of Emin Deli's broad back, the passenger was a tough, big-boned, muscular Turk of medium height with a mass of long black hair upon his head and a huge, bushy handlebar mustache beneath his prominent nose. His name was Mustafa Aydin, but he was called, by those who knew him in the back country, Mustafa from Kilis. It was the old style of address dating back to Ottoman Empire when men were called only by their first names and the hundreds of thousands of Mustafas in Turkey were differentiated by adjectives which described their birthplaces or occupations. When Turkey turned westward and became a republic, the government decreed that each citizen adopt a family name. The people obeyed. They took surnames, but in the back country they continued to call one another by the more traditional forms of address. Logic and reason were on the side of the government, but habit was habit and the customs of one's fathers were not to be discarded lightly.

Mustafa from Kilis was a name of ready identification in the opium-growing land of Afyon. Kilis was a small town on the Turkish-Syrian border where law and order had not yet established a firm grip and smuggling was the chief and most profitable industry. "If you are born in Kilis, you were born a smuggler." It was a familiar expression among knowledgeable Turks. Nothing more need be said. Mustafa from Kilis was a smuggler by trade.

In the opium business, Mustafa was a commission man, a sort of independent contractor. He worked directly for Ahmet Baykal, who was his cousin, born and raised like him in Kilis. Between the two men, Ahmet and Mustafa, there was a blood bond of inviolate family trust. Ahmet had become the "businessman" in Istanbul, dealing with foreigners who came to buy

Turkey's opium on the black market. Mustafa was the field
commander in the operation who knew the terrain as Ahmet
would never know it. Ahmet, with his citylike ways, would find it
difficult to approach and deal with the farmers of the back country, and any foreigner, like Levonian, would find it impossible.
Mustafa, a proud and independent man, considered himself in-
dispensable to Ahmet's operation. His commission on each kilo
of opium he bought was set at ten liras, but there was also a tacit
understanding that if he could buy the opium at less than the
maximum price set by Ahmet, the extra profit would be his.
Ahmet, of course, paid all expenses.

Thus, on this one order, according to Mustafa's own calcula-
tions, he would make at least five thousand liras or five hundred
dollars, and most probably more. It was a good profit, this five
hundred dollars, about three times as much as the average man
in Turkey earned in a whole year.

Mustafa had arrived in Afyon inconspicuously by bus, an
uncomfortable but cheap twelve-hour ride from Istanbul, where
his cousin Ahmet had given him the order for five hundred kilos
and they had made their arrangements. The torn half of the lira
note, which he would use later for identification and a receipt,
Mustafa carried in a money belt tied around his waist. Mustafa
had wasted no time in Afyon. He enlisted the help of Emin Deli
straight away. Though he himself could have made the rounds of
the farmers, Emin was a local man. He knew which farmers had
opium hidden away to sell to the smugglers and he knew how
much each of them was likely to have. And the farmers trusted
him for they knew him. His services, at one lira or about ten
cents per kilo, were well worth the price in time and effort saved
to Mustafa. In fact, Mustafa made it a point to pay top prices for
the opium Emin himself had bought and hidden in the old dry
well in the garden behind his house. Emin, with his little motorcycle, had been able to accumulate only 150 kilos prior to
Mustafa's arrival. They still had to find 350 kilos more to fulfill
Levonian's order. Yet neither man anticipated much difficulty.
Emin had pledged his word. He knew where to find opium. From
the nights he had spent in coffee shops in one village after another, from his talks with farmers who had come in for their
evening of relaxation over hot tea and water pipes and a game of

cards or checkers, Emin knew which farmers had opium to sell on the black market, and what they could not buy from one farmer, they could buy from another. After all, this was Afyon. And *afyon,* in Turkish, means opium.

Afyon Province, with its surrounding regions, is the heartland of Turkey's opium production. It cultivates about 80 percent of the country's legal supply, and Turkey is rated the world's largest producer of legal opium, second only to India. While India grows a greater quantity, Turkish opium has a higher morphine content, sometimes as much as 50 percent higher per kilo, and thus is more desired.

The province lies in the center of the western third of Turkey at the foot of the Sultan Mountains on a high plateau, remote and virtually isolated from the nation's leading cities or its borders. While the nation struggled to westernize after its war of independence in 1923, government reforms have only trickled down into the farmlands of the Anatolia.

The people of Afyon lived according to the mores and customs of their fathers and their grandfathers. In this back country, the senior man of the family was the patriarch and his word was law; the law of the government came next. A proud, physically brave, taciturn people, they lived simple tradition-bound lives, inextricably tied to the family welfare and the family-owned plot of land.

Of the half million people who lived in Afyon Province, more than 80 percent were farmers. They were dependent upon the land and the weather. Yet, the land was rocky, and in need of water, only 50 percent of it available for cultivation; and the weather was as cruelly severe as that of Siberia, hot and arid in the summer and ranging from zero to 20 degrees below zero in the depth of winter. Yet, the Afyon farmer eked out his livelihood under these conditions without complaint, resisting any encroachment upon his independence from any outsider, whether it be his own newly elected government or a despotic sultan who ruled Turkey at the turn of the century. No matter who ruled the government, the farmer ran the farm. No matter how unyielding the land or how cold the weather, the farmer knew he would endure. He lived with the pride and dignity of generations who tilled the land before him, and he believed with all his heart in the Afyon saying: "The land is tough and the weather is tough and the people of Afyon are tougher."

From father to eldest son for generation upon generation, the land has been passed on. The farmers raised wheat and barley and some vegetables and perhaps some animals, but few could produce much more than they and the people of the province could consume. The one good money crop was opium. There had always been a market demand for opium, even before the government had created its Monopoly which required by law all farmers to sell their entire opium crops to the government and at government prices. Still, it was a law the government could never wholly enforce. There were 150,000 independent farmers growing opium in Turkey, and a man could, if he so desired, manage to keep some of his opium from the government to sell to an entrepreneur at a better price.

But opium was more than a money crop, too. It had a mystique which the farmer himself found difficult to explain. It was the one crop that was more than food alone. The milky white sap of the plant was a God-given elixir which, taken in small doses, was a natural medicine. You could eat it or apply it directly to the skin like a mustard plaster and it would cure most of the common ailments: upset stomachs, colds, fever, aches, pains, sprains. But taken in large amounts, it was worse than alcohol (forbidden to all Moslems), for not only would it cloud the senses, it would rob you of your sexual prowess, and nothing in Turkey could more destroy a man's dignity than impotence. Thus, because of the mystique and tradition as much as religion, Turkish farmers lived among the opium poppy fields and never succumbed to the temptation of pleasure offered by opium, while in the neighboring Moslem country of Iran, there were reputedly opium addicts in the millions—so many in fact that in 1955 the Iranian government was obliged, at great financial sacrifice, to outlaw and destroy all opium cultivation in that country.

Of the 150,000 opium farmers in Turkey, not one of them, as far as is known, devoted his entire tillable land to that one crop, despite its potential earnings. The peasant farmer is a religious man. He holds an abiding belief that God in His wisdom has set a limitation on the measure of good things meted out to man and that He has set such a limitation upon the growing of opium. If this were not so, all farmers in Turkey would cultivate acres and acres of opium and all would become rich. Surely, so goes the belief, Allah had designed opium to be one of the most difficult crops to raise.

Of all farming ventures, opium cultivation is the riskiest. Any number of misfortunes can destroy the delicate crop, and only a very foolish and greedy farmer would chance starvation by planting nothing but opium. Besides, the size of an opium crop is limited, not by how much is planted but by how much can be harvested in one day. In the whole year, there is only one twenty-four-hour period in which an individual field of opium can be harvested, and the crop must be gathered in laboriously by hand. Not susceptible to mechanization, opium farming is carried on today as it has been over the past hundreds of years.

First, of course, the land must be plowed. The farmer, with the help of one or two of his grown sons, walks behind an oxen, leaning his weight upon the plow handle as a single steel shaft at the end of the plow turns over rows of earth. Then as much fertilizer (usually dung) as the farmer can spare must go into his opium field. The poppy plant is hard on the soil and needs much nourishment.

In October the field is seeded by hand. This is, more often than not, women's work. And by mid-November, the first green shoots of the poppy plant emerge from the earth. Now the farmer must look to the skies. As the November days advance into December, the weather turns cold and colder and still colder. If it snows before it freezes, he will have a good crop. The snow will blanket the tender young plantings and protect them from the winter's harsh, freezing temperatures. But if the frost comes before the snow, his whole crop may be wiped out.

Then he will have to plant again in the spring, in March or April, when the earth once again turns soft. He will get an opium crop at harvest time at the end of June or the first week in July, just as he would with the autumn planting, but the morphine content of this spring opium will be considerably lower. And the value of the crop will be lower too, for the price of opium is based upon its morphine content.

However, if the crop survives the winter, the farmer will hoe it again in March or April, weeding out the plants which grow too close to one another to thrive. Nor are these uprooted plants wasted. Their broad leaves, which taste like bitter lettuce, are used for salads at the farmer's table.

By mid-May, the poppies have grown to a height of about three feet, their stems emerging about a foot above the highest leaves, and they begin to flower—white, pink or purple. The flowers are delicate, shaped like tulips which gently open to the warmth of June. They are beautiful to see, a field of vivid colors swaying in unison with the wind. Some farmers plant a small patch of opium poppies as a decorative flower garden near the farmhouse. They have the disadvantage, however, of an unpleasant fragrance, which increases in strength as the poppies mature.

The flowers bloom through May and oftentimes through June as well, depending upon the warmth of the spring. Then the petals begin to fall, exposing the pod beneath the flower at the top of the long stem. It is bluish green, shaped like a small, flattened apple. Each day it turns a bit more blue than green in color, a bit softer to the touch.

This is the crucial period. The harvesting must begin at precisely the right time.

Several times a day now the farmer walks among the poppies, feeling the unripened pods, estimating the right time for harvesting his money crop. The rule of thumb is that two or three days after the petals fall off, the opium pods are ready; but it could be four days. The farmer knows that he must either cut the poppy pods at night and collect the opium the next morning, or cut in the morning and harvest at night. But whenever he cuts, he must collect not more than ten hours later. The important decision is when to cut. If he cuts too soon, the milky latex of the plant, which is the opium, will be too thin and it will spill out on the ground. If he cuts too late, the natural aging process of the plant will change the morphine to codeine, which is a similar alkaloid but feebler in its potency content.

When the farmer, as patriarch, decides the time for cutting is right, the whole family, everyone above the age of fifteen, turns out in the field early in the morning. They can harvest only what they can cut and gather within this twenty-four-hour period. Sometimes a farmer can arrange to have a neighbor's family help with his harvesting in exchange for his own family's help, but only if the two men can agree on different days for gathering the crop. The exceptional, rich farmer can afford to hire help among the migrant opium harvesters in Turkey, men who travel to Afyon from the western provinces, where it is warmer and harvesting time comes earlier. They work swiftly and well, but they will manage to steal so much opium in the process that only the rich farmer with a ten- or twenty-acre field can afford the loss. For 98 percent of the farmers in Afyon, the harvesting is a family affair.

Each one in the family, the farmer, his wife, their grown sons and daughters and any relatives living in the household, is equipped with a *cïzgï biçak,* a cutting knife shaped like a scalpel with a small prong, about one thirty-second of an inch, protruding from the edge of the curved blade. It is an ancient, rudimentary instrument, but perfect for the job for which it is used.

Incising the opium poppy correctly and quickly is a skill close to an art. It requires practice, experience and a certain sense of touch. You hold the poppy pod in one hand and with the other you take two sweeps of the knife to draw one continuous incision three-quarters of the way around the circumference of the pod. The art is in making the incision neither too deep nor too shallow. You must slice through the thin skin of the capsule, thus severing the minute veins which carry the life-giving opium juice of the plant from the roots to the flower, without piercing the fruit itself. If you cut into the fruit, its juices will dilute the opium; if your incision is too shallow, you will not get the maximum opium the plant has to give.

One quarter of the poppy capsule is left uncut to sustain the life of the plant. In another two weeks, it will fully ripen, providing another crop of seeds and shells.

It is a hard, long, laborious day, that twenty-four hours in which a poppy field must be cut and harvested for opium. Thousands of poppies must be incised individually and with care. How long it takes and how many people are required to do a field is difficult to estimate, for there are so many variants. No one keeps a stop watch on an Afyon farm. But, roughly, an acre of opium poppies would keep ten grown men and women at back-breaking work all day.

Children under fifteen are never allowed to help in the harvest, not because they are not strong enough but because they are not tall enough. The poppies at harvest have grown to three and sometimes almost four feet in height. People in the field keep their heads well up in the wind or, if the wind is lacking, they wear cloth masks. When the poppies are incised, the milky-white opium bleeds to the surface and coagulates on the shell of the pod, slowly oxidizing in the air. The fumes can be overpowering. The doors and windows of the farmhouse are shut tight for the period. Small children are kept away from the field. The farmers well know the stories of infants who have been overcome and suffocated in poppy fields. The fumes, heavier than air, cling to the ground. They induce drowsiness, and anyone lying down in a poppy field at harvest time is quite likely never to rise again.

Some farmers start cutting at four or five in the morning and they scrape from 2 P.M. until nightfall. But most men prefer to cut in the late afternoon and harvest the following morning in the belief that more opium will ooze from the capsule during the cool of night than in the heat of day. The difference is miniscule, but so is all of opium farming. The entire opium yield of one poppy pod is no more than the length of a cigarette ash.

When the poppies are cut in late afternoon, the farmer will find the following morning a small glob of opium, which has oxidized from white to a dark reddish brown, along the length of the incision. Now each member of the family wields an *algi biçak,* a scraping knife, shaped like a square wooden trowel with a small, dull steel blade about an inch long, inset into the wood. Grasping the pod again in one hand, a sweep of the steel blade scrapes the opium onto the wood trowel. When enough poppies have been scraped to fill the *algi biçak,* the opium is emptied into a small copper cup each harvester carries on his or her belt. The cup is lined with the broad leaf of the poppy so that when the cup is full, the opium can be extracted easily and emptied onto a large tray, at which one person sits as collector. This is usually the farmer himself, the patriarch, or his wife. The collector strips as much of the leaf off the opium as possible and mashes and kneads together the various lumps of opium until it grows to the size of a small volleyball. It will weigh about two kilos, or four and a half pounds. Some leaves and bits of stems not removed from the sticky opium are kneaded in with the opium, adding weight to the ball. Perhaps more leaves and stem twigs than are strictly unavoidable will become enmeshed with the opium. But this sort of "honest cheating" must not be overdone, lest the quality of the opium be reduced. The "dishonest" farmer will go farther, deliberately adulterating the opium with small quantities of animal fat or figs or prunes. Or he may soak and waterlog the opium, for the added weight which brings in more money. But if he is found out, he risks a heavy fine or possible loss of his license to raise opium.

When the opium is gathered, the farmer waits another fifteen days or so until his fields of poppies ripen and turn brown, and then he has another crop of poppy seeds and shells. This harvest will bring in as much or almost as much money as the opium itself.

The seeds, which contain no trace of opium, may be white, black, blue or yellow. The blue and the black seeds usually are sold for export to Holland and Germany, where they are used in pastries, breads and other culinary delights. The white and yellow seeds, which predominate, are brought into the village to be crushed and pressed for their content of oil. Poppy-seed oil is used primarily for cooking throughout the Afyon region. The people prefer its thick, heavy texture in all their cooking to any other kind of vegetable oil or animal fat. It is so heavy that it would make any food unpalatable to anyone not accustomed to it, but in the opium heartland of Turkey, poppy-seed oil has been a staple of the diet for centuries. More recently, it has been found to be excellent as a substitute for turpentine in oil-based paints. Seeds mixed with sugar and water and gelatin make a popular dessert in Afyon for those with strong stomachs. And finally, of course, the seeds provide next year's crop of opium and poppies.

Nor are the shells and stems of the poppy wasted. A growing industry in Turkey, particularly recently, is the export of thousands of tons of empty poppy shells to Holland, Belgium and a few other countries, at twenty-eight kurus, or three cents, a kilo. The shells, which have been incised only partially, still contain a sufficient amount of the alkaloid to permit the chemical extraction of morphine from the shells themselves. It is estimated one-fourth of the world's legal supply of morphine is derived from the poppy shells, although the United States, France and England, the leading importers of raw opium, do not favor this system. On the other hand, the Turkish government now is studying the possibility of producing morphine itself for export, something it has not done to date.

Some villages in Afyon specialize in exporting poppy shells but most of the 495 villages of the province use the shells for fuel or for mixing with mud as a building material. Some feed the shells to the farm animals in small amounts to get them "drunk" and increase their appetites.

While there are no restrictions upon the seeds or shells, the farmer has only until the end of September to sell his opium to the government Monopoly at any one of the eighty-six regional buying stations in Turkey. Thirty-six of these buying stations are located in the Afyon region, since this region produces four-fifths of all the opium grown in Turkey.

The regional stations are open from July 1 to October 1, after which date the possession of opium is illegal. A government agent determines the price to be paid for the opium, either eighty or ninety or one hundred liras per kilo, according to its quality. Judging the quality by its texture, its odor and its color, the government agent looks at the opium ball, bounces it in his hand, sniffs it, and in little more than a moment, he sets the price. Afyon opium almost always is rated B-quality: ninety liras per kilo. Only one area in northern Turkey, near the Black Sea, produces A-quality, which brings one hundred liras, while several scattered opium areas can produce only C-quality. The quality of opium is one of those mysteries of nature, depending upon more than the seed, the soil, the climate and fertilizers.

The farmer does not necessarily have to accept the government agent's price, but he almost always does. The agents are respected as fair and impartial. The farmer's alternative is to send his opium to the Monopoly office in Istanbul where it would be tested for quality in a laboratory and the agent's price undoubtedly confirmed.

However, the independent and proud farmers of Afyon as well as those throughout Turkey have a far better and simpler method of getting higher prices for their opium crop. They simply divert part of it. They may sell five kilos of opium to the government Monopoly and hide away two other kilos, waiting until a smuggler like Mustafa appears on the scene and offers them more money.

Diverting part of the opium crop from the government inspectors has been a way of life for Turkey's farmers since the government Monopoly was established in 1933. Ostensibly, the Monopoly was designed to stabilize the price of opium paid to the farmers in a fluctuating world market. In reality, the Turkish government was acceding to the League of Nations' efforts to control the illegal traffic of narcotics. It was a constant embarrassment to Turkey to be accused by other nations of being the source of so much of the illicit opium being trafficked to the Western nations. Yet, on the home front it was next to impossible to police 150,000 independent peasant farmers. Not until 1953, upon the pressure of the United States, which was pouring billions of dollars in economic and military aid into Turkey, did the government impose new and much more severe restrictions upon opium. The farmers all were licensed for the first time, and they were obliged to file two sworn declarations each year to the government, one stating how much opium they had planted and their estimated harvest, and the other, at harvest time, stating how much opium they actually had raised. If they turned in to the Monopoly less opium than they had estimated in their first declaration, then they had to explain why or face the penalties of fines or possibly jail. If they turned in more, no questions were asked.

The reactions of the farmers were obvious. Not only did they resent government interference, but as a matter of self-preservation they submitted the lowest possible estimate of the future crops and they concealed the surplus. In doing this, the Turkish peasant felt no more like a criminal than the American businessman does who underestimates his income and exaggerates his expenses on his income tax. To the Afyon peasant, the government paid only ninety liras a kilo for his opium, and what he did not sell to the government he could sell for more money to a private person (like Mustafa). He saw no real harm in this. While he knew that opium makes people sick, he had never seen either an opium or a heroin addict. To him, the private person paid more money and with that money he could buy his wife a new coat for the winter.

Even with the new restrictions, the government could not police 150,000 farmers growing opium. And, more to the point, it could not even effectively check on the accuracy of the farmer's declared estimates. It is impossible for a government inspector, for instance, to know how much opium will be raised on any one acre of land. The crop can vary from as much as two to eight kilos, perhaps even more, depending on how many seeds are planted, how many plants are hoed out, how much fertilizer is put in, how much rain falls, how effectively each of the poppies is incised. No one knows. And, so long as no one knows how much is grown, no one truly knows how much opium is diverted from the government Monopoly to the smugglers who roam the Anatolian highlands. The government itself estimates that 10 percent of the opium grown is diverted to illicit channels. The United Nations Commission on Narcotics has estimated the figure to be as high as twenty-five percent. It may be higher. But no one knows. The individual farmer diverts as much as he can get away with. Opium also has a particularly good lasting quality. It does not spoil like a fruit. What the farmer does not sell one year, he can sell the next. It just depends upon when a private buyer comes to the farm.

Hasan Gokmen's farm in the village of Surmenli, twenty kilometers from the city of Afyon, covered twenty-five acres of tillable land. Three acres of it were devoted each year to opium. Yet the eye could not judge Hasan's wealth, for the boundaries of his property were marked only by stones at each corner rather than fences, separating it from that of his adjoining neighbor. His farmhouse was freshly whitewashed, his barn large and the farm tools moderately modern.

Emin assured Mustafa that Hasan was considered the wealthiest farmer of this village. Not only did he have opium to sell from his own farm but he had opium from the smaller farmers in the village, who had sold or pledged part of their opium crop even before the harvest in exchange for a needed farm animal or implement which they could not otherwise afford.

Arriving at Hasan's farm, Emin and Mustafa received the welcome and hospitality traditional in almost all peasant or homestead farms around the world. In Turkey particularly a farmer's social status was measured by the extent of the hospitality he could extend.

"Would you have some tea?" inquired Hasan, after Emin had made the formal introductions in his usual laconic manner. He was known as Crazy Emin because in the village or in the city he would never acknowledge having met a farmer with whom he had done business on the farm. He would refuse to say more than yes or no to a direct question. He would sit for hours in a coffee shop listening to those who would speak to him and to the conversation of others, but never himself uttering a needless word. Yet, somehow, he would forever be getting in trouble by fighting, usually when he was drunk and silent and imagined someone had glanced at him crossly. But on the farm, always, he was sober, not silent but laconic, and a trusted go-between for buyers and sellers.

Buyer, seller and go-between trooped into the farmhouse, followed by Hasan's son, Murat, the eldest of three sons and two daughters. Hasan led his two visitors into the guest room, which would be considered the parlor in most Western houses. In Turkey, it was completely devoted to the entertaining of guests. The son stood at the doorway, not entering the room, ready to serve his father and his guests, as was traditional in a Turkish farmhouse. The women of the house, quite aware of the visitors, confined themselves to the kitchen, out of sight. The men seated themselves at a table in the center of the room which was bereft of other furniture except for benches three feet wide which lined the four walls, upon which the men could sit or recline after eating. What made the guest room special was that the floors and the benches were covered with thick oriental rugs; the floors of all other rooms were bare wood.

First came the pleasantries before business. At a word from his father, the son brought into the room a washbasin with soap resting in the raised center and a pitcher of warm water. The guest soaped his hands over the basin while the son poured water. And then the strong Turkish tea, served in small glasses, sweetened with sugar, was brought to the table with small cakes. At tea, the men talked business. Before, the host Hasan and the guest Mustafa had discussed the weather and the crops and the meddling government. All the while they had sized up each other. Emin, silent, waited for the proper, polite moment to bring the business to a head.

"My friend here, Mustafa from Kilis, he is here in Afyon to make a large purchase of opium," Emin stated at last.

"Yes," concurred Mustafa, taking up the cue. "I would like to buy all you have on hand of this year's crop."

"This year, you know, there was not a good crop," Hasan bargained. "You will find it difficult to find opium."

"Difficult, but never too difficult," Mustafa replied. "I have been in this business since I was fourteen years old and there is always enough opium to be found here or there. How much do you have?"

"What will you pay?"

"I always pay a fair price, higher than the next man's and that is how I do business," Mustafa said. "Emin knows me well and he will vouch for the truth I speak." Emin nodded his head and Mustafa continued. "I pay according to how good your opium is."

Hasan signaled his son at the door. The young man disappeared while the older men talked on and he returned a few minutes later to hand his father a small lump of opium. It was light brown in color, indicating that it was fresh.

Mustafa, who was as expert as any government opium agent, felt the texture, sniffed it, and then, with his pocketknife, cut into the sample to a depth of about an inch, sensing the feel of the blade slicing into the opium. With his hands, he broke the sample into two distinct parts. If it had crumbled into several small pieces, he would have known the opium was stale, last year's crop. But this was fresh, moist opium, and broken in two, he could see the cross-section which would reveal any adulteration.

"All your opium is of this quality?" asked Mustafa, for it was important in all bargaining not to reach the essential point too quickly.

"Of course," replied the farmer. "It is the finest grown in this region."

"Well, then, I can give you 120 liras for each kilo you have," Mustafa declared. This was one-third above the government price. The farmer rubbed his gnarled, leathery hands and looked hard at Mustafa and then at Emin. He saw two poker faces. He beckoned to his son to pour more tea for his guests, and then he said flatly, "I am sorry but I do not have any opium to sell at that price."

"I am a poor man," Mustafa responded. "I cannot pay more and make a profit for I have many expenses—"

"And I am a poor farmer who works hard for a large family," said Hasan. The two men, who had bargained like this year after year, talked price for the better part of half an hour, each one estimating how far the other would give in. Opium prices on the black market are never stable. They vary with the weather and the established government price, which has increased, almost doubling, over the past ten years.

Hasan asked 180 liras a kilo, the equivalent of twenty dollars, or double the legal price, and Mustafa raised his offer slowly. The farmer's eldest son stood at the doorway, listening and learning. One day he would own this farm and he would be doing the trading.

The traders reached agreement at 150 liras a kilo.

The farmer disclosed that he had thirty-five kilos in his barn, all equal in quality to the sample shown, and there were smiles and handshakes once more.

He led them out to the barn, the son walking respectfully in the rear. At his father's bidding, the son cleared away part of a haystack in a corner of the barn, dug a few inches into the soft earth and removed a wooden cover and, reaching deep into the hidden hole, came up with three burlap bags of opium.

Mustafa cut into and carefully inspected each ball of opium for quality, weighed them, and, satisfied, returned them to their burlap bags. Another handshake concluded the deal. Mustafa tied off the tops of the bags. He sealed the knot of the rope with melted wax and on the wax he made his personal mark. That opium was his: No one could change or adulterate the opium he had inspected without disturbing the mark he had made in the wax. In a small notebook, he jotted down Arabic symbols to denote farmer Hasan, the amount of his opium and the price. The opium was his, but, as was customary, Mustafa would not pay for it until it was delivered at the agreed-upon place and time.

Delivering the opium, as well as concealing it past the legal time limit, was also the risk of the farmer.

Emin promised to inform Hasan of the time and place to bring the opium and Hasan recommended two other farmers nearby who also might have opium to sell. After cordial good-bys, Mustafa and Emin left the farm of Hasan and journeyed to the first of the two farms he had recommended.

And so they went from one farm to another, traveling from village to village, and by the end of two weeks, Mustafa Aydin had bought and put his personal mark upon one-half ton of Turkish raw opium.

# 3

# The Trip from Afyon

The night had been well chosen. The cloudless sky seemed so high that the stars gave off little light. It was black, close to midnight, when Emin Deli led the group of farmers toward the rendezvous with Mustafa Aydin. Emin himself had chosen it, a desolate spot upon an unmarked, unnamed dirt road on a hillside beyond the sight or hearing of the nearest village. He had gathered the farmers at a crossroad some five kilometers from the village. Then, after checking that there was no danger of being followed, he pointed the way up the road. He scouted for the file of farmers and their mules like a wagonmaster of the old West searching out any evidence of an ambush.

The opium was all there, 350 kilos, or more than seven hundred pounds, loaded upon the backs of seven stout mules. The sweet, pungent aroma of the opium, like wet hay, scented the air about the men. As they trudged silently up the incline of the road, Emin counted twenty-two farmers who had come to guard the opium and the transaction with Mustafa. Some of them, like Hasan, had come with a son; others had entrusted their opium to friends who would collect the money for them. Each of the farmers was armed with either a rifle or a pistol, some new, most ancient, and they would not hesitate, Emin knew, to open fire if anything went wrong.

Once there had been trust and implicit safety in selling opium to the men who came to Afyon to buy. Emin, who was fifty-two years old and had been a smuggler for as long as he could remember, longed for the old days. Ten years before, up until the end of the 1950's, one could deliver opium in broad daylight in any one of a number of remote spots so long as it was out of the eyesight of the gendarmes. The police in those days seemed seldom to know where to look to find the illegal deliveries. Emin himself had driven illegal opium in a covered wagon through the center of a village and even once through the main streets of the city of Afyon, and no one had been the wiser. A favorite ploy in those days was to transport opium through a village or the city in a casket, draped in black. It made a story to tell, the sight of people and police on the street lifting their hats and saluting in respect as a coffin of opium went by.

But those days were gone. Now it was a dangerous and risky business. Nowadays, deliveries were made always at night, never in the daytime, and always with guns. Now all the farmers had heard that Interpol, the international police, had come to Turkey and were working with the gendarmes against opium smuggling. The farmers realized that more and more men were being caught and more and more valuable opium was being captured. Everyone, for instance, had heard of the big seizure near Konya, the capital of the province to the south of Afyon. There, on March 31, 1963, some fifty farmers had been ambushed by Interpol and the Turkish police as they were making their delivery on a remote road. Three had been wounded in the gunfight and captured. The others escaped but lost their opium, one ton thirty-seven kilos. It had been the largest single opium seizure in the history of Turkey and the tale had traveled far.

Not only were the police cracking down, but the penalties had been substantially increased by the famous new law which had been posted in every village on September 19, 1959. That law had made the illegal possession and illegal sale of opium punishable with jail terms up to ten years along with heavy fines. Before that, the 1953 law had applied only to professional smugglers and those who manufactured morphine base or heroin from the opium. The penalty for these men, if convicted, ranged from ten years' imprisonment to death. Several men, in fact, had been sentenced to death since 1953, although the extreme penalty had never yet been carried out. In Afyon Province over the past year, nine men had been sent to jail in opium cases. One of them, a local smuggler-commission man like Emin, had been sentenced to seven and a half years' imprisonment, plus another seven and a half years of forced residence in a far-off province chosen by the authorities, plus a fine of five million Turkish liras or an extra three years in jail.

The farmers therefore had acquired great respect for the combination of Interpol and the increased activity of the gendarmerie. Somewhat analogous to the National Guard in the United States, the Turkish gendarmerie, about eighty thousand strong, served in peacetime under the Ministry of the Interior and was responsible for border control, the coast guard, and the peace and tranquillity of citizens outside city limits. Under national conscription, a Turkish youth could choose between two years in the army or three years in the gendarmes. The pay was the same: fifty cents a month plus food, shelter and clothing. Afyon, for instance, had a regular police force for the city itself and a gendarmerie of five hundred privates and fifty officers, commanded by a colonel, to enforce the law in the eleven districts and thirteen subdistricts of the province. Ninety percent of the half million people in the province lived in the farmlands and villages outside the city limits of Afyon City.

The farmers, of course, had long lived with the gendarmes and the local police, but they stood in awe of Interpol. They imagined Interpol agents were everywhere, ready to spring a trap at the precise moment illegal opium was being delivered. Their anxiety over Interpol was based upon their lack of knowledge, the mystery attached to the organization and a widespread misconception.

There were no Interpol secret agents or international policemen in Turkey. Interpol has no police force of its own anywhere. It is nothing more than a secretariat, like that of the United Nations, an administrative agency, through which the police of one nation can communicate and cooperate with the police of another, without the usual red tape attached to formal diplomatic relations. Interpol itself has only sixty-eight permanent employees, not one of them the James Bond type. They do desk work in a musty old nineteenth-century mansion on a quiet, narrow street in Paris. Yet Interpol's accomplishments have been extraordinary in fighting international crime. That musty three-story house contains an elaborate radio and teletype system which link the police forces of ninety-two participating nations. Established in 1923 and expanded after World War II in order to pursue criminals and criminal conspiracies over national borders, Interpol can radio a request, say from the United States, to identify, follow, question or pick up a fugitive, to any one of the ninety-two member nations of Interpol. No longer can the clever criminal expect automatic safety by fleeing the borders of the country in which he has committed a crime. Interpol handles about forty thousand such requests a year.

Interpol's headquarters also boasts an elaborate system of 740,000 individual files on criminals and cases. Suspects can be identified by fingerprints, photograph, specialty in crime or method of operation. This is the laboratory of an international police force, used by sovereign police agencies within their own country.

A by-product of Interpol's daily routine, which is possibly its greatest achievement, is the growth of international cooperation between national police forces. In its annual meetings since 1946, ranking police officers of various countries have come to know and trust those of other countries on a basis of personal friendship, enhancing progressively their mutual cooperation as the years go on. At the annual meetings themselves, the police report on the new stratagems of criminals and plan their counter-strategy. Only in this way can the police hope to keep pace with the inventiveness of the criminal mind.

Interpol's chief concern is not with espionage. The organization is strictly forbidden by its own constitution to undertake any activity of a political, military, religious or racial character. The crime at the top of Interpol's list, involving the most requests for help, is the smuggling of narcotics. The illicit worldwide traffic in narcotics is the most profitable, the most prevalent and the most insidious of all international crimes. Interpol's roster of international crime, after narcotics, includes counterfeit money and traveler's checks, blackmail, and diamond and gold smuggling. So, while Interpol can be described as a secretariat, a communications center, a police laboratory, a police congress, it is not a police force. It enforces no laws; it makes no arrests.

What the farmers in Afyon and elsewhere in Turkey mistook as Interpol activity was in reality the spectacular work of one man, a single agent of the U.S. Bureau of Narcotics, operating, since 1960, with the consent and cooperation of the Turkish government, out of a small, one-room, back office in the American Consulate at Istanbul. Before 1960, the Turkish government cooperated with American agents who wanted to follow a special, specific case into Turkey. But in that year, it agreed to allow an American agent to be stationed full time in Turkey on a permanent basis. That agent, from late 1960 until he was reassigned back to the United States in 1964, was Joe Coppola, the son of a supermarket owner in Springfield, Massachusetts, who chose police work over his father's grocery business, became a traffic patrolman in Washington, D.C., and then, at the age of twenty-five, joined the Bureau in 1957.

It was Mr. Joe, as Coppola became known, who introduced American methods to help Turkish police crack down on opium smugglers and farmers who were diverting their opium crops to the black market. It was only in 1960 that the Turkish national police established its own central narcotics branch in Ankara, headed by Halit Elver, a cheerful, energetic, westernized career officer. Elver, who served as Turkey's representative to Interpol, attended the Bureau of Narcotics training school in Washington, D.C., and then returned to Ankara to set up Turkey's first central filing system on narcotics smugglers and suspects. In 1963, the Istanbul city police established for the first time its own narcotics squad of twenty-five, who were ready and eager to cooperate with Mr. Joe, the American narcotics agent.

Mr. Joe had no police powers other than that of an adviser, but he had the American money with which to pay informers. The informers, who were usually retired smugglers themselves, were instructed to set up deals with smugglers or farmers in the "boondocks" of Turkey which would lead to arrests and seizures of opium. The actual arrests and seizures were coordinated through Halit Elver in Ankara and made by the Turkish national police and the local gendarmes. For Turkey, the arrests served as a deterrent to law-breaking farmers and smugglers. For the United States, each seizure of illicit opium meant that much less heroin reached the United States, at considerably less expenditure of tax dollars than it would cost to seize a similar amount of narcotics in the United States. By financing an undercover trip to the back country with from $50 to $250, Mr. Joe might stop a million dollars worth of heroin from reaching New York. At a lonely post far from home, without a knowledge of the language, and at considerable hardship and personal risk, Joe Coppola established a spectacular record in Turkey before he was reassigned back to the United States in 1964. His greatest coup was the single seizure of 1,037 kilos of raw opium near Konya in 1963, a record which still stands today as a challenge to his successor agents in Istanbul, who must devise new ploys to trap today's more sophisticated smugglers like Emin Deli, who, in turn, in order to remain free, have learned from the past mistakes of others.

Emin led his band of armed farmers along the empty, winding road, to a spot where he had cached his own 150-kilo supply of opium the night before. The farmers moved off the road and waited behind a huge boulder which shielded them from the road.

This was not, for safety's sake, the spot where Emin had arranged to meet Mustafa. The rendezvous was about a half mile further up the road, at a crest in the hillside from which he could observe the approach of Mustafa's vehicle coming up from the other side. With Hasan's permission, Emin took the farmer's son with him to the meeting place.

Emin had chosen the rendezvous himself and had led Mustafa to the location from another approach on the afternoon of the previous day. He had shown Mustafa the way only after all five hundred kilos of opium had been bought and marked and Mustafa had assured him that his truck and the money had arrived in Afyon. Between the two men, there was a certain degree of candor, tempered by caution. They had done business before, but neither could be certain that this occasion would be the same as the last. Either man, Emin or Mustafa, might have changed from smuggler to police informer for any number of reasons not known to the other; either one could have had a financial or even emotional setback tempting him to try to cheat the other. For men in the narcotics business, at whatever stage, there is that great temptation: to take the narcotics without paying money or to steal the money without giving up the narcotics. It is this temptation which makes narcotics a risky and dangerous business. The danger point comes almost always at the crucial time of delivery. It is then that narcotics and the money are at the same place at the same time. It is also then that the police prefer to pounce.

Emin and Mustafa were obliged to negotiate the method of the opium delivery with great care.

"You must come with only one truck and only you alone," Emin demanded.

"One truck, yes, but I will come with my driver," responded Mustafa. "There is plenty of opium to be loaded, even with you helping. You have nothing to fear, you will have your farmers there with their guns."

"I fear nothing myself," Emin insisted, upon his dignity. "It is just that the farmers do not like it when they are facing guns. Someone might shoot. You should come without your gun."

"I go nowhere without my gun." Mustafa lifted his sweater to reveal the butt of his revolver.

"Don't you trust me?" Emin asked.

"Oh, I trust you, all right, but not with my life." Mustafa laughed, reassuring the shorter man. He refused also to show Emin the money or the truck before they met at the point of delivery. The less known about the description of the truck, the safer would be the journey to the border, and he had assured Emin when he had arrived in Afyon that the driver, not he, always carried the money, thus removing that temptation.

"You will see the money and the truck when we get there," said Mustafa. "You needn't worry. I'll have the money. But remember, you stay close to me at all times. It is much money and if anyone starts to shoot, you will be shot first. Remember. If I don't get back, I have friends who will come for you."

Mustafa had misled Emin into believing that the truck was coming from Kilis and that the opium was to be driven to Izmir. Such matters were no business of Emin's. The truth might only endanger the operation, Mustafa thought. The truth was that when the five hundred kilos of opium had been bought, Mustafa had telephoned Ahmet Baykal in Istanbul with the prearranged message: "I bought the sheep today at seventy liras each—all of them—they can be shipped in three days."

No need to say much more, not even his name. Baykal at the other end recognized his voice, understood the opium had been bought at 170 liras per kilo, and knew where to send his truck, a driver and the money. "Good, I'll make all the arrangements at this end," was all he had had to say.

Baykal also guessed that Mustafa probably had lied about the price in order to make a bit more than the ten liras' commission they had agreed upon. But how much more, he could not know. Nor did he care much about it, since he figured his own profit was adequate at the 350-liras price Levonian would be paying.

Two days later, a ten-ton Bereford truck, British made, loaded with empty olive barrels, was parked on the side of the highway on the outskirts of Afyon City. The driver lifted the hood and removed the distributor head from the engine. Now the truck would not run and he could wait there for Mustafa without suspicion. To any inquiring gendarme, he could say, "The truck broke down and I'm waiting for my partner who went to get the distributor fixed."

The truck, in excellent repair, moved slowly and easily up the rutted dirt road toward the rendezvous. Mustafa, sitting next to the driver, recognized certain landmarks which assured him he was on the right road. As it approached the meeting place, it went by Hasan's son, who then rose from his hiding place and flicked on his cigarette lighter. Emin observed the signal flame.

From his vantage point Emin could see the headlights of the approaching truck, but he was wary of the police trick of having a jeep, full of gendarmes, follow the lead truck bumper-to-bumper without telltale lights. Hasan's son had been posted ahead to guard against this contingency.

The rendezvous spot was marked by a shirt hanging from the branch of a tree. When the truck arrived, the driver flicked off the headlights. The night was pitch-black. Accustomed to the darkness, even Emin could not see more than silhouettes and shades of blackness beyond ten feet.

"Emin!" came the call from the truck.

The squat smuggler beamed his flashlight at Mustafa and stepped out onto the road. A light from the cab of the truck shone in his face and Emin came forward with his flashlight in hand. When he reached the truck, he noticed for the first time the barrel of Mustafa's revolver leaning on the ledge of the window. "Where's the opium?" asked Mustafa.

"Oh, it's up the road a bit, but wait, there's another man here who will want to ride." Emin inspected the back of the truck at a glance, assuring himself that there were no men hidden there.

When Hasan's son reached the truck, they moved forward again slowly until Emin told the driver to flick his headlights twice to signal the farmers.

At the second meeting spot, the farmers came forward one by one with their opium, and by the light of several flashlights, Mustafa inspected his wax seals on the bags of opium; he weighed them on a shoulder scale, and the farmer then lowered the bags of opium into larger nylon bags held open by Mustafa's driver. Into each of the nylon sacks, the driver stuffed camphor balls to mask the pervading odor of the opium. Then, and only then, did Mustafa pay off the farmer.

The men worked smoothly and carefully, without undue fear of interruption. In this remote spot, far from the nearest village, they were in little danger of any police patrol. One by one the farmers brought forth their opium and were paid in cash. Mustafa kept count of the growing heap of bags of opium and the amount of Turkish liras being handed out. When they were paid, the farmers moved off in groups back down the road toward their own villages or farms with extra money in their pockets.

When the farmers had gone, the three men who were left there paused to rest, to light cigarettes, to congratulate each other on the success of their venture and to admire their horde of opium. Mustafa particularly felt the professional pride of a man who knew he had performed well and was being well rewarded. He had before him a half ton of raw opium, 1,100 pounds, which stood in a pile six feet long, six feet wide and four feet high. It had taken them just a bit more than two weeks to accumulate this amount. They all had reason to be satisfied with their work. Emin had seen Mustafa pay the farmers an average of 150 liras a kilo, some more, some less. He himself was happy to receive 24,000 lira ($2,400) for his own 150 kilos of opium. His profit came to almost three thousands liras, or three hundred dollars, and in addition, Mustafa paid him another seventy dollars, representing two liras for each of the 350 kilos he had helped purchase.

When they had rested, Emin helped Mustafa and his driver unload the empty barrels from the truck. They packed the nylon bags of opium into barrels which they then covered and reloaded onto the truck. The nylon bags, with camphor inside, retained the opium odor. The loaded barrels were indistinguishable from the empties on top of them. A huge tarpaulin covered the whole cargo.

Emin was dropped off at the bottom of the road, closer to the village, and Mustafa, alongside his driver, was on his way to the Syrian border with his valuable cargo.

From Afyon to Kilis on the border by direct route was about 530 miles, but the zigs and zags in the more roundabout journey preferred by Mustafa stretched the trip closer to six hundred miles, with long stretches of secondary roads. Mustafa resigned himself to almost two full days of driving nonstop, except for fuel and food, as he and the driver took turns at the wheel. The practice of Turkish truck drivers' sleeping in their vehicles by the side of the road was considered too high a risk for the dubious comfort involved. The trip was arduous but not particularly dangerous. There was little likelihood of their being stopped on the road by any patrolling gendarmes. The truck had the appearance of so many others on the road: neither new nor very old, but in excellent running condition. The truck had been rented in Istanbul under a fictitious name by a lackey of Baykal's, and could be abandoned if necessary. Both Mustafa and his driver were traveling with false identity papers and fictitious names. They had stories prepared in the event they were stopped: They were going to Gaziantep, near the border, to pick up a cargo of olives for a businessman in Istanbul; they themselves were merely itinerant drivers, who had been given the truck and its cargo of empty barrels for this one trip. If the police found anything other than empty barrels, the two truck drivers would indeed be surprised.

Actually, they had made this trip before, and other trips from other places; never once had they been stopped by the police, nor did they expect to be stopped this time. Nevertheless, their stories were ready.

They headed south and eastward from Afyon, over long stretches of dismal, semi-desert plains, through the small, dead towns of Cay, then Aksehir, and on to Konya, which is perhaps the most important city in the center of the Anatolian Plateau, some 3,770 feet above sea level. A large agricultural center of about eighty thousand people, Konya was surrounded by wide stretches of small, low, terraced homes with gardens enclosed within high, whitewashed mud walls. The center city, or old town, of Konya was believed to have been settled three thousand years before Christ.

Beyond Konya, Mustafa decided against the main highway leading directly to Adana near the Mediterranean coast. He chose instead the more southerly route, a secondary road only partially paved, hilly and winding, which took them through the Taurus mountains to the coast of the Mediterranean at Silifke, a sleepy village of four thousand people about 315 miles from Afyon. This southerly route was more arduous, took more time, but had the advantage of no police patrols. Mustafa and his driver rambled by historic landmarks and remnants of the ancient Hittite Empire, the Holy Roman Empire, the Crusades and other past glories of this land. But their attention was not upon biblical sites or ancient history. Their eyes were upon the road ahead of them and the safe arrival of their cargo of 1,100 pounds of raw opium.

At Silifke, they changed the license plates on the truck so that it could not be identified as coming from far-off Istanbul. With Gaziantep plates, the truck became a local carrier, unworthy of any police suspicions. From Silifke they picked up speed and time on one of Turkey's modern asphalt highways along the coast of the Mediterranean toward Gaziantep, another 250 miles away. They passed through Adana, a small crowded city of almost 200,000 which was the commercial center of southern Turkey, and forty-seven miles beyond Adana they came to a fork in the highway. If they turned right, southward, the highway continued through Antakya, over the border, through Syria, into Lebanon and on to Beirut, which Mustafa understood was the destination of his cargo. The opium would be worth almost twice as much in Beirut as it would on the Turkish-Syrian border. But that route, which hugged the eastern shore of the Mediterranean Sea, was for legal cargo only. Customs checks at the border were thorough, and searches were the rule rather than the exception. Mustafa, a wise and experienced smuggler, knew his limitations. He would take the opium only up to the Turkish border. To carry 1,100 pounds of elicit opium across the border required an expert. Mustafa had a business arrangement with the best of them, and his employer, Baykal, was quite willing to pay the price.

Mustafa now was approaching his home ground. He followed the left fork in the highway and continued eastward to Gaziantep, the capital of the province, a modern city by Turkish standards, situated on a huge plain between two hills. Famous throughout Turkey for its pistachio nuts, Gaziantep housed the headquarters and main garrison of the two and a half brigades of gendarmes, some 3,700 men, who guarded the 545-mile Turkish-Syrian border. They protected it not so much against the implausible likelihood of invasion but against the continuous waves of smuggling in both directions which went on day and night, year around. Despite the prevalence of gendarmes and police, Gaziantep itself was as safe for criminal operations as any large city around the world, safer in a way than the small village. In a bustling city of 150,000 people, Mustafa's truck passed inconspicuously through the crowded streets and into the closed courtyard of the home of a friend on the outskirts of the city. There the truck came to a dusty rest in safety and out of sight. There it was unloaded.

Only the last leg of the journey remained. But carrying the opium from Gaziantep to the small border town of Kilis thirty-seven miles away held more danger than all of the preceeding 565 miles from Afyon. In Kilis, every vehicle and particularly trucks were suspect. The move was accomplished, however, not by truck but rather in a series of sorties at night in a battered station wagon which had been converted to a sort of panel truck, its side and back windows painted opaque.

Mustafa himself drove the opium to a farmhouse several

kilometers southeastward of Kilis and, by prearrangement, turned it over to an old and trusted friend, known as Celebi, who was perhaps one of the five most successful smugglers in Kilis. Tall and lean, over six feet in height, with a sharp beaked nose, Celebi was a proud, high-living, vivacious man. He was a professional border smuggler of considerable repute. He undertook no other work. Not yet fifty, he was considered a veteran among the smugglers of Kilis, for he had the experience and wisdom of men older than himself and the physical stamina of men many years his junior. He knew the border better, could run faster and farther, could outshoot, outdrink, outwit any of his contemporaries. In him, Mustafa had complete faith and confidence.

Having given over the opium to Celebi and having made the necessary arrangements, Mustafa himself crossed the Turkish-Syrian border quite legally. Carrying the half of the lira note in his pocket which Baykal had given him as his identification, he made his way to the little coffee shop in Azaz. There he would make contact with the receiver of the opium, the man with the other half of the lira note, and then he would wait patiently for the message from Celebi. The barbed wire, the police patrols, the machine-gun posts and the explosive mines which guarded the border, they would not stop a man of the caliber of Celebi. He would come to Syria, along with the whole half of a ton of opium, he would come.

# 4

# Crossing the Border

He was called the Jack Rabbit by his cronies who worked and played with him. On foot he could outmaneuver a gendarme on horseback. He could run a swift zigzag course, fall flat on his face or somersault and come up shooting. They told stories of the gendarmes on the border he had either killed or wounded. He was fearless. His word could be trusted; he was an honest man. He worked at night and lived day to day, spending the money he earned at night, for a smuggler's life can end quite abruptly.

Celebi's days were spent at the national pastime, drinking tea or coffee and playing cards in one of the many coffee shops in Kilis. His prowess with women and liquor he proved in the evenings when he drank raki and frequented the public houses of Kilis. Celebi the Jack Rabbit was a typical Kilis border smuggler, perhaps superior to most others, but typical: He could run and he could shoot.

While other men bragged of their wounds in a town where the loss of a foot to a border mine was a symbol of a man's bravery, Celebi had no need to boast. He had a reputation. Like most men of Kilis, he carried a revolver in the waistband of his Arabic trousers. Under the tacit code of the area, an insult would oblige a man to draw his gun and shoot. A man's dignity and pride are his most prized possessions in Kilis, as in most of Turkey, where he owns so little else.

The parallel of this life with that of the old American West of perhaps one hundred years ago is obvious and striking, particularly to the Turkish people who see so many ancient grade-B Westerns made in Hollywood. For them, the whole area of the Turkish-Syrian border is known as the Texas of Turkey. It is their Wild East. And of all the small towns and villages on that 545-mile frontier, Kilis is the Dry Gulch, where the only true law exists in the hearts, guts and guns of the men of the town. To the police, Kilis is the Marseilles of Turkey, just as for the Paris Sûreté Marseilles is the Chicago of France. Thus, the reputation of a place lives long after those men who, like Al Capone, have made that reputation.

Kilis sits on a hilly section of a vast plain, hot most of the year and bitter cold and rainy for a few winter months. In appearance, it hardly differs from any other remote town in Turkey. Half the size of Afyon, it has one main street of hand-laid cobblestones, scorching in the summer, slick and muddy in the winter, with tiny stores and coffee shops lining the main square. Farming is the chief (legal) industry and unemployment the most prevalent occupation. Its particular geography makes a difference to its fourteen thousand inhabitants. Kilis lies on the edge of the border to Syria, and it is said (although no one has counted) that everyone, or nearly everyone, is involved in carrying things across the border, from one country to another, back and forth, depending upon national scarcity: coffee, tea, tobacco, foodstuffs, alarm clocks, razor blades, playing cards, gold, household wares and, most profitably, opium. For as long as anyone can remember, smuggling has been a way of life in Kilis.

Among the variety of ways of taking contraband across the border, the simplest and perhaps oldest method was to bribe a customs inspector or a guard at one of the legal exits. Along the border there were forty-nine transit points for vehicles and pedestrians and thirteen regular customs controls for trucks and caravans carrying legal merchandise. However, the Turkish government was continually improving its policing of these exits, posting rewards for seized contraband, and no smuggler could be assured any longer that bribed guards would remain faithful to the bribe.

Perhaps the most frequent method used was to employ one of the numerous farmers who had police permits allowing them to cross the frontier daily because they either owned or worked on farms on both sides of the border. They lived, in effect, in both countries. Nor did they consider this unusual. The farms had been passed down from one generation to another long before the border had been drawn separating Syria from the old Ottoman Empire. Although these farmers and farmhands were seldom searched, they could carry across the border only what they could conceal without suspicion on their bodies or in a small parcel.

Celebi, as a professional, knew all these methods and others and he realized, as did his friend Mustafa, that so valuable a cargo as half a ton of opium would need to be run across the border after midnight. Crossing the border was for Celebi a sort of game, a contest with challenges and danger, but a game he was accustomed to winning.

There were different ways to play the border game, but Celebi had a favorite which he reserved for his more important assignments, such as this cargo of five hundred kilos of opium. At the preferred time of the month, when the moon was in the first quarter and the nights dark enough for concealment and yet light enough to see one's way, Celebi chose the suitable night for the crossing. He picked fifteen of his trusted cronies and arranged a rendezvous. They would have to cross and recross the border twice in one night to deliver a thousand pounds of opium. For that, each man would be well paid: sixty Turkish liras for one night's work, the equivalent of six American dollars.

Celebi himself worked for a flat fee, based upon the cargo and the number of crossings rather than so much money per kilo, which he had negotiated with Mustafa Aydin. Because he would plan, direct and lead the crossing, Celebi had demanded and received 1,200 liras ($120) for the night's venture, the equivalent of ninety dollars to pay fifteen couriers and the equivalent of thirty dollars for himself. By the economic standards of Kilis, that was a great deal of money, but then again, everyone knew that the most highly paid people in Turkey were the smugglers.

Besides, Celebi would have his wife out on the mission also, and she worked for nothing.

Because the authorities at the border had taken to using informers, paying men of no integrity to reveal the plans and routes of smugglers, Celebi sent a trusted friend to misinform and misdirect the gendarmes. If the gendarmes believed this informer, they would go out on a wild goose chase miles and miles from the point at which Celebi intended to cross; if they disbelieved him, they would do nothing. He sent another messenger across the border to Azaz in Syria to tell Mustafa where and when to meet. That night he briefed his couriers.

At the very end of that day, midnight, on the Turkish side of the border, a short, stout woman dressed in black led an old thin horse across the railroad tracks which marked the beginning of the forbidden zone of the frontier. The woman stepped gingerly over the railway ties, keeping pace with the horse. After some fifteen yards, she came upon flat land. The earth here had been raked and smoothed out that morning, as it was every day, by the gendarmes in the hope that they could detect the points at which the border had been crossed the night before. The woman, however, did not seem to take notice. She walked on at a moderate pace, yet with care, for she knew the way which had been pointed out to her before. Even the horse seemed to know the way, stepping so quietly. The horse carried an innocent sack of flour, nothing else, except for a hemp rope knotted loosely on its saddle horn. The rope trailed behind the horse and yet it did not touch the ground.

It was a long rope, as much as two hundred feet in length, perhaps a bit longer, one end tied to the horse and the other end held up by Celebi and his fifteen hired runners behind him. The men walked in a crouch, each like a Santa Claus, bent over and close to the ground, one hand holding the rope line and the other clutching a gunnysack of opium slung over the shoulder. Each sack weighed fifteen or sixteen kilos, or about thirty-five pounds. For these men it was a light burden. They could have carried a hundred pounds or more for miles and miles, were it not for the loss of mobility in an emergency that the added weight would entail. Mobility, flexibility and stealth plus intimate knowledge of the terrain were the ingredients of success. The men walked single file, the last two of them trailing their jute sacks on the ground to obliterate the footmarks of the men ahead of them.

The woman and her horse walked on through a stretch booby-trapped with anti-personnel mines, but she followed a path in which the mines had been detonated some time ago by a small herd of sheep driven through the area. This was only one of the several paths through the mine fields which Celebi had marked out as his own. Every smuggler's stock-in-trade is the routes he knows across the border. A good smuggler has four or five current ones, so that he can choose the safest one for each particular night according to his information of gendarme activity, his experience of the past and his own intuition.

Celebi, following the lead of the rope, was sure of himself this night. This was a route he used only infrequently for the most important cargos. The gendarmes might come upon him only by pure chance. But he feared no informer, for he had implicit trust in the men behind him and in the woman up ahead leading the horse. She was his wife. As a good Moslem spouse, she obeyed her husband; the wife of a smuggler, she was a smuggler, too. Her role in the border crossing was simple. She followed the path laid out by Celebi, and if the gendarmes approached her, she dropped her end of the rope from the horse and she explained that she was on her way to visit a sick relative in Syria.

If the rope fell to the earth, the slack would inform Celebi what was happening two hundred feet ahead, although in the black of night he could not see the scene. But neither could the gendarmes see him. If they believed his wife but took her in to the post for further explanations, then Celebi and his men would continue safely across the border. If the gendarmes suspected the trick and retraced his wife's steps back to him, he and his men would turn and slip silently back into Turkey just as swiftly as the gendarmes followed.

Celebi's wife allowed the horse to take the lead as she walked by its side through the stretch of mine fields. By Turkish standards, she was a handsome woman. Dark-skinned as most southern Turks, she was a large woman, about five feet six, with broad shoulders and an ample bosom. She outweighed her tall, sinewy six-foot husband, but there was no flab upon her body. She was almost as strong as a man. Although she had given birth to five children and had raised the three that lived, she thought nothing of jogging miles in her husband's business of border running.

At the barbed-wire fence, she deftly snipped the remaining strands, left there purposely the night before. The barrier parted with a twang. Beyond the fence, there was more raked land to reveal footprints and, further on, more anti-personnel mines. This area for miles on either side of Kilis was the most heavily mined sector of the entire border. Justly so, because Kilis was the major point of departure for smuggling. At one time the border had been mined to a depth of 350 meters, or about 380 yards, the mines being planted indiscriminately. But that had proved too dangerous for the gendarmes as well as for the smugglers. Since 1960, the mines were planted with greater concentration and care in several strips of ten or fifteen yards depth, separated by blank land and barbed-wire fences to a total depth of one hundred yards. Because the smugglers always seemed to discover the location of the mines, the government brought in army engineers to plant the new mines each year, selecting only men who lived in the interior, far from the border, so that they could not pass on to the smugglers any information on how to detect the mines. The gendarmes posted at the border were under strict orders never to enter the mine fields. Anyone wounded or killed in the mine fields, it was understood, was left there to rot. The one and only location plan of the mines was kept in the safe of the commander of the counter-smuggling and intelligence division of the gendarmerie in Ankara.

Beyond the hundred yards of mine fields lay a stretch of land patrolled by gendarmes on horseback. Celebi and his band moved cautiously but steadily forward with Celebi in the lead, holding taut the rope which led to his wife ahead. He felt the signal on the rope, two sharp jerks, at about the same time he heard the sound of hooves in the distance. He held up his hand and the line of men behind him stopped in their tracks. Up ahead, though he could not see her, Celebi knew his wife was standing still, quiet and listening. The hoofbeats stopped and there was silence in the night, broken only by the sighing of the wind. The gendarmes on horseback had stopped. Whether or not the patrol had spotted his wife in the night, Celebi could not know. He waited. Then came the sound of the horses again, but this time the hoofbeats were receding in the dark. Celebi could not tell whether the gendarmes had seen or heard or suspected anything. It did not matter so long as they went on their own way. Nor was it surprising that they had chosen not to investigate. Unless a patrol chanced directly upon smugglers, there was little likelihood of any gunplay. Most of the gendarmes, aside from the officers, were young recruits, serving out their conscription at fifty cents a month. They had scant desire to engage in a gun battle with experienced smugglers, unless it was absolutely unavoidable. Yet, when the two forces met, there were gun battles. In 1964, for instance, five gendarmes were killed and seventeen badly wounded in skirmishes on the Syrian border. Many more smugglers are killed and wounded each year, according to the gendarmerie, but the exact number is kept secret.

The point is, however, that men like Celebi must be prepared to die on any night they cross the border. They must be prepared to shoot it out with the gendarmes, knowing that if they kill or wound a policeman and are found out, they must flee. If you kill a Turkish gendarme, you must flee to Syria, and if you kill a Syrian soldier, you must escape to Turkey.

Once past the area controlled by the gendarme patrols, the smugglers came upon the actual political border between Turkey and Syria. This is a buffer zone three miles wide, a no-man's-land, forbidden to both nationals, in which any man seen can be shot on sight. The topography is the same on both sides of the border as it is in the buffer zone: gentle rolling hills of brushland. At the crest of some of these hills on the Turkish side of the border, spaced from a half mile to several miles apart, are machine-gun emplacements manned by as many as twenty-five soldiers, but never less than three, for fear that adventurous smugglers might try to overpower the post and steal the machine gun. Throughout Turkey, guns are a prized and valuable possession. In Kilis, more than elsewhere, the men would risk or trade almost anything for a revolver or a rifle. The machine-gun emplacements, pointed toward the border buffer zone, serve mainly as a deterrent: Only the rankest amateur would be so stupid as to come within firing range of the lethal machine guns.

Celebi and his band jogged through the buffer zone, emerging in Syria, relatively safe. They ran single file on the edge of a road for another four miles to their meeting with Mustafa at a desolate, unmarked spot about halfway to the town of Azaz. With Celebi leading the way, the men ran tirelessly at a good pace, their gunnysacks of opium joggling against their backs. The runners were of all ages but equally fit, for in this part of the country age made little difference. A man of sixty could run as long and as fast as a boy of fifteen. From the farmhouse near Kilis to the meeting place outside Azaz was little more than eight miles, a modest distance for these experienced runners. Even with the added caution necessary in sneaking through the mine fields and past the patrols of gendarmes, the trip one way took them no longer than ninety minutes.

At the rendezvous, Mustafa Aydin greeted his old friend Celebi with genuine affection. The runners heaved their sacks of opium upon the ground and Mustafa presented a bottle of *raki* which the men passed from one to the other, each runner taking a single swig, until the bottle made a full circle back to the host who drank with them. Two canteens of water then made the circuit. The men rested only for a short while and then, full of smiles, they trotted off in the dead of night back down the road toward the farmhouse in Kilis and the second half of their load.

Mustafa sat back upon his haunches at ease, his body leaning against a tree trunk, for he realized that he had two and one half to three hours to wait for the return of the runners. The hour was two o'clock in the morning and the night was cold. For warmth, Mustafa had his bottle of *raki,* and for conversation he had with him the Syrian courier of the buyer of the opium. This courier, called Abdul Abdurahman, was a short, dark-skinned Arab wrapped in countless layers of clothing. Their conversation was desultory, for they had little to say to one another. One represented the buyer and the other the seller of the valuable horde of opium at their feet, and neither cared to divulge any more information than was necessary for this operation. Camping about a mile from them was a band of men hired by the Syrian to cart off the opium when he gave the signal. Until the full load arrived, Mustafa and Abdul had nothing more to do than to weigh and count the opium on hand and to wait.

The opium resting on the ground in front of the two men in Syria now was worth at least twice as much as Mustafa had paid the farmers for it in Afyon. Mustafa had paid the farmers 150 T. L. and had charged Baykal in Istanbul 170, but here in Syria, so close to but yet over the border, the opium would bring 350 liras or even 400. And yet Mustafa was no more tempted now than he had ever been before to try to sell the opium himself. Successful smuggling, he knew, was more than bringing contraband across a border; one had to accomplish the final step of finding someone across the border to whom to sell the contraband. And there was the rub. Mustafa knew no one well enough to trust who would have the 350 or 400 liras a kilo to buy these five hundred kilos. The Syrian sitting next to him, he knew full well, had nothing near that money. Mustafa suspected correctly that he was a chemist of sorts, who knew how to convert the opium to crude morphine. But he was no more in business for himself than was Mustafa. He was a hired hand. Neither would this wily little Syrian be trusted by the buyer, whoever he was, with the money to pay for the opium. He had only a receipt to give Mustafa in exchange; the buyer himself would pay Baykal whatever was owed when Baykal presented the receipt, proving the opium had indeed been delivered. Mustafa was but a cog in a wheel, a gigantic wheel of secret dealings, the whole of which was beyond his comprehension. Yet, he did have the satisfaction of a man who does his job well. His commission of twenty liras a kilo from Baykal and his fudging on the price for another twenty, added up to a grand commission for Mustafa of twenty thousand Turkish liras, the equivalent of two thousand dollars, and in the social strata of his own circles that was a fortune.

With the patience of a peasant, Mustafa waited for the return of the border runners. The border, as he well knew, was a beehive of activity this night as it was almost every night. But how much opium in all crossed the frontier that night or on any night, or what was the average for the whole year, neither Mustafa nor anyone else could say. A successful operation goes undetected and uncounted in the statistical tables of the authorities.

Although Kilis was a favorite smuggling depot, there were other points of exit in Turkey for opium destined for the Western market: over the Saman Daği mountains at Antakya into

Syria, or by boat from Iskenderun or from Izmir direct to Beirut or to Marseilles. In recent years, despite the heavier jail penalties meted out for dealing in morphine rather than opium, some men were doing the conversion in Turkey and shipping morphine the long and expensive route overland by car through Bulgaria, Yugoslavia, northern Italy and into France. How much illicit opium is smuggled out of Turkey in all? No one knows precisely. No one knows exactly how much opium is grown on an acre. The estimates vary here as much as 50 percent and more, and thus no one can tell how much is diverted. The legal production of opium in Turkey varies considerably from year to year. For instance, in 1962, the annual production was 310 tons; in 1960, it was 365 tons; and in 1958, it was 162 tons. But in 1964, because of a particularly harsh winter, the annual production was only about seventy-three tons. How much more opium was diverted? The Turkish government admits to about 10 percent. The United Nations Commission on Narcotics estimates the figure may be as high as 25 percent. The federal Bureau of Narcotics estimates that approximately sixty thousand active heroin addicts in the United States use between one ton and one and one-half tons of heroin each year, which would mean that about ten to something under fifteen tons of opium smuggled out of Turkey reach the United States in the refined form of heroin. But the United States is only one customer of Turkish opium. Two to three times as much opium is smuggled from Turkey to its neighbor Iran, where the number of opium eaters and smokers stagger the imagination. No one counts because there is no method of counting. Estimates of Iranian opium addicts ran from one to five million men and women up to 1955, when the government, in desperation, outlawed any and all poppy cultivation in Iran. Since then the estimate of addicts in Iran has declined to fewer than a million. But how many fewer, no one knows.

Despite the efforts of cooperating nations around the world in the struggle to control the flow of illicit narcotics, no one can truly tell just how much black market opium is smuggled out of Turkey. There are intelligent guesses and estimates, but time and again the experts are obliged to say that nobody knows. All agree, however, that the lack of information is due to the intelligence of the principals who control the clandestine traffic of narcotics throughout the world. The Turkish police perhaps express it more simply: "The smugglers are smarter and always one step ahead of the police, and, besides, there are more smugglers."

No one knew, for instance, not the police of Turkey or Syria or America, of the exploits of the burly, semi-illiterate smuggler named Mustafa Aydin, who in a matter of three weeks had transported half of a ton of raw opium from central Turkey to a roadside within the Syrian border. His job was completed and successful when the runners had returned with the second half of his load, and the opium had been weighed and stacked, tied and secured upon the swaybacks of a dozen dirty Syrian donkeys. The parting formality was the exchange between Mustafa Aydin of Turkey and Abdul Abdurahman of Syria of the two halves of the Turkish lira note each man had carried in his pocket. In their business, torn currency was tendered as a bill of lading.

# 5

# Cookout in Azaz

Equally by day as by night they remained safe, for there was no one about to see them. Their camp site was in the mountainous brush country somewhat more than thirty miles from the roadside near Azaz where they had started. This was God-forsaken country. Neither roads nor trails led to this plateau three thousand feet above sea level. It was wild country, rocks, dry brush and dusty desert land, good for nothing, neither farming nor grazing nor mining. Less than 30 percent of all of Syria's land is arable and this area was the worst. No one wanted this land and no one came here. Nevertheless, each end of the camp site was guarded by a lookout, armed with a rifle. They were bored men and they dozed as time passed so slowly. Yet, they were on guard.

From the air, if a chance plane had passed, the camp site would have looked like just another encampment of a nomadic tribe. Two tents had been set up for the men who could not find accommodation in a nearby cave. The mules were tethered at the end of the long lines which allowed them to graze as best they could on the brush and bits of grass near a small but flowing stream. The only difference between this encampment and that of any of the Kurdish tribes roaming the area was that this one had two fires ablaze instead of one, and the fires burned around the clock. Balanced on tripods over each of the fires was a large fifty-gallon oil drum, and cooking inside each of the huge black pots was opium. But that, of course, could not be seen from the air. And the lookouts, albeit dozing, guarded the approach from land.

The process of converting opium to morphine base, or crude morphine, is quite simple. The morphine is an integral part of opium and needs only to be extracted. Any cook can do it, man or woman, by following the recipe. However, in Syria, such knowledge is so rare that the man called Abdurahman considered himself a chemist. After all, he had been taught how to get the morphine powder out of the mess of opium during a week-long visit to Marseilles. The trip had been a high point in his life. He had been shown how to use the chemicals on a small amount of opium. And then he had been taken to a place near Beirut, and another man had watched him working on a larger amount, and now he was trusted to work by himself and to report to the Frenchman who looked like a Lebanese. His had been the only name given to him of all the men he had met, and, on pain of death, he had been warned never to reveal that name, Léon Levonian.

Since he had won the trust of these Frenchmen, Abdurahman had put more money in his pocket than he had ever earned before. He was paid five dollars for each kilo of morphine base he produced from the opium and to him this was a great deal of money. Before, he had run errands and delivered packages for a pittance and before that he had starved when he could not steal. He understood that his chemistry in the mountains was against the law but he had risked going to jail all his life for considerably less money. Besides, it had been explained to him that so long as he followed instructions and did nothing beyond what he had been told to do, the risk was not very great. The danger he faced was the temptation of trying to cheat the men who paid him.

The greatest risk involved in this operation had passed when Abdurahman reached the camp site he had selected as his laboratory. In the thirty-mile trek through the hills, he had run the danger of encountering marauders who might steal his cargo of opium. To guard against this, Abdurahman had hired fifteen men to accompany and protect him and the mules. Their rifles all were old, most of them Italian of World War I vintage, but they could be fired. The men were chosen for their bravery and loyalty. Abdurahman had promised them good pay, a dollar a day for their time, so he could be reasonably certain that they would not run off at the first shot of a gun battle. It was well known that in the vast stretches of desert and brush country of Syria, any caravan not adequately protected was open to attack from any tribe of superior numbers or fire power. It was not unlike sailing in the days of old when pirates attacked merchants' ships for whatever unknown riches they might carry.

Abdurahman's luck had held. He had made the thirty-mile trek without incident, setting up camp near the needed supply of water, and he had gone right to work.

The wood had been gathered, the fires firmly established and banked, the empty oil drums cleaned and filled to the three-quarter mark with opium and water to half the level of the opium. Abdurahman, the "chemist," kept a constant check on the fires, for this was essential. In a laboratory, he might have had a thermometer, but here in the wilderness he used his longest finger. A quick dunk into the solution, and his finger would inform him if the water was hot enough to melt the opium but below the boiling point which would destroy the morphine. If too cool, he would order a man to add a few more sticks to the fire; if too hot, he would add cold water.

To the warm water, he then added straight lime and watched the water turn a milky white as the lime, once in contact with the water, changed chemically into a crumbly mass of calcium hydroxide. Lime is so inexpensive and easily available, it is often used as a fertilizer. But to the Syrian peasants watching over the fifty-gallon drum, the reaction of this white chemical upon the blackish-brown opium was a sight to behold. Chemically, the lime precipitated the mixture. It dissolved the mass of opium in the pot, separating from it the morphine and a little bit of the codeine that was in the opium. The peasants could see the black stuff—the botanical segment of the opium—settle down to the bottom. With it went quite a few other alkaloids contained in the opium, which they could not see.

Abdurahman stood over each oil drum, making certain that his man kept stirring the mixture. The process continued for an hour, until the water once again became clear, with perhaps only a tinge of the color of weak tea. He then poured off the watery solution. It was the liquid, not the sediment, which contained the morphine.

He poured the tealike solution ever so slowly through a stretched segment of cloth into another empty oil drum. In a laboratory, special fluted filter paper would have been used over the mouth of an Erlenmeyer flask. But in the hills, woven cloth served well as a filter.

Once again the solution was heated over the fire, with the temperature controlled, and to this solution, the Syrian "chemist" added another common chemical, ammonium chloride, which is nothing more than a concentrated form of the household cleaning agent, ammonia. The odor was powerful and unmistakable. Abdurahman poured the ammonium chloride at arm's length and sparingly, bit by bit, while another man gently stirred the solution. When the right amount of ammonia had been added, it caused the morphine along with a little bit of codeine to precipitate from the water. The morphine, again with a small quantity of codeine clinging to it, crystallized and became a solid. It could be seen clearly as a great cloud of grayish-white mass in the water.

Again, the men filtered the solution through a cloth, and this time the valuable part of the solution remained on top of the cloth. It was brownish-gray in color and it was crude morphine, commonly known as morphine base.

They poured the remaining water through another cloth to filter out whatever morphine they had missed the first time and could catch the second time around. The wet, powdered morphine was then put out on the cloths in the sun to dry, sheltered from the prevailing wind, and the process was started again: heating the water, filling the drum with opium, adding the lime, filtering, adding the ammonium chloride, filtering and then allowing the resulting morphine base to dry. In the sun, the drying might take five or six hours; without the sun, it would dry overnight or perhaps sometime during the morning hours. To the men in the Syrian mountains, the resultant product of their labors appeared quite innocuous. Bitter to the taste, it looked like highly refined brown sugar; its crystals were tiny and granular, light brown in color. Only Abdurahman had some concept of the value of this brown bitter sugar and the use to which it would be put. The simple men who worked with him knew only vaguely that what they were doing was indeed against the law, but they had never seen a heroin addict nor could they be privy to the machinations of the merchants in organized crime who dealt in drugs.

The crude morphine was carefully brushed from the cloths into waxed-paper bags and sealed, ready for delivery. In a laboratory, a good chemist would purify the morphine with ether, removing much of the codeine and other impurities remaining in the morphine. Opium is considered a fruit containing some thirty alkaloids, the most prominent of which is morphine. It also contains codeine, papaverine, narotine, narceine and other alkaloids, each of which comprise less than one percent of the weight of opium. However, unlike lime or ammonia, ether is expensive, and the underground "chemists" of Syria, Mexico and the Far East do not bother with this final purification.

Just how much morphine Abdurahman and his helpers extracted from the five hundred kilos of opium at hand depended, of course, on how much morphine the opium contained in the first place and upon the efficacy of their simple and crude methods. Raw opium from Turkey is so desired by the worldwide net of merchants who supply the Golden Market because it yields 12 to 15 percent of its weight in morphine. Only Yugoslavian opium is known to be of equal quality. All others range from 5 to 7 percent morphine, including opium grown in India, China, Burma, Egypt or Mexico. When the raw opium is treated and prepared for export by the Turkish government Monopoly, and the leaves, twigs and other gross impurities are peeled away, the morphine content rises to an average of 20 percent of the weight of the opium. But with the crude methods used in the hills, the average morphine content extracted from raw opium averaged only about 10 percent.

That was all Léon Levonian expected: fifty kilos of morphine base from five hundred kilos of raw opium. Abdurahman did not measure or weigh the total amount of morphine he accumulated in the large waxed-paper bags, although he surmised he had about one hundred pounds of the narcotic. Abdurahman still was new at the game. He was relatively a beginner, satisfied with the $250 he would be paid for his work, eager to please his exacting employer, and not fully aware of the opportunities his work offered him. Only later would he learn enough and sufficiently overcome his fear of reprisal to venture a bit out on his own. Only when he knew the routine of his own job well enough, would he learn how to cheat. Then he would weigh the morphine before turning it over to the customer who paid him, and if he produced eleven instead of ten kilos of morphine from every hundred kilos of opium, he would keep that one extra kilo and sell it himself. That one kilo of morphine in Beirut would bring him more money than he was paid for his six days' work in converting all five hundred kilos of opium for another man. He might do this sometime in the future, but only if he were brave enough. Selling morphine base in Beirut was lucrative but dangerous. Abdurahman had been warned. By selling the extra morphine base he could steal from Léon Levonian and the Frenchmen in Marseilles, Abdurahman could become a rich man quickly. But if he failed and was found out, he could be a dead man.

Abdurahman knew his way around Syria, where the national police and the gendarmes did not concern themselves particularly with narcotics. The authorities in Damascus cooperated with the American police when asked, but they maintained no special forces to combat the traffic in narcotics. Syria was only a transit point in the flow of illicit drugs; the traffic presented no integral problem in the country itself. And so, Abdurahman had little fear in transporting the one-hundred-odd pounds of brown powder, which was so easily concealed, through his own country, even to the nation's capital. But to take it to Beirut was another matter. Beirut was a city of intrigue, too complicated for a simple Syrian like Abdurahman to venture into alone.

# 6

# Deal in Beirut

At the edge of a cliff of rock on the road to Tripoli, Léon Levonian leaned against the parapet of the roof garden of the Casino de Liban and gazed down the long coastline at the night beauty of the city he loved the best in the world. From the height and distance at which he stood, he could view the whole expanse of the city, sparkling with vivid lights like a jeweled tongue thrust out in the quiet dark waters of the Mediterranean. It was the Paris of the Near East: Beirut.

For sheer dazzle, New York's Time Square might compare, if the rest of Manhattan Island were blacked out as was the countryside outside Beirut. Las Vegas, neoned by night in the midst of its Nevada desert, compared as a zircon to a diamond. By day, its gleaming, high hotels along the waterfront gave rise to the thought that this was probably what Miami Beach was trying to copy. Everyone could see that Beirut was beautiful, but those who knew it well considered the capital of Lebanon to be the most exciting city in the world. It was Léon Levonian's favorite, and like himself, the city was rich, wide open, free and amoral.

The casino blended with the city. Entirely privately owned, it was said to be the largest in the world, bigger than Monte Carlo or anything in Las Vegas. Its subterranean nightclub, featuring

hula, belly and chorus dancers of all races and nations, was
cavernous and soundproofed. Its marble entry hall was of ball-
room proportions. Its two gaming rooms, carpeted and quiet,
were fashioned after the Cannes Casino, decorous and elegant.
Gamblers of all nations and all varieties of wealth gathered here
to test their skill and luck upon the permutations of the wheel
and the flip of a card.

Levonian had left the gaming tables soon after he had spotted
the arrival of Inspector Abou Salim Mallouke of the Criminal
Investigation Division of the Lebanese Sûreté. He was a well-
known man in Beirut and a frequent visitor to the casino. An
inch below six feet, of medium weight, Inspector Abou Salim
was tall by Levantine standards and young, in his mid-thirties,
for the position he held. His entry into the room caused the usual
flurry of activity. He walked about, smiling and acknowledging
the flicked signs of recognition from those with whom he was
acquainted. He was impeccably groomed as always in a dark suit
of continental cut; his shoes were of Italian origin, his hair carefully pomaded, his fingernails manicured and lacquered. Appearances are of high importance in the Levantine world. Yet,
few who had dealt with Inspector Abou Salim mistook his
genial affability for softness or stupidity. He was smart, cunning,
and a powerful man in Beirut.

As the inspector walked through the card room, Levonian
was able to slip away unnoticed and mount the broad stairway to
the roof garden. Used for summer dining and dancing, the roof
was now dark and deserted. Covering the whole casino, it was a
large area broken up by boxed-in air vents, and a man could
easily stand hidden or unrecognized, assured of privacy.

Only by leaning over the parapet into the illumination on the
outside of the casino could Levonian read the time on the face of
his expensive Swiss watch: a few minutes before midnight, the
appointed time for his meeting. Even so, he expected to wait.
Social finesse demanded that a man arrive late for an appointment and the more important the man, the later he was expected
to be. Levonian understood and was prepared to yield the point.
He would wait as necessary because he needed this man for
whom he was waiting, he needed him to bring the merchandise
safely into Lebanon.

There were a variety of ways to smuggle even a hundred pounds of morphine base into Lebanon. The amount made little difference. The size of the border between Syria and Lebanon, however, was small, and there were few roads and fewer people to trust. Levonian had learned long ago that smuggling methods must be designed to fit the customs and circumstances of each country, even each locality involved. Turkey was different from Syria and both were quite different from Lebanon. This was, in its way, one of the most sophisticated countries of the world—at least Beirut was. While the peasant population of the hinterlands was as backward and tradition-bound as the Arab world, the heart of the nation was its largest city of half a million people, Beirut, and the Beiruti took pride in their heritage as sophisticated traders and merchants without equal. They were descended from the Phoenicians, the first traders of antiquity who invented bookkeeping and money as we use them today. Lebanon is a tiny nation which has virtually no natural wealth, no industry, and yet is one of the most prosperous lands in the Middle East. Its chief industry is trade. Geographically, it is the trading center between East and West, the commercial and banking capital of the Middle East. Beirut is a free port, specializing in buying from one nation what it can sell to another at a profit, including money in its gold and foreign exchange brokerage houses. It has more banks than Berne, Switzerland, and rivals the Swiss in handling secret coded numbered accounts, stringently protected by law, with no questions asked. Lebanon banks even pay interest on checking accounts. The money pours in, particularly from the nearby oil-rich lands of Saudi Arabia, Kuwait and others, as well as from precariously perched rulers who use Beirut's banks to squirrel away funds for the day after the fall. But banking, after all, is merely another form of trade; money deposited in Beirut banks is used to buy other money, gold, diamonds or merchandise which can be converted back into money, more money. All this is trade, and little Lebanon maintains its role as the middleman, taking a commission on each trade.

Against this background, narcotics became merely another commodity in which to trade. Lebanon found itself geographically between the opium of Turkey and the heroin of France. Culturally, it bridged the two dissimilar nations. Men grew rich in Beirut beause they could buy in Turkey and sell in France more easily than the Frenchmen could themselves. The service to the heroin makers in Marseilles and in Italy was worth the commission. As traders, the Beiruti saw nothing wrong in trafficking in narcotics. Despite all the narcotics laws, the merchants in Beirut told themselves they were merely performing a service. They were not supplying harmful narcotics to their own people; the drug merely flowed through their own country like oil, leaving only a profit behind. That such traffic in narcotics was illegal merely imposed an added risk on doing business, which naturally raised the prices charged. Good or evil hardly entered into consideration. Culturally, the Lebanese developed quite a different set of ethics than those prevalent in the nations of the Western world. This was a country which had been conquered and occupied through the years by the Egyptians, the Persians, the Turks, the Arabs, Greeks, French and to an extent by the British. Without the strength to combat their oppressors the Lebanese resorted to the compromise, the pay-off, the bribe, the superficial acquiescence to the conqueror. Dignity and pride, so valued by the Turks, Greeks and Arabs, were viewed as expensive and futile luxuries to the Lebanese. There developed in the country the tradition of the bargainer, the peddler, the middlemen, with their traditional distrust, fear and hatred of established authority. Levantine businessmen sought immediate gain and trusted no one. Theirs was the heritage of the trader and the peddler of old, and it has long baffled the Western businessmen accustomed to the legal restrictions governing the honesty of business transactions. This was truly complete free enterprise. The only code of ethics was, "Let the buyer and *seller* beware!" It was said that any smart man walking ten steps in downtown Beirut should be able to find ten opportunities for making money. There were many obvious examples, known to everyone, of penniless men smart enough to become millionaires in just a few years in banking, shipping, trading, real estate, white slavery or narcotics.

Léon Levonian understood the attitudes and trading atmosphere of Beirut in a certain practical sense. Perhaps because of his own Armenian heritage, he had found that he too had an instinct for dealing with the so-called oriental mind of the Lebanese businessman, and in Beirut every man was a businessman, part or full time, whether he traded in buttons and threads, oriental rugs, gold or narcotics. No one commodity took precedence.

Coming from Marseilles and spending a good deal of his time in Beirut, Levonian bridged the gap between the two cities. Being Armenian was a distinct advantage in Beirut which contained a large Armenian colony. He had proved to the men of Marseilles that he could purchase morphine base from the suppliers in Lebanon as well if not better than they could. Once he had learned that part of the business, he had moved on to dealing directly with Ahmet Baykal in Istanbul, thus cutting out the profitable commissions paid to the Lebanese middlemen. From this saving, Levonian was able and quite prepared to pay well for help in bringing his valuable merchandise into and through Lebanon. He considered it good business: A man well paid and satisfied with his share is not so apt to double-cross the man for whom he works.

The night was so black that Levonian could hear the approaching footsteps long before he could make out the figure of the man walking casually toward him. He waited silently. Nor did the other man speak until he was upon him.

"Levon, it is so good to see you again, how are you?"

"Just fine," Levonian replied. "I am sorry to call upon you at such short notice, but we have need of your help once again, and Jean Paul said he especially wanted your help again."

"That is very kind of him and how is everything in Marseilles?"

"Oh, there is no trouble. Jean Paul has a shipment in Damascus which he wants moved tonight."

"Tonight? That will be rather difficult for I have a rather special appointment at the Kitty Kat." He spoke of the girly nightclub with a sneering smile, but Levonian recognized the gambit as merely a bargaining point. "It must be tonight, only tonight," he said.

"You want me myself to go at this hour?"

"Yes, with me, of course, like the last time, and we can bring back the courier with us, if you think that best, or we could leave him behind."

"This shipment, it is a large one, yes?"

"No, not large," countered Levonian, thinking of the price he would have to pay.

"How large?"

"I am not sure. One, perhaps two suitcases, that is all."

"That's what you say, but what you call suitcases, I might call trunks."

"Oh no, they are not trunks, one ordinary suitcase, like the last time," Levonian bargained.

"Must it be tonight?" the counter came. "Why not sometime tomorrow, perhaps tomorrow night?"

"No, the arrangements are already made, and for tomorrow, they would have to be made over completely again."

The man shrugged. "Well, if it must be, it must be, but you know, as I told you the last time, I cannot do this often and not at the price you set last time."

"I do not set the price. You know that," Levonian lied. "The arrangements are made in Marseilles. What I pay, I must report to Jean Paul, and if he does not approve, then they find other ways. But I myself, I like this way. It is simple, it is safe and we have the trust. Do you want to set the price? What do you think we should pay?" Levonian was an excellent trader. He traded not in his own name but in the name of a man and an organization of men in Marseilles who were far more powerful than himself. Jean Paul Savelli was a familiar name to anyone of any importance in the narcotics trade around the world.

These two traders knew each other fairly well from past negotiations. There was no set price for the services asked. Each deal was separate and distinct. Nevertheless, as in all business negotiations, there are guide lines. Levonian knew he must pay this man well, for his abilities were unique and they were needed. If he were dissatisfied or felt cheated, he might turn Levonian over to the police. The name of Jean Paul Savelli was dropped into the negotiations as insurance. It meant that if anyone wronged Levonian, he would be dealt with by Jean Paul Savelli. It also meant that if this man overcharged Levonian, he might incur the displeasure of the Savelli organization behind him and risk all future profitable dealings. Both men understood that the price had to be correct and mutually satisfactory. Each of them knew the guide lines, although a little bargaining always was useful.

"Three thousand pounds!"

"Fifteen hundred!" said Levonian.

They reached agreement on 2,400 Lebanese pounds, or eight hundred dollars, which was a fair price to pay for some five hours of extra-legal work performed by one of the top officers of the Criminal Investigation Division of the Sûreté whose job it was to supress the flow of narcotics in Lebanon. There was no safer way to carry narcotics across the Lebanese border than to have Inspector Abou Salim Mallouke drive the car with the narcotics. It was tantamount to having J. Edgar Hoover's chief assistant drive Willie Sutton to the First National Bank at midnight.

Once the price was agreed upon, Levonian insisted that they start off immediately or not at all. He wanted to leave the police inspector no time for second thoughts on how he might convert this opportunity into an even more profitable one.

They left the casino in the inspector's personal new Pontiac, a car priced at about eight thousand dollars in Beirut, which was more than the police inspector's legal salary for the year but only a small fraction of his gross receipts. The American car made its way tortuously down the narrow winding road from the cliff top to sea level. They doubled back toward Beirut and then headed out on the famous Road to Damascus.

Where St. Paul walked and changed the course of Christianity almost two thousand years ago, an Armenian smuggler and a ranking Lebanese policeman now sped in an American car as fast as the road would allow on a mission designed to fatten their pocketbooks and buy their pleasures at perhaps the cost of their souls. The Road to Damascus today runs alongside the ancient route, sixty-six miles between Beirut and the capital of Syria, a narrow two-lane highway widening only at times to three lanes, constricted by the topography of the land into a long series of climbs and descents, curves and hairpin turns. No stretch of the road runs straight for more than a half mile. No matter how many times the inspector had made this trip, driving on the Road to Damascus demanded his full attention. One never can become familiar with this road, for around any single curve one might come upon a slow-moving truck, another car crossing the center driving line, or a herd of goats crossing the road.

Soon after Beirut, the road wound its way up to the top of the Lebanese Mountains, some six thousand feet high, and for somewhat more than a mile they drove at a crawl through clouds which hung over the peak of the mountain. Descending upon the other side, they entered the famous Bekaa Valley, which extended north and south almost the length of the entire country with the Lebanon Mountains on one side and the Anti-Lebanon Mountains, equally high, on the Syrian side. Enriched by the watershed of both mountain ranges and protected from winds, the Bekaa Valley is reputed to be the most fertile land in all the world. Local legend claims this was the Promised Land sought by Moses. Some say it was the true locale of the Garden of Eden, where all life began. The Bekaa Valley today produces, as the chamber of commerce points out, Lebanon's fabulous citrus crops and grapes. It also produces, as the underworld well knows, the world's finest quality hashish which supplies the most discriminating of the millions who smoke marijuana in Egypt and the Arab world.

Across the Bekaa Valley, some forty miles from Beirut, the Road to Damascus is cut by a massive stone overpass and gateway which serves as the border control of Lebanon, first immigration and then customs. Inspector Abou Salim, as a high-ranking officer of the Sûreté, was well known to all the border guards. He merely had to allow himself to be seen. The men at each control point saluted him and the blue Pontiac passed through.

Five miles further on, through no-man's-land, the sign at the side of the road announced, "Welcome to the Syrian Arab Republic." At the bright blue and yellow gateway, the commissioner and his passenger had merely to show their passports. Diplomatic courtesy was extended. The commissioner assured the guard on duty he was on a short mission, he would be back that night. It was as simple as that.

The guards at each of the Lebanese and Syrian borders were like their counterparts at frontiers around the world, civil servants working long hours at little pay, doggedly searching cars and trucks, luggage and cargos with scant hope of discovering contraband of more than nominal value. On the Road to Damascus, between five and six hundred vehicles, cars and trucks, crossed the border controls each day, and for the inspectors to search each one thoroughly would cause intolerable traffic jams. Thus, as a matter of practical policy, the customs men spot-checked some of the vehicles. A dilapidated old truck of a Lebanese or Syrian peasant would be pulled off to the side and the driver, one who had no political influence at all, would be obliged to unload his varied cargo for a serendipity search. Tourists were passed through usually without even a search of their luggage as a matter of good will. Officials of either country were sent on their way uninspected, inasmuch as a search might imply an insult to the man's honesty. This was not such a lackadaisical attitude as it might seem. Customs searches are meant to serve more as a deterrent to wholesale smuggling than as an infallible means of detecting contraband. Experienced customs men, when alert, can spot the nervous amateur, and occasionally they will find some contraband of insignificant value. But the professional smugglers dealing in narcotics, diamonds or gold are far too experienced to be found out by an ordinary customs inspection. The professionals are caught at the border, except in rare instances, only when the customs men have been alerted about a shipment in advance. Then they know whom to look for, what to look for and sometimes even where to look. For this, customs services at borders around the world pay rewards, which are at times substantial. The informers remain in the background, take their pay, and never come forward. Thus, they can work on and on, making their living on their rewards as professional informers. Without such advance information, customs inspectors would have difficulty stopping smuggling at all. But by using informers, they do a surprisingly creditable job, surprising to the public and to the smugglers as well.

For instance, any one not familiar with customs techniques would think it quite easy to slip one or two pounds of heroin or morphine base past a customs inspection. Narcotics are so small and so valuable for their size that a man could hide two pounds of the powder in a money belt around his waist, or a woman could slip it into her bra, and walk through customs confident that tourists are not subject to a personal search at any border. Such people are amateurs. Because they usually work alone, they think no one knows what they are doing. They overlook, however, the fact that anyone smuggling narcotics must buy it from someone else and also must have arranged for someone to buy it at the other end. Thus at least two other persons have knowledge of the venture. Usually more people are involved, and any one of them might inform to the police or customs for any number of reasons—for the reward itself, to extricate himself from arrest or difficulties with the police, or simply as a means of doing a favor in the hope of future good will. The amateur is always expendable in the narcotics business and he is usually the first to be caught and the last to know the reason why.

Particularly in Lebanon, where the professionals of the underworld were bound with no code of ethics or group loyalty, every man was a potential informer. Nor does a man have to forsake crime in order to cooperate with the police. He could inform one day and smuggle the next, depending upon which was more expedient. In fact, in Lebanon, he might do both on the same day.

These circumstances of doing business were understood and recognized fully by Léon Levonian and Inspector Abou Salim Mallouke. They provided a dangerous undercurrent to the superficial ease of movement on the surface. The blue Pontiac sped on through the night, past acres of farm land, and on up into the Anti-Lebanon Mountains, approaching Damascus. The police inspector and the smuggler gossiped of men, business affairs, and women of pleasure, never disclosing, if they could help it, information which might be too useful to the other. But beneath their conversation lay the elements of their conspiracy.

The ease with which they had passed over the border had been well paid for and well worth the price paid. Levonian was paying the inspector more money for a car ride of a few hours than he had given his Syrian chemist for six days of work. Why? Because the C.I.D. inspector was one of the only two men (the other being the head of Lebanese customs, similarly engaged) who could insure the safe transport of the morphine at the least risk. There were many, many more Syrian chemists available.

Inspector Abou Salim was more than a crooked cop, a policeman on the take, as that position is known in the Western world. He was thoroughly corrupt but he boasted that he was not a hypocrite. He drove his expensive car openly, he frequented the honky-tonks of Beirut, he fondled the girls, he entertained lavishly, he traveled abroad many times a year, and he made no pretense of living on his official salary. He boasted pridefully of his knowledge of what was going on in his city. Far beyond merely accepting bribes for his silence or protection, Abou Salim was an active participant. He operated quite openly, yet no one truly knew the scope of his activities, and what was known could not be proved. His accommodation with Levonian was only one of many. More often, he served as a go-between, in the sense of the ordinary Lebanese middleman, helping a potential buyer and seller get together. Professional traders in narcotics might be hard to find at a moment's notice, for they were always in transit. Inspector Abou Salim, however, worked hand in hand with the smugglers of contraband, and he made it his business to know where they were and what they were doing. So, for a small commission, he would lead an American buyer, strange to Beirut, to the bar where he could negotiate his deal. Abou Salim, considering himself honest and forthright in such affairs, would accept his broker's commission and leave the two men to their business. It soon became known that it was wise to deal through the inspector, for it was to be expected that he protected only those with whom he himself did business. Others faced the possibility that the C.I.D. inspector might catch them in the line of his more normal duties. In fact, the inspector had a fairly good record of arrests for his superiors to note. There was no shortage of criminals in Beirut.

There was, however, one particular irritating thorn in the freedom of the inspector's extracurricular activities in narcotics. Whether or not he discussed this with Levonian on the trip to Damascus is not known, but it was, at the least, a potential danger somewhat beyond the inspector's control.

There was an American narcotics agent stationed in Beirut,

serving as a treasury attaché in the American Embassy on the Rue de Paris. Since the Lebanese government, at a level much higher than that of the C.I.D. inspector, gave the American government leave to assign a narcotics agent to help stop the flow of illicit narcotics through Lebanon, Abou Salim was obliged to work in harmonious distrust with the American agent. At the time, that agent was particularly adept and adroit at adapting his techniques to the complex and intertwining narcotics situation in Beirut and environs. Abou Salim had had his hands full with this American agent, a young, blond man from New Hampshire who had majored in comparative literature and Elizabethan drama at Harvard and who had, after graduation, drifted into law enforcement when a short stint at teaching had bored him. In the Bureau of Narcotics, he discovered the "satisfaction of contributing to something beyond my own well-being while engaged in work which draws upon more than just the routine expenditure of thinking and imagination."

In Beirut, Henry Lambert worked alone, as did all narcotics agents assigned abroad, planning, deciding and taking action on his own initiative. Limited in the number of undercover roles he himself could play, he manipulated informers and informants, worked diplomatically with the local police, and followed cases originating in Beirut to wherever they might lead him in the Arab world. His relations with Inspector Abou Salim, for example, were handled with a delicacy of diplomatic finesse. Henry Lambert, as an American narcotics agent, could not make an arrest in Lebanon. He could, however, hire men to negotiate with traffickers and then call upon the Beirut police to make the actual arrest. Although he suspected the complicity of Abou Salim, he nevertheless had to work with him almost daily. He had learned to work around the Lebanese inspector or to inform him of a case only at the moment before the arrest was planned so the inspector could not thwart the weeks or months of preparation. The two men worked successfully on some cases and were at cross-purposes on the occasions when the inspector had a personal stake in the men under investigation. At one point the inspector had proposed through an intermediary a working cooperative arrangement: If the American narcotics agent would keep him informed of all the cases upon which he was working, then he, Abou Salim, would personally guarantee to hand over at least one narcotics case a month to the American agent. This would undoubtedly enhance the American's career, make his work much easier, and more than fulfill the requirements of his job. It would also allow Abou Salim to operate with a freer mind. To the Lebanese policemen, this was a worthwhile bargain, a compromise by which both police officers would gain. To the American officer, as to the federal Bureau of Narcotics, this was corruption—typical and understandable perhaps, but corruption nevertheless. The offer was rejected diplomatically, through the intermediary, so that the two police officers could continue to work together face to face, as they were obliged to since neither could dispose of the other. The Lebanese was not of sufficient rank to expel the American narcotics officer from Lebanon, and the American, as an invited guest of the Lebanese government, was in no position to bring such serious charges against Abou Salim without proof. The two men, each with a respect for the other's intelligence, went about their police work in their own separate ways as best they could.

Neither Salim nor Levonian had any reason to believe that the American narcotics agent was at all aware of Levonian's activities. And, as usual, they were quite right. Levonian had no arrest record pertaining to narcotics either in Lebanon, Turkey or France. Once, back in 1955, his name had been recorded as a witness to a street shooting in Marseilles which had been part of a feud between two rival Corsican gangs over the profits ($216,-000) from a shipment of 2,700,000 American cigarettes being smuggled from Lebanon to Corsica. Then, once again, in 1956, he had been questioned and fingerprinted by the Marseilles police as the suspected instigator in the murder of a well-known confidence man who himself had a long police record, but nothing could be proved. And so, as far as the police and Interpol files were concerned, Léon Levonian had no criminal record; his name was not on the card index file of narcotics merchants in Sûreté headquarters in Marseilles. He was known in that city as the younger brother of an established businessman. The police thought of him as the young, spoiled son of a close-knit, loving Armenian family, one who still was sowing his wild oats in the bars and night spots of the Place de l'Opéra and who enjoyed the thrill of intimacy with the pimps and prostitutes and gangsters who frequented that district, but who himself had never been charged with a crime. Levonian hoped to keep it thus, at least until he became so well established in narcotics that he could hire others to do what he was doing this night. He had to go for the fifty kilos waiting in Damascus because there was no one else he could quite trust with that huge quantity of narcotics.

Damascus spread out before them as two separate cities, the new and the old. The new city, built since Syrian independence in 1946, had six- and eight-lane avenues laid out in careful geometric patterns, flanked by modern office buildings which blended the latest in modern architecture with arabesque decorations of biblical times. Even at this late hour of night the streets were shining with the fluorescent lamps arched overhead.

Abou Salim's responsibility in this venture extended only to getting Levonian across the border and back again. Once in Damascus, he headed for that city's favored nightclub, La Cave du Roi, and turned the car over to Levonian.

"Be careful with my car, Levon!" he warned.

Levon headed for the old city on the hill, built in pre-Roman times, where all the cobblestone streets, save one, were narrow and crooked and crowded, hardly able to accommodate this huge American automobile. St. Paul had named the one exception The Street that is Straight, and that thoroughfare still stands today, as straight as ever, lined with shops and pushcarts, bisecting the old city which once had been walled in for protection against invaders. Today three of the seven gates of the old wall still stand. Levonian was headed for a section just beyond the Eastern Gate, where Christians and Armenians lived as minorities in a Moslem world.

Levonian parked in front of a large brick apartment house, not unlike the cheerless public housing developments built around the world. He disappeared into the anonymity of the tall building.

In one of the several hundred apartments, he greeted his "chemist," Abdurahman. "You have the silks?"

"Of course, they are all ready for you," the young man exclaimed. He dutifully introduced Levonian to his cousin and his cousin's wife, whose apartment he was using for the meeting, and they, despite the late hour, respectfully offered their guest tea, which he respectfully accepted.

Only following the tea could the two men excuse themselves to transact their business in the privacy of the bedroom. Abdurahman had explained to his cousins that he was selling a quantity of silk to an Armenian from Beirut, a transaction which was somewhat shady but not really outside the norm of law.

On the floor alongside the bed lay five fiber suitcases secured with leather straps, all identical. Levonian's eyes glowed with pleasure. He could not tell the suitcases apart.

Without hesitation, Abdurahman lifted first one and then a second suitcase to the bed, unstrapped and opened them, revealing inside of each a number of sealed calico cloth bags. Levonian opened each bag in succession, opening the nylon bag within the calico bag to reach the grayish-brown powder. Despite its dullness, the morphine gleamed in his mind's eye like gold. He tasted a sample from each of the bags with the tip of his moistened finger, assuring himself that he was getting morphine and not some worthless substitute. Then he weighed each bag—fifty in all—with a small spring scale Abdurahman provided. Afterward, it would be too late to check on any thievery. But now, assured of his treasure, Levonian congratulated his chemist upon his fine work. Having paid him in advance the expenses for chemicals and for the hire of the men he needed, Levonian now handed over one thousand Syrian pounds, the equivalent of $250. Levonian then accepted from the young Syrian the half of the lira note he had handed to Ahmet Baykal in the Istanbul nightclub. It had come full cycle now and appeared hardly the worse for its travels. Levonian sighed, thinking of Ahmet Baykal with the other half of the lira and of their meeting set for Geneva in the future. When they fitted the two halves together, perhaps over drinks in a hotel bar, and then destroyed the lira note, it would mark the complete success of this venture. Meanwhile, there was a great deal of work still to be done.

Levonian picked up the two suitcases filled with morphine. They were worth fifty thousand dollars in Beirut. Abdurahman hefted the three dummy suitcases, filled with personal clothing, and followed Levonian down to his automobile. Levonian carefully placed his suitcases on the floor of the trunk of the car and

Abdurahman loaded his suitcases on top. Levonian expected to get through the border without the locked trunk being opened, but if it were, then he had to rely on the complacency of the border guards faced with five suitcases in a policeman's car at an ungodly late hour.

# 7

# Mixed Cargo

Speeding back toward Beirut in a shiny new American automobile, Léon Levonian was smuggling narcotics in style and comfort. The engine of the big car purred luxuriously as the miles slipped beneath the tires, and the car's heater took the chill from the night air. Levonian and the police inspector still were dressed in their evening clothes, their shirts still white and clean, the silk ties still knotted up to the collar. They might have been on their way to a party.

Neither mentioned the morphine in the trunk of the automobile, and whatever fears either felt at the risk of passing through customs were not expressed. Each of the two men had nerve; otherwise he would have been in another business. Léon Levonian felt he had done everything right in this venture: He had paid attention to the details; had taken every precaution; had paid the police inspector enough money; and had kept to an absolute minimum the number of men who knew that he was carrying morphine on this road this night. The guards at the frontier would have no reason to stop Inspector Abou Salim Mallouke from driving through tonight as he had so many other times, no reason to insult his integrity by demanding to search the car.

As the car sped along, Léon Levonian worried more about

the possibility of losing his valuable merchandise than of being arrested. He felt confident that even if the morphine were found in the car, he could somehow talk his way out of going to jail. Salim, of course, would deny any knowledge of what was in the back of his car. Levonian would put the blame on the Syrian chemist, insisting he was taking his luggage to Beirut as a favor. He might have to pay his way out on bail while the case was pending and that would cost money, but the real calamity would be that he would lose the narcotics. He would have to pay for that loss, pay heavily in money and reputation, and he would have to make good to the men in Marseilles for their share of the merchandise. And yet, there was no better way to smuggle narcotics across the Syrian and Lebanese border than in the automobile of the inspector in the Criminal Investigation Division.

There were many ways, of course, to carry narcotics across the border, and the methods were becoming more and more sophisticated as the years went on. Each innovation in smuggling held the promise of a fortune for the man smart enough to think up something new. Thirty years ago, opium and sometimes morphine was smuggled in the Middle East in camel caravans. They were still used in some places more remote than the environs of Beirut. The narcotics were put inside sealed metal cylinders and forced down the throats of the camels who walked them across the border. When the customs authorities caught on, they installed X-ray machines at the border checkpoints. So the smugglers switched to double rubber bags which could not be detected by X-ray. But the rubber bags sometimes burst inside the camel's stomach and the luckless, doped beast would stagger up to the border like a drunk. Then, the customs agents began to purge suspicious camel caravans at the border. It was a risky and expensive business, for the camels usually had to be slaughtered in order to remove the narcotics intact from their stomachs. It is said that in those days some smugglers substituted unwanted babies for camels, the infants being cheaper to buy and to slaughter than were camels, but these stories, passed on by word of mouth, are not susceptible to verification or proof.

Smuggling methods took a leap forward with the advent of the motorcar in this part of the world. Secret traps and hiding places were built inside and beneath cars and trucks, in the fenders, the gas tanks, inside the upholstery or within the spare tire. The outside of the vehicle always looked the same. Trucks were preferred to automobiles simply because they were bigger and offered more hiding places. On the Road to Damascus, with its heavy traffic of trucks carrying farm produce, a favorite ploy has always been to bury bags of morphine amongst one or two hundred crates of fruits or vegetables carried on a single truck. The sheer work and time involved in searching through such a cargo would deter even the most conscientious border guard. When possible, realistic smugglers went one step farther: They hid their narcotics amongst a truckload of uncured animal hides. The stench of the raw skins was most dissuasive. The latest innovation has been to secrete morphine base in airtight containers deposited inside one of the many oil-tank trucks which ply the roads daily. Detection is next to impossible. The only countermethod available to the police is the informer. There are two distinct types of men who give information to the police, and both are considered essential to police work, whether it involves narcotics, smuggling, robberies or killings. The first, whom the police call an informer, is the type best known to the public: the man who "squeals" on his colleagues and friends for whatever gain it will bring him. He is without loyalty, a loathsome creature, despised and distrusted by both the criminals he betrays and the police who take and use his information. The second type, whom the police call an informant, is less widely known: the man who gives his loyalty to the police and, at their request, infiltrates the underworld and serves as a listening post. He is used by American narcotics, FBI and secret service agents outside of the United States in situations where they themselves cannot penetrate a foreign criminal society. Usually he is a man on the fringe of the criminal world who is a police buff but not qualified by education or background to serve in law enforcement. To the criminal, the informer and informant are indistinguishable from one another. To the police, one is a trustworthy ally paid with rewards for his help and the other is a man to be used when possible, but never trusted. There is one more type of informer, far more dangerous than either of the first two, and that is the woman scorned. Like most men, amorous criminals are often loquacious in bed, unable to resist boasting of their worldly accomplishments. Some of the most spectacular police cases have been initiated by women, once loved and then rejected, who have turned vengeful. They come to the police ready to tell all they know, to cooperate fully and fearlessly, and in return they want no money, no favors, nothing but vengeance.

Many supposedly smart criminals, following the precepts of their trade, have stumbled into the hands of the law without ever knowing where and how they misstepped. The informer, the informant, the vengeful woman equalize the odds in life's game of cops and robbers. It would seem at first glance that the robbers have the advantage of surprise. How can the police know where they will strike or smuggle or escape? But then again, with anyone a potential informer, how can the robbers know what the cops know or don't know?

The large American automobile, containing the high-ranking officer of the Lebanese Sûreté and the unsuspected Armenian narcotics smuggler from Marseilles, stopped only momentarily for the courtesies first at the Syrian control and then at the Lebanese frontier. Then it sped on in the night toward Beirut, its cargo of morphine base in the trunk unsearched, undetected and undisturbed. When one is successful, it is so easy. It is as simple as going through the border without contraband—sometimes, perhaps even most of the time, but not always.

Down the mountain, across the Nahr River, and into Beirut where the Rue al Nahr and the Rue Gouraud led to the central downtown shopping area. The car slowed as it circled the central plaza of the Place des Martyrs, and Levonian pointed out the little side street he wanted. Mallouke parked the car before one of the many cloth and textile shops on the narrow street. Levonian slid out of the automobile, stretched his limbs, and peered in both directions. With a key from his pocket, he unlocked the front door of the darkened shop and returned to the car. Abou Salim, remaining at the wheel, with the engine of the car idling, handed him a separate key to the trunk (which he had been prepared to tell any demanding guard at the frontier he had lost). Levonian lugged all five pieces of baggage into the shop and locked the door behind him. He carried the two important suitcases with him around the counter and behind a hanging drapery into the tiny room in the rear of the shop. A small lamp glowed in the room.

Two men there gazed at him, smiling in anticipation. *"Tout va bien, eh?"*

"Yes," Levonian whispered. "These two are the ones. Check them first and then take them. The other three leave here."

Levonian carried the other three suitcases into the back room and hurried outside. The whole operation had taken perhaps a minute.

Inside the automobile once more, he heaved a great sigh of relief and patted Salim on the arm. "Well, we have time now, let us go somewhere and I can buy you a drink."

Salim headed the car back toward the tourist area on the waterfront and the Kitty Kat Klub, where he favored the dancing girls and the hostesses. He understood without being told that Levonian wished to have him in sight until the narcotics could be removed from the store to another hiding place which he, Abou Salim, would not be able to find. For any intelligent man in this business, it was standard operating procedure.

Thus, before the inspector and Levonian reached the cabaret, the two suitcases of morphine were out of the store and on their way. By the time the inspector and Levonian were cheerfully responding to the *"Bonjour, chéri,"* of the cabaret's hostesses, embarking on what remained of the night's pleasure hours, the morphine cache had reached the safety of the Nahr District of Beirut. This was the Armenian ghetto of Beirut, stretching for several miles along the Nahr River on the northern edge of the city. Its streets were narrow, crooked and dirty; its houses were made of crumbling stucco, its shanties constructed of flattened-out oil drums. Here countless thousands of Armenians lived, poor, traditionally clannish, split by ever-erupting internecine conflicts but loyal to the group as a whole. Most of them were refugees, honest, hard-working and oppressed, but the ghetto was also the haven for the criminal element of the city. This element ruled it by force. Criminals of all sorts were so entrenched that the Beirut gendarmes seldom if ever dared to venture within the Nahr District boundaries. The honest but suspicious citizens of the ghetto refused to talk or cooperate with the police; the criminal element met the police head on with revolvers, rifles and submachine guns. This was their territory. It was not unlike, except in degree, New York's Harlem or Chicago's South Side or Philadelphia's North Side of some years back.

This then was the sanctuary that the Nahr District provided for Léon Levonian's cache of crude morphine in Beirut.

Within this sanctuary, the house to which the morphine was brought was like so many of the houses in the area that it was indistinguishable. Made of white stucco, with the paint peeling, two stories high, protected from observers by a high wall, it was typical of the area, poor on the outside, well apportioned within. The morphine base was brought to this house most casually. The two men from the store parked their car in front, took the two suitcases from the trunk, and marched inside. How could anyone seeing them know what was inside those two ordinary suitcases?

The two men entrusted with the narcotics were close confederates of Léon Levonian. One was his cousin, Elias Faroukian, a young, sensual man with piercing black eyes and a long nose which seemed to hook over his upper lip. He owned the small textile shop but longed to become an impresario of a troupe of dancing girls. He envisioned not only control of the pretty dancers but an excellent means of transporting narcotics, stowing them within the girls' luggage as they traveled from country to country. Customs officials are not likely to challenge a troupe of flirtatious females traveling with trunks and trunks of stage costumes. But until he had the money for this venture, Elias was happy and willing to take orders from his more experienced cousin, Levon. The other man, the one carrying the suitcases, was a Corscian from Marseilles.

Pierre Trigano, born in Marseilles thirty-five years before of parents who had come from Bastia, Corsica, was Léon Levonian's best friend and business partner in narcotics. A good-looking man with the broad shoulders and flat stomach of a welterweight fighter, he might have been handsome but for the small pockmarks which had blotched his face since childhood. He had had a hard life up to the time he had turned to crime. Failure had dogged his every effort, always striking at the time when his hopes were at the highest. He left school at the age of thirteen and was apprenticed to a coppersmith in a maritime shipyard in Marseilles. He became a telegraph operator in the postal service at sixteen, only to be conscripted two years later into the youth labor force organized by the Nazis occupying France. From 1942 to almost the end of the Second World War in 1945, Trigano served in what was tantamount to slave labor in Austria, while other, "smarter" French youths, like Léon Levonian, managed to avoid the conscription. After the war, he operated a small bar in Marseilles which failed. He then bought a tiny coffee-roasting shop on Rue Navarin, at which he nearly starved. His one success was his marriage to a beautiful blonde Marseilles girl of Italian parentage, but then he was forced to resume his craft as a coppersmith in order to make a living. The final blow came when a pressing machine smashed his finger. The first phalanx of his right index finger was amputated. Pierre Trigano then closed his coffee-roasting shop and gave up. He found his way to the Place de l'Opéra and offered his services to narcotics traffickers he met there at the bars. With his past experience as a coppersmith who worked on ship boilers, Trigano had entrée to almost any merchant ship in the harbor. He served a new apprenticeship. Only after he was tried and tested on small errands was he entrusted to carry narcotics on board ships docked in Marseilles or Le Havre. With the excuse of working on the boilers, he could walk aboard almost any ship and make his delivery in the engine room. He became a reliable courier, a man who could be trusted to follow directions, to do what he was told, to deliver narcotics from one place to another. He had not the brains or imagination for the long-range planning essential to an entrepreneur in narcotics, but he and his kind were needed also. As a courier, Trigano soon accumulated more money than he had ever had before. He reopened his little coffee shop and put his wife behind the counter; he bought a small grocery store for his mother and father; and he began to enjoy the company of men who were becoming rich by doing little but special work. It was Trigano who introduced and vouched for his friend, Little Léon, to the powers of the narcotics business. Léon had helped him during his lean years with the coffee shop. Léon had not only purchased coffee for his grocery business from Trigano, he had loaned him money. To the little Corsican this was the truest test of friendship. When Léon later displayed an eager interest in the Corsican underworld of Marseilles, Trigano had taken him along and introduced him. Levonian soon had proved able and willing, more intelligent than his friend Trigano, and also that he had his own money to invest in narcotics enterprises. Thus, over a period of almost ten years, Pierre Trigano and Léon Levonian had grown closer together as trusted friends and business partners in narcotics.

Trigano carried the two suitcases of morphine into the house. He would not allow the hospitable Elias to handle them, for now the narcotics were his responsibility, and such responsibility put him on edge. The endless possibilities of what could go wrong assailed him always when he was handling contraband. He was nervous, but he was professional and efficient, too. This was his part of the operation, as a partner of Levonian's, for it involved the sea.

The necessary arrangements had been made beforehand. The ship was anchored in the harbor, the courier briefed, the time of delivery agreed upon. All Trigano had to do now, the day before delivery, was to recheck and repack fifty kilos of morphine base for a sea voyage.

The merchant ship, with the French colors on its stacks, lay quietly at anchor in the bay a mile or so off the northern edge of Beirut. It showed only its two masthead lights and its starboard green running light to the shore. Its hull, from far off, was as black as the night sea. The hour was far past midnight, and the crew, with the exception of one sole lookout in the wheelhouse, was supposed to be asleep in their bunks or somewhere on liberty ashore. There were no special watches, no special lookouts or guards, for this was not wartime and nothing out of the ordinary was to be expected. The ship was scheduled to dock later that morning to take on its cargo. Access to the ship would be far easier then, and that is what made this time, just a couple of hours before dawn, so appropriate for the task at hand.

Elias had come along only with the greatest reluctance. Physical danger, however slight, was as repugnant to him as physical labor. He had arranged for a boat with a small outboard motor, but only Levonian's insistence had persuaded him to accompany Trigano in the small craft. The morphine base lay in the bottom of the boat, secured now in four separate wrappings all tied together with strong fishing line. In the unlikely event of their being stopped and questioned, Elias, who spoke Arabic, had a story ready. They were going fishing, and they had two fishing poles with them to prove it.

They approached the dark ship with the use of the outboard motor. When they were close enough for Trigano to make out the dim light in the porthole in the side of the ship, he took to the oars. Their boat was nothing more than an oversized rowboat, frequently used for fishing in these waters. It moved ever so slowly with only one man rowing, but it moved silently. Closer still to the freighter but not too close, Trigano flicked a series of dots and dashes with his flashlight. He waited, his eyes on the porthole. Back came the return signal.

He turned in his seat and rowed steadily. As he came alongside, a door opened in the side of the ship. Trigano corrected his course towards the open door. When he reached the ship, he shifted the rowboat around so that its stern faced the gigantic black wall of the vessel's side. Only dimly could he see the opening in the side of the ship and the figure of a man standing there. From the opening somewhere about halfway between the waterline and the open deck, a line came down, played out hand over hand, to the small boat bobbing in the sea. Trigano grasped the line and swiftly tied it around his precious cargo. When the package was secured, he tugged twice on the line, and up and away it went. The door in the side of the ship closed silently and Trigano took up his oars and rowed quietly away in the dead of night, back towards the lights on the shore of Beirut.

On any seagoing freighter or passenger ship of average size, there are said to be more than thirty thousand places in which to hide narcotics. Customs and police experts, who have devoted their careers to searching out contraband aboard ships, might possibly know twenty-nine thousand of these hiding places, but never all thirty thousand. Large quantities of narcotics are transported across the Mediterranean or the Atlantic more often by ship than by airplane, because it is a "safer" way to travel. There are so many more shipping companies and so many more hiding places aboard each ship, that it is impossible for customs agents to search every ship reaching Marseilles or New York. Unless tipped off in advance by an informer, routine customs searches almost never uncover narcotics. Even forewarned, the odds are with the hider rather than the seeker. A ship offers extraordinary hiding places besides the usual lockers, closets, lifeboats, storerooms and cubbyholes. Men have secreted narcotics in the walls, beneath the flooring or above the ceiling of cabins, or inside the hollow places of complex machinery, or within an unused section of piping. Almost everything within the hull of a ship can be taken apart and put together again, and so, with a screwdriver and a bit of privacy, a crewman can stash narcotics away almost anywhere on a ship and defy anyone to find it in a practicable search, short of stripping the ship down to its hull.

The seaman who took aboard Léon Levonian's fifty-kilo cache of morphine for the voyage across the Mediterranean was a Corsican named Georges Seca who had a lifetime of sea duty behind him. Now in his fifties, he was sailing on this ship as a supernumerary assistant cook. He had paid the regular crewman to call in sick so that he could replace him for this one voyage. As a regular courier for Jean Paul Savelli in Marseilles, Georges Seca earned enough money in smuggling narcotics so that he now went to sea only when there was a shipment to be handled. He had the union seniority and the friends to assure him a place on any vessel of his choosing, and in this way no particular ship was used for smuggling more than any other.

Georges Seca, being not unlike most other men, preferred to go to no more trouble or work than was necessary, and on this Mediterranean run from Beirut to Marseilles, he saw no need for any of the more esoteric hiding places. Having taken the fifty-kilo package aboard at the ship's side port nearest the galley, Seca deftly slipped it into a burlap sack ordinarily used for potatoes. He shouldered the load to the potato locker on the deck beneath the galley, and in the privacy of the storage locker, where only he came to fetch the day's supplies to the kitchen, he tucked the sack of morphine among a ton of potatoes. Only he knew which sack of "potatoes" was different from all the others. It was simple and safe, and the narcotics, as long as they remained in this locker, could not be traced to him. Anyone might have put that one bag there. Nor would he have to touch it until it reached its destination. It was tucked beneath some other bags in the rear of the locker, only its top flap showing, and that flap was discernible only to someone who could recognize it. He, for instance, could see the flap each time he opened the locker; anyone else taking potatoes from the front end of the locker would not notice it.

Seca padlocked the potato bin and ambled up to the galley for his first cup of coffee of the morning. He had only a half hour to wait for the start of his regular morning watch.

Two mornings later, the freighter, having taken on a mixed cargo, sailed from Beirut. On deck, as the ship left the pier, an assistant cook waved a large white handkerchief, and on shore, a short, Italian-looking Frenchman with a pockmarked face observed the departure through binoculars, and then made a telephone call. Léon Levonian smiled. His merchandise had come a long way, some six thousand miles, and now it was going home. Marseilles was the home of narcotics, the hub of the business.

# 8

# Marseilles

Léon Levonian's cargo, despite its potential
value of more than ten million dollars if and when it reached the
streets of New York, arrived unannounced and quite inconspicuously in the Port of Marseilles. In the daily commercial flow
of the largest and busiest harbor facility in France, the fourth
most active port in all of Europe, one-hundred-odd pounds of
brown powder was an insignificantly small item, no matter what
its ultimate value. After all, the Port of Marseilles, which
stretched for miles and miles along fully half of the city's border
on the Mediterranean, handled more than 35,000,000 tons of
cargo and some twenty thousand ship movements in and out of
the port every year. Only the consignees of Levonian's fifty kilos
had made plans for this particular shipment.

By mid-morning, the big incoming freighter, one of about
thirty ships to arrive that day, had tied up at its pier in the Bassin
de la Grande Joliette. The pier was crowded with the busy activity of machines and men unloading the vessel when Assistant
Cook Georges Seca, who had taken Levonian's narcotics aboard,
strolled off the ship, clean. Carrying nothing but his own belong-
ings, he submitted to the inspection by the customs guard at the
shipyard entrance with complete nonchalance. The morphine
remained aboard.

Seca had made it a point not to come in contact with the burlap bag of narcotics after he had placed it in the potato locker. From the door of the locker he checked it visually each day at sea, but he did not touch it. Before leaving the ship, however, he pointed out the hiding place and that particular burlap bag to one other man, a deckhand who had signed on that morning for the next voyage. He would take it off the ship.

It would cost Levonian's associates a bit more money. But this extra link in the chain of those handling the merchandise was considered well worth the protection it gave. Seca might know the source of the morphine but he would not know to whom it was to be delivered or its true owner. The new seaman would know the collector but not the owner or the source of the morphine.

Once ashore, seaman Seca reported to his only contact, Trigano; he had completed his particular task. Trigano, in turn, telephoned Jean Paul Savelli, and after they had met, Savelli made his arrangements with the chemist who would convert the morphine to heroin. Business was not discussed on the telephone. The calls were limited to arrangements for meetings. Each link in the operation was clearly separated so that if one man were to be caught by the police, he could not, even if he wanted to, lead the police further than one link in the complex chain of conspiracy in handling the narcotics. The couriers, for example, knew Trigano's role, but not that of Levonian, and none of them knew which chemist in Marseilles would receive physical possession of the merchandise. Jean Paul Savelli knew all the men and arrangements involved, but then, of course, he himself did not touch the merchandise.

The day was given over largely to making the final arrangements for the safe transfer of the morphine from the ship to the chemist. Meetings were held in guarded places, usually in the back of a neighborhood bar where every patron was known and a venerable alcoholic was paid to stand lookout for any unfamiliar face. Telephone conversations were coded in generalities which only the conspirators could interpret correctly. It was assumed by these merchants of heroin that the Marseilles police dogged their every footstep and monitored their phone calls and so, whether a phone conversation or a particular trip pertained to business or was completely innocent, evasive action always was taken as a matter of course. Trigano's phone call to Savelli, for example, went something like this:

"Hello, this is me. How are you?"

"Yes, I was expecting your call."

"I need to see you . . . I am there now, can you come?"

"No, I can't go up there . . . what if you come down?"

"Okay, I'll come down in a half hour, is that okay?"

"Yes, half an hour. Did you see the guy?"

"Who do you mean?"

"The guy we saw together before your trip. You know, the tall one."

"Yes, I understand. I saw him and he's fine, just fine."

"Good, then I'll see you in half an hour or so."

What could the police learn from that conversation, unless they recognized Trigano's voice, knew that he had flown to Beirut a week before, knew that Seca was the tall one mentioned, and knew where the men had prearranged their meeting place? The conversation could refer equally to an arrangement for an innocent meeting or for a conspiratorial one. How could an outsider differentiate? The police might, if they were fast, try to follow Savelli from his apartment, if they knew he were leaving it, but the odds would be stacked against them.

Savelli left his apartment by a rear service exit, but he did not take his own large automobile. He pulled away from a side street in a friend's car. He drove three blocks from his apartment house and then circled that block twice, and at the end of one long side street, he double-parked for a quarter of an hour while he observed if anyone was following him. He was an expert at this. He went through similar, although not exactly the same, maneuvers almost every time he left his home, even when his mission was a package of cigarettes at the corner tobacco shop.

The Corsicans who dealt in drugs in Marseilles were proud of their reputation as the cleverest criminals in the world. They took positive joy in confusing the police for the sake of the joke alone. They realized intuitively that the creative element in a career of crime is the variety of operational methods. In their every move, criminal or innocent, they sought to avoid any pattern which the police might read and use. The first thought of a

Corsican narcotics merchant upon rising in the morning, it is said, is, "What did I do yesterday and how can I do it differently today?" If he went downtown in his own car the day before, he would take a taxi today. If he used one route today, he would take another tomorrow. If he met with a co-conspirator one day, he would be sure to be seen with nine nonconspirators that same day.

If only because they so outnumbered them, the narcotics merchants of Marseilles were able to keep better tabs on the police arrayed against them than the other way around. The Narcotics Squad of the Sûreté in Marseilles numbered only twelve detectives, and this was a fourfold increase over their force during the 1950's. The Central Bureau for the Repression of Narcotics in Paris also consisted of only twelve men, but then narcotics addiction was not a social plague in France as it is in America. It was considered in France a commercial crime.

In Marseilles, the professionals among the narcotics traffickers knew the narcotics police officers by sight, and they posted men outside Sûreté headquarters to check the cars and the license plates of the cars the detectives used.

The Narcotics Squad knew the leading traffickers just as well, and by various means at their disposal they kept abreast of the trends and the practices of the narcotics trade. The difficulty was in catching the practitioners in the act of the crime. The Marseilles Narcotics Squad keep cross-reference files listing more than twelve thousand names of men who at one time or other have been involved in or suspected of trafficking in narcotics. But a special list covers fewer than one hundred who are thought to be currently active and significant in the flow of heroin from Marseilles to America.

For as long as anyone can remember, Marseilles has been the hub of the worldwide flow of opium-derived narcotics. It is a venerable city, proud and traditional, beautiful and friendly, situated in the Mediterranean, so near the Atlantic, at the junction of sea lanes which crisscross from Asia, the Near East, Africa, South America, and in part from the United States and Canada. Ships, supplies and sailors pour into Marseilles from all parts of the world. Its enormous waterfront became over the years an international oasis for the adventurers, the homeless, the woebegone and the criminals whom the sea has washed to its shore. Marseilles' waterfront became a criminal's hideaway, a smuggler's paradise, a revolving marketplace for contraband where a sailor could buy, sell or trade any item, large or small, stolen or smuggled from any part of the world. Extralegal activities on the Marseilles waterfront expanded in time from mere smuggling and barter in stolen valuables to traffic in narcotics, white slavery, prostitution, counterfeit money, gambling, gunfights and gang warfare. As a great seaport, whose heart was its commerce, the tentacles of its criminal octopus reached far beyond the borders of the city itself.

Domination over these various lucrative crimes and rackets was won eventually by various means, including wits and guns, by a single group of men in Marseilles—the Corsicans.

Marseilles is sometimes described as the largest city in Corsica, for there are perhaps four times as many Corsicans living in Marseilles as in Bastia, the largest city of that rocklike island which lies in the Mediterranean halfway between France and Italy. The Corsicans are one of the proudest groups of men in the world, with the national characteristic, if there are any such things as national characteristics, of sincerely believing they are naturally, by birth, better than any race of men. They flocked to Marseilles and to southern France because Corsica itself was too poor to support them, and although Corsica is a *département* of France, just as Hawaii is an integral part of the United States, the Corsican never describes or thinks of himself as a Frenchman. The average Corsican might spend all of his adult years in Marseilles, but he returns to Corsica for the "important moments" of his life: He is born there, he marries there, his wife returns there to have his children and he retires and dies there. His godhead is Napoleon and the Emperor of France was a Corsican, and so he sees no need to forsake his rich heritage. He lives in Marseilles as part of a clan, proud of and loyal to his own people.

Despite their pride, however, the Corsicans came to the mainland of France years ago like any minority—in waves of immigration like the Irish, Italians, Jews and Puerto Ricans came to America—and found only the most menial jobs open to them. In Marseilles, the sea offered the most available employment; crime offered the greatest opportunity; narcotics offered the greatest profit. They fought the Frenchmen, the Arabs, the Algerians and anyone else disputing their control over the spoils of crime, and they secured over the years their absolute monopoly over narcotics and their control over white slavery and prostitution.

The actual number of Corsicans who turned to crime, of course, was a minute percentage of the hundreds of thousands of islanders who came to France to live honest, hard-working and productive lives there, but they banded together in a fraternity as close-knit as that of the Sicilians who turned to crime in America and became known as the Mafia or Cosa Nostra. They maintained the same code of loyalty to one another and silence to outsiders, on pain of death. Just as did their "Sicilian cousins," they fought internecine wars, some of them based upon old village rivalries, others fought over territorial or spoils jurisdiction, such as the "Combinati Affair" in the 1950's in which thirty-five men were killed in street ambushes over a disputed boatload of stolen American cigarettes. But such feuds, reminiscent of the gang wars of the 1920's and 1930's in America, gave way in France more recently to a new sophistication in organized crime which parallels the most modern business methods.

The Corsican lords of crime in Marseilles began to work more in concert than against one another; an enterprising man was taken in as a partner rather than fought as a competitor. Meetings and conferences are held so often in the bars of the Opéra District of Marseilles, that the district near the Old Port has become known familiarly as the Little Vatican or the Vatican of Crime. The decisions made at these conferences are considered as binding as a religious edict. There is even a man in the Little Vatican who is known as The Pope. A retired narcotics smuggler, he acts as an impartial arbitrator in all disputes taken to him and his decision is regarded as infallible. In one instance not long ago, he found an accused narcotics trafficker guilty of stupidity and poor judgment rather than betrayal in hiring a courier who lost $120,000 worth of heroin to the police, and he "decreed" that the accused sell the two hotels he owned within forty-eight hours and turn over the proceeds to the group which suffered the loss. The hotel owner cleared eighty thousand dollars, which he paid over immediately, discharging his debt, and he continues in the heroin business today, a healthy but poorer man.

Of all the men who frequented the Little Vatican, this little city within a city, perhaps the best known and reputedly the most powerful was Jean Paul Savelli. The Sûreté, in an official report on the narcotics situation in France, had said of him, "He should be considered not as a single link in a chain, but as one of the great ones in this special commerce." Savelli's fraternity was considered to be the most powerful one in Marseilles, and by reputation in his own milieu, he was thought of as the executive vice-president of the General Motors of narcotics. The police knew Savelli well, and he knew them, too. "When you catch me," he told one narcotics detective who had trailed him for two months, "when you catch me, then, you will be The Pope—but you will never catch me because I would know your face in a hundred. Now, let me buy you a drink and then you can go back to your little office."

The police had a thick dossier on him going back almost ten years, but not once (thus far) had they been able to gather the precise and complete evidence required by French law with which to indict him. A familiar, handsome figure in the Marseilles underworld, Savelli resembled to a certain degree Rudolph Valentino. He had regular features, a dark complexion, piercing dark eyes, broad shoulders, flat stomach and long, polished black hair. Born in Corsica at Olmeta di Tud in 1920, he grew up in the island's largest city, Bastia, and came to Marseilles at the age of seventeen to work as a hairdresser. He worked in Marseilles, but he returned "home" to marry in 1942, and again to see his first daughter born in 1944. After the Second World War, he divided his time between Corsica and Marseilles and going to sea. From seaman to smuggling to narcotics, from 1950 on, Jean Paul Savelli never did a day's honest work again. He left his wife with the beauty salon in Corsica and lived openly with his mistress in Marseilles. He accounted for his money and lavish style of living by insisting that he had won six million francs in a national lottery and that he earned fifty thousand francs a week by gambling. The police could neither prove nor disprove his claims that he had been a part owner of three gambling casinos in Havana under Batista;

that he had financial interests in several Marseilles bars; that he made a good deal of money at the races and casinos; and that he could afford to live and travel as extravagantly as he did. His varied activities and interests made it impossible to prove that his wealth came primarily from narcotics. Savelli, to be sure, was on the list of narcotics suspects in countries around the world. He was *persona non grata* specifically in the United States, Canada, Cuba and Mexico, but he had not, at least up to this time, ever been in jail.

Although his travels were somewhat curtailed, he was now in a position to pay others to do what he himself had done before. Like an executive vice-president, he was concerned with the management; he no longer found it necessary to work on the assembly line itself.

In their planning, Savelli, Levonian and Trigano assigned the first day in port of the freighter to the crew members of the ship: Let them carry ashore their own contraband when the guards were most punctilious in their searches. Everyone leaving any of the Marseilles shipyards was given a routine search, particularly ships' crews. It was well known that merchant-marine men around the world augmented their meager ship pay by smuggling. The opportunity came with the job. Anything that could be bought or stolen in one country and sold in another at a profit was stock in trade—silks, artifacts, gold, watches, transistor radios, pharmaceuticals and illicit drugs. Virtually every experienced sailor took his chances from time to time, if not on a regular basis, at walking past the shipyard guards with something illegal in his possession. Some were solitary entrepreneurs, others worked on salary for regular combines handling black market and stolen merchandise. To an extent, this smuggling by seamen was tolerated philosophically by the authorities, for they realized that it, like prostitution, was a way of life and could never be completely eliminated. Of course, the more valuable items such as narcotics, diamonds or gold were not on anyone's "tolerated" list. But how could the police or customs differentiate what one sailor was sneaking ashore from that of another, without stripping every man who walked by a shipyard gate?

Narcotics, being small, easily concealed and extraordinarily valuable, topped the list of desirable contraband handled by seamen who were experienced and nervy enough to get into that trade. Some stashed a kilo of morphine or heroin or hashish or even opium in their handbags or inside their clothing and hoped for the best when walking by the customs men. Others sewed the drugs into the lining of their kapok jackets. Leather hassocks sold throughout the Near East could conceal five or even ten kilos of morphine in the stuffing. The guards at the gates usually nodded the familiar hassocks through, sometimes in exchange for a gift of one, since it was clearly impractical to take apart and put together each souvenir carried by a sailor. When hassocks became temporarily suspect, there were dolls, stuffed animals and a hundred other items which could serve as makeshift containers. It was not too difficult to devise a way of getting something past the customs guards.

But with a larger cache such as fifty kilos, rather than attempt to go past the guards, one goes around them. It is dangerous but not too difficult; if one is caught, he is caught usually with the evidence in his hand and there is no escape from jail. But the shipyards are vast, impossible for the guards to patrol effectively.

After dark on the second night the ship was tied up in port, seaman Antoine Guidano moved Levonian's fifty kilos from the potato locker to a hiding place in his cabin. Guidano was an able-bodied seaman approaching middle age, a stupid brute of a man whose only apparent pleasure was to get roaring drunk at irregular intervals. When sober, though, he had the instincts of a wild animal. Like a rat in a warehouse, he could sense when danger lurked near him or where a trap had been set in anticipation of his escapade. He had been chosen for this task now, as before, because he could be trusted to do what he had been told and nothing more, because he would adhere to the code of silence if he were caught, and because he was expendable. The most dangerous jobs, vis-à-vis the police, were given almost always to the least important men in the operation. This is not to say that these men were anything less than capable. For a seaman like Guidano, stealing things off a ship was like child's play, more natural to him than the simple tasks he performed as a deckhand aboard ship.

Inside the burlap bag, he found the four separate packages

bound in waterproof paper and tied securely. One of the packages he slipped into an ordinary seaman's handbag. With this in his hand, he strolled to an open deck of the quiet ship and surveyed the pier, piled high with cargo and ship provisions. The path from the ship to the dockyard gate was lighted in a fashion, but otherwise the pier was dark and deserted and silent. The open decks of the ship also were safe, for the few men who remained aboard in port were engaged below decks playing cards, in bull and bragging sessions, or sleeping off the first night's revelry. Anyone who might encounter a fellow crew member would hardly question his activities on deck. Guidano walked carefully, his senses alert, down the ship's aft gangway to the pier. He picked his way between the stacks of packaged wares to a high load of lumber which he had chosen before. For an ordinary man, that walk from the ship to the hiding place against a background of minor sounds and imagined footsteps in the dark, with ten to fifteen kilos of narcotics in hand, might have rubbed the raw edges of his nerves to the point of excruciation. At any moment, one might be confronted with a voice of authority. "You, there! What are you doing there? What have you got there in that bag, eh?" Just that and it would be all over. One might run, to no avail, or one might try to explain that he was new to the ship and just happened to find this bag containing a fortune's worth of morphine. But Antoine Guidano had the steely nerves of an experienced burglar, not those of an ordinary man.

Guidano tucked his package beneath an overhang on one of the piles of lumber, and then, having zippered up his bag once again, he walked nonchalantly back to the deck of his ship. There he once again surveyed the surroundings and checked the silence which signaled safety. Then he made another trip, from his cabin to the deck, to the pier, to the pile of lumber, then back to the ship and his cabin again. Four trips in all, and the hundredweight of morphine, enough by itself to set up a man in the illicit drugs business, was safely deposited on one of the hundred-odd piers in the Port of Marseilles, which was itself separated from the city by an eight-foot wire fence and whatever customs or police officers might be on patrol that night. For Antoine

Guidano, the first part of his job was finished. Now he had to wait for the right time.

There are some men, on either side of the law, among the experts on the subject who describe the flow of illicit narcotics as moving not from hand to hand or from one man to another, but rather from one hiding place to another. In their view, these fifty kilos had traveled not from a group of farmers in Turkey to Emin Deli to Mustafa Aydin to Celebi the Smuggler to Abdurahman to Levonian to Trigano to Georges Seca and to Antoine Guidano, but rather from various hiding places in barns in and near Afyon to a garage in Gazientep, to a farmhouse in Kilis, to a roadside near Azaz, to a cave in the Syrian Mountains, to a house in Aleppo and an apartment in Damascus, and on to a shop and then a house in Beirut, and a storage locker on a ship, and now a pier in the Port of Marseilles. This movement from hiding place to hiding place gives a fundamental advantage to the smugglers over the police, customs and narcotics agents who try to stop them. The police must find the narcotics in order to produce the evidence against the smugglers. The narcotics are the *corpus delicti* of the crime. And it is considerably more difficult to find a small hiding place than a man. The difficulty is that the man who traffics in narcotics, no matter at what level, will lay his hand on the *corpus delicti* of his crime only when he is certain in his mind that the police are nowhere around. The final and ultimate trafficker in the worldwide conspiracy in narcotics is, of course, the addict. He puts the narcotics in his arm and there it remains beyond police scrutiny forever.

At this stage of the journey, however, the fifty kilos of morphine was hidden on the pier as Antoine Guidano sat in his cabin checking his wristwatch for the appointed hour. If anything went wrong now, if anyone spotted his movements, if any police or customs men should appear on the scene, then he would not approach those four packages on the dock again. He would walk into town and make a single telephone call and then they would send someone else to make the pick-up tonight, tomorrow, tomorrow night, anytime it once again became safe.

Guidano climbed to the deck of the ship again and looked around. The raw sea air went right to the bone. It was dark and damp and cold. But it was quiet and safe, too. Guidano walked off the ship, past the packages under the woodpile, and waited in the dark near the wire fence, empty-handed.

At precisely the appointed hour, he heard the quiet engine of the Citroën approaching. The black car seemed to slide to the curb in the quiet of the night. He could barely hear the click of the latch as the driver opened the door. Nor did he slam it shut. He gazed up and down the street and quickly approached the gate.

"Antoine?"

"Pierre?"

"Yes, quickly now."

Guidano moved swiftly indeed. In two short trips, he brought the four packages to his side of the gate. It was ridiculously simple. He could reach his arm to the top of the eight-foot gate and hand over each package. Pierre Trigano relayed the narcotics into the trunk of his car, covered the four bundles with a blanket, shut the lid firmly, and drove off. The whole transfer, that moment of danger, took hardly more than a minute.

Proceeding at a lawful speed and paying special heed to the traffic signals and the traffic abroad on that night, Pierre Trigano headed back towards the Boulevard de Paris and the center of Marseilles, skirting the Old Port and the Opéra District, where one might almost always come upon police. He worked his way along the intertwining avenues and boulevards to the quiet Castellane District in the sixth arrondissement. Only an act of God could disrupt the success of this carefully planned venture, he thought, for here he was, Pierre Trigano, a man without a police record, the son of a retired policeman, lawfully married, the father of a darling daughter, driving a lawfully rented, perfectly ordinary automobile. Yet, anything could happen for whatever reason. Trigano recognized his own nervousness although he knew he masked it from those who observed him. He knew that he performed well and that of late he had risen in the organization and in the esteem of the men who entrusted him with more and more important tasks. His status had improved constantly since he had brought in Little Léon to work with him. There had been hints that something new, something bigger than anything they had done before, might be proposed to them both at a meeting scheduled for the next day.

Trigano turned off the Avenue du Prado onto the narrow residential Rue Flaque and parked the Citroën in front of a gray limestone house, the number of which he noted. He carefully locked and checked the doors and the trunk of the car before he left it, and then he strolled around to the Rue Edmond Rostand where he had parked his own automobile, a tiny sports convertible, of which he was inordinately proud. Trigano drove back to a particular bar in the Opéra District where he was to meet Levonian. He did not look around as he walked, although he was sure that someone else was somewhere within sight and that before he had had his first drink with Levonian, the Citroën with the fifty kilos would be on its way to its destination.

The Narcotics Squad of the Marseilles police would have traded ten Triganos if they had been able to follow the man who drove the Citroën from the Rue Flaque to where he was going.

# 9

# The Clandestine Laboratory

Early the following morning, not long after dawn, in the village of Aubagne, about seventeen kilometers east of Marseilles, a tall and exceedingly thin middle-aged man completed his preparations for a motor trip. His manservant carefully laid his expensive suitcase in the trunk of his Mercedes 300SE, and as the engine of the big coupe warmed up in the morning cold, the tall man gazed with affection upon the beauty of his estate. Box hedges ten feet high lined the frontage of the property. Flower beds of prize roses offset the gleaming white of the two-story house in which his wife and two daughters lay sleeping. The swimming pool was empty for the winter and the tennis court lay idle, too. The master of this estate was quite content with his present station in life. He had been born a poor man, receiving no formal education beyond grade school, but he had made his own way in life.

"If Madame Paoli asks, tell her I said I hope to be back in four days, not more than five," he informed his manservant. "I am off to Lyons." The small man nodded and went to unlock the gate which guarded the privacy of the estate. The big Mercedes rolled through and onto the service road which led to the double-lane highway beyond.

Aubagne is a town of some 18,000 inhabitants which some people consider a suburb of Marseilles, located on the Expressway East which leads from Marseilles to St. Tropez, Antibes and Monaco. It is surrounded by good hunting country and those who live there are either very rich, owning large estates, or quite poor, eking out a living by pottery work or serving those in Aubagne who are rich.

Josef Paoli was very rich. In the $100,000 home he had just left, he had a library of first editions and rare books worth perhaps sixty thousand dollars, though he could barely read. He liked to show off his expensive volumes, such as the *Works of Dante* as illustrated by Salvador Dali, and to challenge his guests to estimate the price of each book. Similarly, he took a childish pride in a magnificent crystal chandelier in his dining room, which had cost seven thousand dollars. Each piece of furniture in his home, selected with the help of the finest decorators and antique experts, gave Josef Paoli happiness and pleasure.

He had spent almost one million dollars so far in converting a nine-hundred-acre hunting estate in the Basses Alpes region, north of Marseilles, to farming and sheep-grazing land. But this he considered an investment. He meant to retire soon, when the right moment came. Meanwhile, the Basses Alpes provided the best game-hunting ground in all of France.

Josef Paoli thought of his retirement almost always. He made plans and he put them off. For all his money, he could not buy fat. Just over six feet tall, he could not get his weight up to 150 pounds for more than a week or so. It would always fall off again, and his skin, a dark sickly yellow, seemed to hang on his bones. Despite his big car and his tailored clothes, he looked like a cadaver of a man. He was not well and he knew it.

He drove carefully along the quiet road which led to the Expressway, checking his rear-view mirror constantly. Three miles from his home, he stopped, waited a minute or so, and then he turned back, driving about one mile in the direction from which he had come. Then he pulled off to the side of the road. He lifted the hood of his car and feigned an inspection of the engine, but he looked up and down the road. Slamming down the hood, he took binoculars from the front seat and checked the road again. Only when he was certain that the road was deserted as far as he could scan in both directions did he reenter his car. The engine caught with a roar and he drove several hundred yards further and on to a dirt road which led to the mountains. Dust billowed up over the shiny Mercedes for the quarter mile to the bleak wall of another Aubagne estate, not more than two miles from his own. Even before he beeped his horn, his arrival was greeted with the snarling yowls of the dogs on the other side of the wall. They were ferocious beasts, those six German dogs, trained to attack any trespasser, but Albert Guerin, their master, was there at the gate, as arranged, waiting to admit Paoli inside without delay.

The excited dogs surrounded the slow-moving car, ready to pounce. "Shut up, shut up now!" Paoli called from the window and the dogs subsided at the sound of the recognized voice. With the compulsive care he gave every task, Paoli drove the Mercedes into a vacant stall of the garage. The garage, almost the size of the house, stored the large truck, the two panel trucks and the three or four automobiles needed in the establishment. The house itself was a one-story ranch model painted a deep barn-red offset by white shutters, with two dormer bedrooms added in the attic. Although smaller than Paoli's own home, this too was an estate, for its property lines extended far beyond the walls. Albert Guerin was the owner on record, but it had cost Paoli a good forty thousand dollars to buy this establishment for him. This too was an investment. This was Joscf Paoli's place of business, his heroin laboratory, the largest and best equipped of all the secret, illicit laboratories in France. He was the true, secret owner of the villa, and he insured Guerin's loyalty to him with the promise to give the small man the mortgage as a gift when he himself retired. Guerin served not only as his front for the villa but also as his chief assistant in the laboratory; the in-service training would make him in time Paoli's professional successor.

Josef Paoli was known in his narrow milieu as the best heroin chemist in France and hence the best in the world. He was at the pinnacle of his life's work. Born in Corsica in 1915, he had gone to sea as a teen-ager, become a bartender on several passenger liners, and then had been taken in as an apprentice by his half brother, who was in his time one of the three most successful heroin chemists in Marseilles. Paoli worked for his half brother as Guerin now worked for him until his half brother, after twenty years of illicit chemistry, had been indicted and convicted for manufacturing heroin although the Marseilles police never once located a single one of his clandestine laboratories. His half brother had forfeited his bail to flee from France, and although he was living comfortably where he was, Paoli intended to retire before he was caught; he meant to spend his remaining years as a gentleman farmer in the Basses Alpes. Over the past four years as an independent chemist, he had stashed away money enough for that retirement, but business was so good, he could not bring himself to quit. They knew of him by reputation in America, the Sicilians who bought heroin wholesale, and they wanted his particular product because it was the best on the market. He was considered an equal of the very top men in the narcotics business, men like Dominique Benucci and the others. Everyone in the trade who knew him treated him with respect. After all, it was the chemist who made Marseilles the hub and nerve center of the international flow of heroin. Without the chemist, the merchants would have no product to sell in the Golden Market of New York. Others had tried to match the quality of French heroin, of course, and they continued to try in Turkey, in Lebanon and in Mexico, but their product was considerably inferior. In Italy, the police had long ago cracked down on the existing laboratories there, and in the Far East, the local demand for smoking and eating opium consumed virtually all of the production. The French chemist was in a class by himself, Paoli knew, and deserved his high prices and the respect of his peers for his specialized knowledge. Paoli considered himself a man of stature, a professional man no matter how illicit his enterprise. Albert Guerin, his laboratory assistant, doted upon him as would a student upon a Nobel Prize scientist; only the milieu in which they labored was different.

Paoli had set a precise routine for his laboratory which Guerin followed impeccably. When the chemist had parked his Mercedes, Guerin closed the garage door to hide the automobile from anyone who might spy over the villa walls. Alongside the Mercedes sat the rented black Citroën, which Guerin had used the night before. At a nod from Paoli, he opened the trunk of the car for the first time since the previous night so that Paoli himself could inspect the number of packages delivered.

Each of the men carried two packages through the back door of the garage to the house and down into the basement. Here was the laboratory: a large room enameled white, brightly lighted, and superbly equipped with multiple gas burners, running water, balloon flasks and tubing, suction pumps and the best paraphernalia that money could buy. The superiority of this equipment as much as his own skill was the secret of Paoli's reputation as the best heroin chemist in France. Most other heroin laboratories were temporary affairs, hastily assembled for a specific job, either in an old and vacant country home or in a trailer or on a boat, and then, when a specific amount of heroin was made, the laboratory was disassembled and hidden away or moved so that the police would not have time to pinpoint its location. Paoli's innovation was to change from the temporary, movable lab he had used before to this permanent workroom, in which he could operate with the best equipment on a regular weekly basis and store vast quantities of the chemicals needed to convert morphine to heroin. This laboratory was successfully kept secret, for no one—not even his best customer, Dominique Benucci—knew of its location. Albert Guerin and a second laboratory assistant, Francesco Maneri, and their wives lived on the property, but they were accomplices in the operation, just as vulnerable as he himself. The wives were responsible for keeping up the house and for preparing the meals. Paoli worked the laboratory only three and occasionally four days a week. Any more he considered injurious to his health, but for those three or four days he remained inside the villa at all times, eating and sleeping there. It reduced to the absolute minimum the risk of accidental detection of his coming and going. Moreover, it shrewdly misdirected his customers as well as the police: One would hardly guess that a man would take a three- or four-day trip to a place of business only two miles from his home.

Josef Paoli was optimistic that the police would never find his cherished laboratory. He trusted the two couples who worked for him. They lived quiet lives here, never entertaining, remote from Marseilles, one of several hundred similar walled-in estates, protected by a Frenchman's traditional high regard for the privilege of privacy. Yet, Aubagne itself was small enough for word of any unusual police inquiries or activity to reach him or the Guerins in time to clean out the laboratory—or so Paoli devotedly wished. A fatalist, he believed he had done everything possible to protect his operation. More than that he could not do. The odds were that he would retire before the authorities stumbled upon the biggest laboratory in all of France.

The work routine at the laboratory was well established. The four packages of morphine base, supposedly representing fifty kilos, were unwrapped from their waterproof bindings only when Paoli was on hand to inspect and weigh each of the plastic bags of brown powder. He called out the precise weights to Guerin who noted each figure on a sheet of paper. At the end, he added up the columns of measurements. Anything under fifty kilos, Paoli would report to Benucci before opening the plastic bags. Any fraction over the stipulated amount would be tucked away in Paoli's private stockpile, as a bonus rightfully earned by his more delicate scales. Besides, Paoli knew that contrary to popular belief the chemical process of converting morphine to the highly refined heroin increases the weight of the finished product. Because the process of conversion is that of chemical synthesis, one kilogram of morphine base will normally produce 1,217 grams of heroin. Thus, the chemical molecular weight of heroin (diacetyl-morphine) is 369; morphine has a molecular weight of 303.

Paoli inspected the quality of the morphine delivered to him and sneered. He invariably held the morphine makers of Turkey and the Near East in disdain. Always before beginning the conversion process he was obliged to repurify the morphine base. This was a simple process of mixing the morphine with acetone in large enamel basins and allowing the mixture to stand for several hours. Guerin and his helper alternated in stirring the mixtures while Paoli himself went upstairs to have a second breakfast. Keeping the stomach full was important to a chemist working with morphine and Paoli was an exacting man. The acetone worked to separate the morphine from the other alkaloids of opium, such as papaverine, narcotine and narceine, as well as the impurities which had not been removed by the crude extracting methods used in the hills of Syria.

Paoli returned to the laboratory to supervise the filtering of the mixture. Ordinarily, this would be a prolonged process, the dripping of the fluid drop by drop through fluted filter paper into a flask, but Paoli used a suction pump to speed up the operation. Occasionally, if the morphine base was of particularly poor quality, Paoli would further purify it with tartaric acid and bone black. But this time he had only to dry out the mixture to have suitable morphine free of impurities and secondary alkaloids. For this drying out and evaporation process, he used a specially designed heating closet, a costly little apparatus which more than paid for itself by the time it saved.

With a relatively pure form of morphine, Paoli now was ready to make heroin. The actual conversion process is not particularly complex or difficult for a trained chemist with the proper equipment. Yet there is an expertise required which is beyond the scope of anyone unfamiliar with the properties and reactions of certain chemicals. Amateurs with inadequate training are usually able to turn out only low-purity heroin, and that at the risk of blowing up themselves and their laboratories. In Turkey, Lebanon, Mexico and elsewhere, explosions in clandestine laboratories take their annual toll of ambitious but amateurish men who practice illicit chemistry. In Italy in the early 1950's, the police cracked down on those perfume and plastics manufacturers who moonlighted in heroin conversion; the Italian underworld, it seemed, had little heart for chemistry. In France, the heartland of heroin production, the clandestine laboratories were run after the Second World War by bona fide chemists and laboratory assistants who had, for one reason or another, turned to crime. But these men soon ran afoul of the law or the code of the underworld. Their place was taken over by certain adept Marseilles criminals. It seemed that it was easier for an experienced criminal to learn the skills of the chemist than for a bona fide chemist to acquire the skills of a successful crook. Paoli had learned his particular brand of chemistry from his half brother who had acquired his know-how from a German-trained chemist who had been murdered attempting to cheat an irate customer.

The semiliterate Paoli, former seaman, laborer and bartender, had become fascinated with the intricacies of chemistry, and he read and reread snatches here and there in an extensive library of chemistry books he kept in his laboratory. He sought to improve his knowledge and his skills beyond what he had learned from working experience. He considered himself a dedicated chemist, a skilled technician, a professional man: He had status.

He prided himself on not only knowing how to convert morphine to heroin, but also delving into the whys and wherefores of the chemical process. Pure morphine is transformed chemically into a crude or impure heroin by a process known as acetylation. That is, the morphine is treated with acetic anhydride, one part morphine to two parts acetic anhydride, and heated double-boiler style at 85 degrees centigrade for six hours. Acetic anhydride is a common type of acid used widely in chemistry laboratories as a reagent, particularly in the production of plastics, film, and synthetic fabrics derived from cellulose. It is a colorless, pungent and extremely corrosive liquid which must be handled with considerable care. Being a form of pure acetic acid (household vinegar contains only about 6 percent acetic acid), its strong, acrid smell is overpowering. Paoli had every window in his laboratory equipped with ventilator fans and he and his helpers wore gauze dust masks, but still one had to grow acclimatized to the smell of acetic anhydride to remain in a room with it for any length of time.

The most important factor in the process of heroin conversion, as Paoli emphasized to his two assistants at the start of each day of work, was the supervision of the brewing of the morphine and acetic anhydride. As with a soufflé, the chef must hover over the stove. Paoli worked with large balloon flasks, each of which could accommodate two kilograms of morphine and four kilograms of acetic anhydride. So great was the demand for his product, he had expanded his laboratory so that he and his assistants could "cook" four balloon flasks at one time, thus preparing eight kilos of heroin in a single operation. The morphine and acetic anhydride were double-boiled in the flasks, which were immersed in water inside large metal containers, called *lessiveuses,* commonly used in France for boiling laundry, similar in shape to modern household garbage cans. Each flask, a spherical ball of glass with a short stubby neck, was topped with serpentine glass tubing so that the vapors could be condensed rather than dissipated, in much the same way as alcohol is distilled to make whiskey. Each flask also contained a thermometer so that the temperature of the morphine mixture could be kept as nearly as possible at a constant 85 degrees centigrade, or 15 degrees below the point of boiling. This required the skill of a chemist. There was a leeway of only five degrees on either side of the optimum point. If the temperature fell below 80 degrees, the process of acetylation ceased; if it rose above 90 degrees, the morphine itself would be destroyed; if it reached the boiling point, there was the danger of explosion and the whole laboratory could be destroyed. To make the process even more difficult, the amount of chemicals used also was critical, for they could change the boiling point of the mixture and bring about a most unexpected explosion.

Making heroin is long, unpleasant and tedious work. One can neither relax nor allow one's attention to wander. The fumes emitted by the cooking morphine and acid, despite all the window ventilators in the laboratory, are both noxious and highly inflammable.

After six hours, when the brew was finished, the excess acetic anhydride distilled off and the chemical synthesis of morphine into heroin accomplished, the flasks were removed from the heat and allowed to cool. Paoli now had impure heroin in solution, or what the chemists would call diacetyl-morphine-acetate. The conversion was still not complete. The acetate and certain unwanted salts formed in the chemical process of making the heroin still had to be removed. But at this point Paoli called it a day.

The following morning, each kilo of impure heroin was washed with a mixture of ten quarts of water and a half pound of bone black. The bone black purified and decolored the heroin, giving it the pure white color for which the best French heroin is known to addicts around the world. The mixture then had to be filtered from the excess bone black and water, then precipitated with carbonate of soda and dried and sifted again. This too, despite the use of suction pumps and other apparatus, was tedious work.

Now in its white crystalline form, the heroin had to be processed all over again to remove certain salts and other impurities.

This time it was washed with water and tartaric acid, then whitened once more with bone black, filtered, precipitated, then completely dried out and sifted again.

Paoli at this point carefully tested his product for purity. Here his own pride and reputation were at issue. He knew it was impossible to produce absolutely pure heroin. Traces of some of the other alkaloids of opium as well as certain chemical salts cling to the heroin. A purity of 85 percent is considered average, and anything below 80 percent would be considered substandard on the French, though not the Mexican, market. Paoli insisted on a purity of 90 percent, sometimes achieving as high as 98 percent; any product which fell below 90 percent would have to be repurified before Paoli was satisfied.

At the desired purity, the heroin was put through one more process: hydrochloration. Paoli had to make it soluble in water so that the ultimate user, whoever or wherever he might be, could dissolve the heroin and inject it into the bloodstream. For this, each kilo of heroin was poured into two quarts of boiling acetone; into this bubbling broth Paoli added exacting amounts of hydrochloric acid and an equal amount of 90-degree alcohol. When the chemicals had interacted upon one another, the now soluble heroin was taken off the heat and allowed to cool for twelve hours. Then, of course, it had to be dried out once again in the low-heat drying closet, and, finally, the heroin crystals had to be pulverized into a fine powder and sifted.

The result was the finest quality heroin that money could buy on the illicit market. A fine, fluffy, snowy-white powder, it looked like baby's talcum powder. In reality, it was one of the most powerful depressant drugs in the world, some twenty times more potent than the morphine sulphate used medically to relieve the worst bodily pain.

While the first batch was left to stand and cool for the necessary twelve hours, Paoli started all over again, brewing another eight kilos of morphine base with sixteen kilos of acetic anhydride.

With the best of laboratory equipment and the true expertise which comes from experience, Paoli, the illicit chemist, could and did manufacture sixteen kilos, or thirty-four pounds, of heroin in three or four days, but three or four days is all he would work in any single week. A careful, cautious man, he realized he needed the other half of each week to detoxicate himself. He put in ten hours a day at the laboratory, and despite surgical gloves and dust mask which he wore for perhaps three-quarters of the operation, he knew full well that he still breathed in noxious acid fumes and traces of heroin powder which wafted in the air. He knew that the corrosive acids he handled ate into his fingertips and threatened infections. And so he took exemplary care of himself. He forced himself to eat full and substantial meals, though the laboratory work made food obnoxious to him. He drank quarts and quarts of milk each and every day and he bathed his hands delicately in milk after each laboratory session. Each afternoon he took a nap and he set aside for himself at least eight hours of sleep every night. Rest was essential.

The prime danger he feared was that he himself might become addicted to heroin. Paoli understood the chemistry of the body as well as that of heroin. Heroin is toxic, a poison which taken in a large quantity can cause immediate death by depressing or stopping the action of the central nervous system. Absorbed in small, minute quantities, however, it allows the body to adjust and adapt its own internal chemistry to accommodate the poison of heroin. But once the body has changed, its new chemical balance must be maintained at that level of heroin. The body demands it. At this point the person is addicted; the need is beyond his control. If the body is then denied heroin, after the slow and steady intake, the change is too sudden for any quick readjustment back to the original chemical balance and the body reacts with violence and pain commensurate with the amount of heroin it requires. The addict suffers withdrawal symptoms. The ordinary consumer takes heroin for its euphoric effect, and as his or her body chemistry adapts to it, he or she must take more and more heroin to get the original effect desired, and thus a vicious cycle is established. Paoli, the chemist, however, went to great lengths in the opposite direction, guarding his bodily health and detoxicating himself every week without fail. Heroin addiction, after all, would ruin his life. No one in this business trusted an addict.

The week's output was checked, measured and weighed, sixteen kilograms of high-grade heroin, packaged by the half-kilo in double plastic bags and sealed with Scotch tape. The clearing away and cleaning of the laboratory, the storing of all equipment and chemicals in locked closets—all this was left to the two assistants and their wives. In the stealth of night and the rural quiet of a Marseilles suburb, Paoli drove safely home to his wife and children.

The amount of actual work he did in those three and a half days was not to be underestimated. At the end of the job, he was a fatigued man. But he was a rich fatigued man. He made the best heroin available and he charged the top price for his services: 3,500 new francs (seven hundred dollars) a kilo. For this week's half-week of work he would be paid $11,200.

The figures clicked through Paoli's mind with the precision of a computer. For converting the fifty kilos on order, his friend Dominique Benucci would pay him, on delivery, $35,000. Of course, that was not all profit. He had expenses. He paid premium prices for the chemicals he needed, in order to keep those purchases as secret as his clandestine laboratory, and there were the salaries, and the upkeep of the trucks and cars, and incidentals. But, all in all, he did well. He took in close to fifty thousand dollars a month, and after expenses his net profit averaged out each month to $36,000. Yes, it was a good, satisfying personal income, secret and untaxable, for a man without education who knew one particular chemical process: $360,000 a year, with a two-month vacation.

# 10

# The Corsicans

"You are a smart young man with a good head and both of you have done quite well, but, you know, of course, bringing the morphine to Marseilles, that is only half the journey." He was addressing both of them, but looking at Levonian. "Now you have a choice to make because I am going to put opportunity in your way and you must choose to take it or not to take it."

Levonian focused his attention now on the speaker, who talked on and on, using more words than seemed necessary, as though he preferred to creep up to a point rather than reach it directly. The young Armenian could not shake a feeling of self-consciousness despite the comfort of his chair and the snifter of brandy in his hand. This was the first time he had been invited to the home of Dominique Benucci and the invitation signified in France that he was being accepted as a social equal of the host. Yet, Levonian felt more like a captain of the field summoned to the headquarters of his general. Trigano sat upright on the edge of his chair, silent and nervous, like a schoolboy in class.

Savelli had brought them to the apartment at a moment's notice that night, although there had been hints of such a meeting since the morphine had been brought in safely a week before. Dominique Benucci himself had answered the door. Levonian guessed that the family was occupied elsewhere in this large, beautiful apartment while the men met alone in the library. Perhaps it was the elegance of the room that was so overpowering. The furniture seemed to be all priceless Directoire period, polished to a high gleam, and the opposite long walls were lined halfway to the ceiling with rows and rows of leather-bound books, arranged according to size.

The host, in this setting, looked less imposing than Levonian had imagined him to be from his reputation. He was shorter than Levonian, a little fat man with a receding hairline and an unmistakable potbelly accented by a thick gold watch-chain he wore across his vest. He had monopolized the conversation like a garrulous old man from the moment the three men had arrived. He chatted about the weather and mutual acquaintances and inquired of their families and refilled their brandy glasses. To see him like this, one would hardly suppose he was the Dominique Benucci who held the reputation of being the most important man in all of the Marseilles underworld. But then, as Léon Levonian realized, you cannot know a man from his appearance.

Dominique Benucci lived two lives, each of them separate and distinct from the other. He owned two hotels, several bars and cafes, and one of the city's finest restaurants, a chic meeting place in the Old Port. He was an important figure in the political and social circles of Marseilles. His wife served on several charities, his one daughter attended the city's best Catholic school, and he frequently entertained visiting celebrities in Marseilles. He was a charming and gracious host and people came away generally impressed with his veneer. But beneath that surface was a wholly different man, whose inner thoughts often were masked by the easy banter of his conversation.

The underworld, with its social hierarchy as rigidly drawn as that of society on the right bank of Paris, knew a different Dominique Benucci, one who commanded the loyalty and allegiance of men like Savelli and Albert Beltramino, tough, hardened men who dipped their fingers into the most lucrative of all France's crime. Dominique Benucci, by reputation and in fact, was at the very top of the very best rackets: narcotics, prostitution, smuggling, counterfeiting, anything that brought in money.

He had the wealth to finance any size operation; he could call on a small army of men to do his bidding; gunmen, professional killers, strong-arm men were ready to heed his command at a price—he had only to give the word to his lieutenant, Savelli. Perhaps even more important than his wealth were his contacts in America: He dealt with the very top men in the Mafia in Italy and in America. He had the customers for heroin in America. He also knew more ways to smuggle narcotics safely into the United States than any other man in Marseilles. Not only did he have a band of regular couriers among French seamen, but he also enlisted airline pilots and stewardesses and certain diplomats and entertainment celebrities. It was Dominique Benucci who first thought to provide special entertainment, like high-stakes gambling or sex, for otherwise honest men who crossed his path, and then to have his lieutenant, Savelli, blackmail the compromised and susceptible ones into becoming couriers of heroin. He was a shrewd manipulator and a man of power, the extent of which no one could fully assess, and it was these qualities more than anything else which carried him from his beginnings as a poor Corsican seaman to the acme of criminal power in Marseilles. And he seemed like such a nice man, so talkative, so gracious, so charming.

"So, I give you this opportunity to go to America because I have faith in you, faith that you can do what I have in mind with no great risk to your own safety," Benucci said, coming at last to the purpose of this meeting. His tone of voice was as casual as that he used in discussing the weather. "You two would go together and there you would be my collectors, handling the money, because it is no longer wise for Jean Paul Savelli here to be seen over there too often. I will tell you everything you have to know, who to see, what to say, and what arrangements to make."

Benucci explained that his shipments of heroin went to one Vic Dinella in Montreal, and that on special occasions it would be necessary for either Levonian or Trigano to go to Montreal to see that everything was working smoothly, to iron out any complaints or differences which might arise. They would not have to handle the narcotics and they would not have to carry large amounts of money over the border. The payments would be made somewhere in New York, separately from any delivery.

For their services, they would be paid 2.5 percent of all the money they collected. In fact, they would just take their cut off each payment before depositing the money in a bank, to be transferred to a special account they would open in a Swiss bank. That 2.5 percent would earn them more money at less risk than all their previous ventures in Turkey and the Near East. Benucci loquaciously explained what he would have them do in America, mixing detail where necessary with generalities which prevented the two young men from knowing the whole operation before they accepted his mission. Interspersed throughout his talk were his assurances that they need not accept this offer; they could reject it and continue operating as they had before with no ill feeling on his part.

Nor was there any need for them to make a decision immediately, Benucci went on. They should think this over seriously for it was a most serious decision. This would be a big step for them, moving to America, and there were many more risks because the American narcotics agents were everywhere on the lookout for the traffic. But then, there was much more money to be made, and it would be safe enough so long as they worked within the pattern which he had set with his Sicilian friends in Canada and America. Some of his heroin went directly to New York, but most of it went first to Montreal, because it was easier to get it into Canada than directly into the United States. The Canadian organization had its own methods for shipping to the States. But all this, Benucci said, he would explain later, when necessary. Right now they should only consider the proposition, ask questions if they had any, and come to a decision in one week's time.

Levonian could hardly contain himself from replying on the spot. His mind leaped ahead. In his daydreams for some time past he had envisioned himself among the opportunities and easy money in America, for he had heard stories of the prices heroin brought in New York. Yet, he instinctively realized that he should not appear too anxious before Dominique Benucci. Besides, although he knew he would succeed in the end, he still had to convince his friend, Pierre, who had been in past discussions a good deal less enthusiastic than he about crossing the Atlantic.

"Would it be possible, if we did go to America, to do more

than just collect for you?" Levonian ventured. Silence hung in the room after the question. Levonian feared instantly that he had broached a sensitive subject too soon. But then Benucci laughed.

"Ah, it didn't take you long, my eager friend," the older man exclaimed. Then turning to Savelli, he added, "You see, Léon here has the brains, he is thinking all the time, and that is good, that is what I want; you see, I was right." Turning back to Levonian, he said, "I know what you are going to say, but you say it, I want to hear it from you."

Embarrassed, Levonian suggested that while he represented Benucci in America, he could also sell his own heroin there. His arrangement with Savelli and Benucci up to that moment had been a half-and-half partnership. Of the opium he bought in Turkey, half belonged to Benucci and Savelli and half to Levonian and Trigano. Levonian had advanced his own money in Istanbul, and now that the merchandise had been delivered safely to Marseilles, Benucci and Savelli would pay the second installment due to Ahmet Baykal. While they had not risked any money, they had supplied the important contacts with Baykal and the couriers from Beirut to Marseilles, and they had stood behind him with the power of their names and their organizations. And so, half of the fifty kilos of heroin belonged to them and half to Levonian. On the first shipment they had bought Levonian's share in Marseilles, but now Levonian saw the opportunity of selling his own twenty-five kilos in America.

Benucci appeared amused, as if dealing with a child, at Levonian's suggestion. "And who would you sell your stuff to in America, eh?"

"To anyone," Levonian replied, adding hurriedly, "anyone you suggested."

"Ah, not to anyone!" exclaimed Benucci in mock horror, "but only to the man or men I picked out.

"That is most important," Benucci continued, "because you are a smart man and you know what happens to all those seamen who go into business for themselves. They are all the same, they start off small and they grow bigger and bigger and they think they are smarter and smarter and then, poof, they are finished.

"There was Gaston Ferrandi for example, whom I helped for

ten years." Benucci named the shipping line for which he worked. "He was the son of a friend of mine in Bastia who also learned how to make money on a ship. He smuggled silk stockings and small radios and things, and so I gave him some drugs to carry. I told him it was essence of perfume for a friend in New York and he was young and naive and he believed me. I gave him two hundred dollars to bring this essence to a friend in a bar in New York. He did it well. So, after a few trips, I gave him an extra fifty dollars to bring back a small package to me, the money. For a while he did this and he was happy. But then he got smart. He talked to my friend in the bar and he learned first what was in the package, then he learned how much my friend was paying. Ah, then he saw that he was making two hundred dollars on a package and I was getting two thousand dollars or something like that. So, what did he do? He told my friend to stop buying from me and he would sell him heroin cheaper. So, my friend did that, and Gaston bought heroin here and sold it to my friend in New York. He made a lot of money and then he got even smarter. He found out that all my friend was doing was selling the heroin directly to another man and making even more money. So Gaston found the other man and he sold his heroin for even more money. Then, he found a second customer there in New York and a third. Ah, but the third customer was not a true customer. Gaston could not know that. The third customer was a narcotics agent. So, today, where is Gaston? He is in prison in America.

"That, my dear Levonian, is what happens in America to men who are too smart," Benucci concluded. "You understand?"

"Yes, of course," Levonian said. "I would not sell to anyone I did not know; only to someone you recommended. Believe me, I will keep my word."

"You agree then that the recommendation I give you for a customer is very, very important, yes?"

"Of course," said Levonian.

"So, then, how much should you pay me for this safe customer I am to find for you?"

An intimation of Benucci's subtle shrewdness crept up upon Levonian and for a moment he stopped to consider. The older man was far ahead of him, he realized, as he subconsciously abandoned the impulse to try to outwit him. This was the man who was not only the financier but the brains behind everything, or almost everything, that Jean Paul Savelli did, and while Savelli was considered so important a figure on the street, it was Dominique Benucci who arranged everything in the background. His ambition, the young Armenian decided on the spot, was to become a Dominique Benucci rather than a Jean Paul Savelli, and the way to accomplish that was to work with the master as long as possible, to accept his terms and his advice and his experience.

"Whatever you thought was fair, I would agree to," Levonian replied.

"Good," Benucci exclaimed with a smile of pleasure. "You have the idea. It is better for men to work together than one against the other. There is plenty of money to be made in America, barrels of it, so there will be enough for us to share. It is good for you to work for yourself also. You will work harder and you will be more careful. Yes, it is possible, if you go to America, to sell your own stuff, but only with my help. Do you know the risks? It is much more dangerous over there than here in Marseilles, from the customers as much as the police, and there are more police, more tricks, more traps. Over there you must be much more careful——"

"Yes, I know," replied Levonian. "But I would have you to advise me what to do."

"You must give me your word that you will sell only to those I know personally in America, that you will deal with no new customers without first informing Savelli or me. That is the greatest danger, the sin of greed, with all that American money around, so easy to pick up. Everybody is tempted. You must remember this and give me your word. The police there are not to be underestimated."

All the while that the men talked, Dominique Benucci studied the young Armenian's responses, his reactions and his facial expressions. Much of his own success he attributed to his ability to judge men and to choose those to work for him and with him who were competent, mentally agile and reasonably trustworthy. Like the president or director of any large business, he could not do everything himself; he had to delegate authority, and Benucci had discovered over the years that oftentimes he could pick a man for a specific job who could perform that task better than he himself ever could. Buying and selling narcotics, in Benucci's estimation, was much more a business than a criminal activity. It required the same kind of thinking, only more so, as his own legitimate hotel and restaurant enterprises. To deal in narcotics successfully, one had to make long-range plans, anticipate future events, invest and reinvest money to make more money, put off the immediate gain for the future one. The ordinary criminal did not have the mind or mentality for this; what he wanted, he took immediately by pointing a gun or burglarizing a house or picking a pocket. Benucci and racket men like him looked down on the thieves, the thugs and the gunmen of their milieu. They hired them and they used them, but they did not socialize with them. It was a matter of class. What Dominique Benucci had to decide this night was whether or not Léon Levonian had enough class as well as wits to deal with his customers in Montreal and in New York. Whether or not the young Armenian was smart enough to smuggle heroin into New York, as he had suggested, was up to him, but he would have to prove it before Benucci would give his personal stamp of approval.

Pressing the fingers of his opposite hands one against the other, as if about to pray, Benucci asked: "So, you will soon have your heroin back from the chemist, and I can find you a customer in America, so you tell me how you are going to get that stuff into New York. Do you know how?"

"I have an idea," said Levonian slowly, "but I haven't worked it out yet. I've just thought about it in case I got the chance to go to America."

"Tell me and I'll tell you right away if it is any good, because if I do not think it is good, I cannot give you a customer; my friends trust me not to do anything at my end to endanger them. You understand? So, how would you do it?"

"In my car; I have a Simca sports model that I have been thinking about for this kind of thing," Levonian said.

"But the police in America know all about cars and where to look in them, they know all the places."

"Not this place," exclaimed Levonian. "I think I could put it in my Simca so nobody could find it. You see, there is—"

"No, don't tell me where," the older man interrupted. "Tell me, how many kilos can you put in one car?"

"Twenty or twenty-five, I haven't tried it yet."

Benucci's face gleamed. "Very good, you prepare this car of yours, put in some sand or dirt in this hiding place, and then let Jean [Savelli] here try to find it. Then we shall see. Perhaps even if he does find your hiding place, if he likes it, then I think even then we can do business—that is, of course, if you and Pierre decide you want to go to America."

The men talked soberly long into the night of what Levonian and Trigano might expect if they chose to go to America. Benucci advised them how he would expect them to live quietly, without ostentation, in New York, making trips on his behalf to Montreal and perhaps to Mexico City. Without naming names, he explained what their roles must be in dealing with his customers, warning them to separate their business life from their social activities.

By the end of their meeting, it was fairly obvious to all of them that the two friends would indeed go to America. Trigano had agreed to leave his wife and five-year-old daughter home in Marseilles until he established himself somewhere in New York. Since he had lost the first phalanx of his right index finger in an accident and had abandoned steady work, Trigano had grown accustomed to living on more money than he had ever made as a laboring man. Now he was supporting not only his wife and child, but his own mother and father and his wife's parents as well. His "career" was inextricably tied to that of his friend, Léon.

Levonian left the meeting titillated at the prospect of what lay ahead of him. In quick flashes, he daydreamed visions of great amounts of money and of power. What he had done before was but a prelude. Now he was at the beginning of a new phase of this career, and just as much as he was reassured that he had been right to take to a life of crime, he was now confident that he would succeed at what came next.

Promising to meet with Trigano the next day, Levonian returned to his home on a side street just off the Old Port. He let himself in quietly, taking great care not to disturb his mother, who lay sleeping in the master bedroom of the six-room penthouse apartment in a seven-story modern building overlooking the water. Despite his outside activities and his thirty years of age, he lived at home as a good, obedient Armenian son should, respectful and considerate to his pious, old-fashioned mother, who still dressed only in black and veiled her face when she ventured outside to shop or to go to church. At home, he answered to his Armenian name, conversed in the old tongue and dutifully took almost all his evening meals with his mother. She ruled the roost, and Levonian remained within her confines as a point of family honor: For a son to leave an Armenian home before marriage is thought to cast dishonor and shame upon that house and that family. Nor would he bring the corruption of his outside activities into his own home. Levonian's mother, the head of the household, had not the slightest inkling of her son's true occupation or of his innermost thoughts. She didn't dream that her son might be contemplating going to America.

But that night Léon Levonian thought of nothing else. Too overwrought to sleep, he lay wide awake in bed, speculating on how he would arrange his little Simca car, what he might have to pay Benucci for his help, and the riches, power and fame that awaited him in America.

First he would have to fly to Geneva to pay off Baykal and to make certain other arrangements. He still had his half of the lucky Turkish lira note, hidden now beneath the velvet cushion of his cufflink box. But, after seeing Baykal, he would be off to America. Those twenty-five kilos of heroin he had brought all the way from Turkey he would sell in New York for a minimum of a quarter of a million dollars. That would be the start. He would go on from there—the first man since the Eliopolis brothers (who had been Greek, not Corsican), back in the 1930's, to command a network from the poppy fields of Afyon to the Golden Market of New York.

# Part Two

# 11

# New York City, the Golden Market

When Léon Levonian reached the Golden Market, he entered into a new and different area of the business, but the way had been cleared for him. His friend Trigano was there ahead of him, waiting at Kennedy Airport in a new, cream-colored Imperial. It had been Trigano, reluctant in the beginning to leave Europe, who had come first and alone to New York, to live in a cheap midtown hotel, to mingle and to make friends at a social club for French-speaking people in New York, until finally he had found a suitable, safe apartment in a residential section of Kew Gardens which was neither too far from nor too close to the narcotics arena of Manhattan.

Trigano had suffered the pangs of loneliness which beset him in this strange, new environment full of potential danger and risk, so that Levonian would be spared the mundane tasks associated with establishing a base of operations. Their relationship, tacit but understood in the past, was sealed by Dominique Benucci in Marseilles: Trigano was the front man and Levonian the brains behind him. As the collector in America for the Benucci organization, Trigano followed instructions and did what he was told and nothing more. He did not sell, he did not negotiate, he merely collected. He was the front man; Levonian conducted the actual business on behalf of the Benucci organization and for himself.

In establishing any business in a new territory, the smart merchant surveys the market and the competition. Levonian had been well briefed before his arrival; the narcotics market was established for him, the customers selected, and the competition sized up. In the narcotics business, of course, the foremost competition is the police; they would, if they could, bankrupt you. Levonian therefore was instructed on what to expect in the American market from the police authorities. He studied in his fashion not only the narcotics laws of the United States but also the policies and practices of narcotics law enforcement. Before he left Marseilles, he was told not so much the statistical details but rather the underworld's opinion and attitudes of the activities and working methods of the Federal Bureau of Narcotics.

The professional criminal's attitude toward the police is quite different in the United States from that generally held in Europe. Those in the business of buying and selling heroin in the United States, particularly at the upper wholesale and distribution levels, have a deep, abiding respect and fear of the Federal Bureau of Narcotics. If they err in their judgment at all, it is in overestimating the capabilities of federal agents. They suspect the "feds" are everywhere, around the corner, potentially at the edge of every deal. Of course, they have ample cause for concern. Some of the biggest, best-protected men in organized crime have fallen: Vito Genovese, Big John Ormento, Tough Carmine Galente, Joe Valachi. Well-informed on all aspects of their business, the top echelons of the Mafia and the Cosa Nostra families know the federal "narco" agents are concentrating on them, not on picking up the stupid dope addicts or the cheap pushers on the street. They know that when the federal agents can't get a top man with the merchandise on him, they get him on conspiracy to sell narcotics. Twenty major conspiracy cases over the past ten years had netted the Bureau of Narcotics more than two hundred important gangsters. Others not so big were being sent up all the time. If you counted all the men currently behind bars in the federal penitentiaries, almost 17 percent of them, you would find, were sent there by agents of the Bureau of Narcotics. The prison terms, since the Narcotics Control Act of 1956, are long and hard, mandatory, without benefit of probation or parole. In comparison, the narcotics business anywhere else in the world is a breeze. For any young man embarking on a career of crime in the United States, the enormous and quick profits in narcotics are still there to be grabbed, but, oh, the risk is ever so much greater and increasing steadily.

That is the view generally held by those who control the business of narcotics in America. At the now famous meeting of Mafia chieftains at Apalachin, in upper New York State, back in 1957, it was decided that every member throughout the country would have six months to dispose of his inventories and get out and stay out of the junk business. At the end of that time limit, the "law" was enforced by several brutal murders. But as time went on, some of the members cautiously drifted back into the business; they found they could not make their accustomed living otherwise. Their operation changed, however, as they dealt in heroin only at the topmost levels, maintaining their control over the contracts and the sources of supply in Europe and the Near East. They turned most of the handling of distribution and sales over to others, particularly the Negroes and Puerto Ricans in New York, who were willing to take the risks of long prison sentences.

This fear and concern of the underworld was a tacit tribute to the effort of the Bureau of Narcotics. Actually, the Bureau is not all-knowing or all-seeing. No one within the Bureau, for instance, had any knowledge of Pierre Trigano's entry into the United States or of Léon Levonian's arrival four months later or of Levonian's store of heroin, which came separately and safely shortly thereafter. The Bureau of Narcotics, which is a subdivision of the Treasury Department, is the smallest law-enforcement agency of the federal government. In comparison to the Federal Bureau of Investigation's seven thousand agents, the Bureau of Narcotics has fewer than three hundred. That amounts to about 2 percent of all the law-enforcement personnel in the federal civil service establishment. Nor does the Bureau want more men. It has declined congressional offers in the past, because the Bureau operates differently from all other policing agencies, with the possible exception of the espionage and counterespionage units of the Central Intelligence Agency. It does so of necessity because the narcotics laws of this country are fundamentally different from other federal statutes on crime.

The basic law governing narcotics today is the Harrison Act of 1914, which can only be understood in its historical setting. The invention of the hypodermic needle just prior to the Civil War, the indiscriminate use of morphine to treat soldiers wounded in the War Between the States, the slow but steady spread of morphine addiction in the postwar years, the wide use of opium as the main ingredient of the cure-all nostrums so popular at the time, all contributed to the spread of narcotics addiction through the country. At the turn of the century the sale, the possession, the use of morphine and opium were legal. Anyone could buy morphine pills at the counter of the corner drugstore at about twenty-five cents a pill. More women than men used them. Outside the big cities, maiden aunts and a good many mothers were hooked on the favorite brand of cough syrup or on straight morphine. Heroin pills came on the market, ironically, as a supposed cure for morphine addiction. According to a medical survey of the time, one out of every four hundred Americans was addicted to morphine. No one tried to count the syrup drinkers. Theodore Roosevelt was the first president to recognize this trend as a scourge upon society, and in 1909 he called the first international conference on narcotics in Shanghai. Thirteen nations pledged their cooperation. That was the first step. Then, in 1912, Theodore Roosevelt convened another international conference on narcotics at The Hague, where nations formally signed a treaty pledging to enact laws to control the illicit use of and traffic in opium-derived narcotics.

Congress, in trying to draft a federal law at the time, however, could find nothing in the Constitution which gave it the power to outlaw the use of any drugs. So, instead of a direct prohibition, the Harrison Act of 1914 imposed a commodity tax of one cent per ounce on all opium-derived drugs produced, imported or sold in the United States, and required that all persons dealing in such drugs be licensed and registered with the Secretary of the Treasury. Of course, the Treasury Department licensed only physicians and pharmacists.

The effect of the Harrison Act, as it still stands today, was to make illegal and unlawful the manufacture, sale or possession of opium, morphine or heroin without a license. Subsequent acts of Congress added marijuana and cocaine to the proscribed list. The Harrison Act did not outlaw the use of any of these narcotics. A young man can walk down the street with the telltale railroad-track marks up and down the veins of both his arms, from the elbow to the wrist, and any policeman would recognize him as an addict, but he could not arrest him on a narcotics charge unless he found some quantity of unlicensed drugs on or about his person. A young woman can "go on the nod" against a corner lamppost or on a park bench or anywhere, and technically she has violated no narcotics statute unless she is in actual possession.

Narcotics is one of those crimes in which the victim submits willingly; in fact, he is a party to the crime, with his own misguided self-interest vested in protecting the source of his narcotics supply. In almost all other crimes against person or property, from robberies to assaults and homicides, there is a victim or a relative of the victim who is eager to supply information to the authorities. Police detection ordinarily begins *after* the event, working back to the crime from eyewitness descriptions, fingerprints, clues at the scene, the recovery of stolen property. In narcotics, however, because of the way the laws are written as well as because of the people involved, both federal agents and local police must work their case *before* the crime is committed. Only in that way can they even hope to be on the scene to apprehend a suspect in the act of selling or possessing narcotics. To do this, narcotics agents must be as wily, as devious and as quick as the dope pushers themselves. The result is a battle of wits, well understood by both sides.

From the very start, when the Bureau of Narcotics was established as a division of the Treasury Department in 1930, taking over the enforcement of the Harrison Act from the Internal Revenue Service, the basic *modus operandi* for its agents was undercover work. To catch a heroin seller, a narcotics agent had to pose as a buyer. Then, when he bought heroin, marijuana or cocaine, he could arrest his supplier for selling narcotics and he had the evidence in hand. As the years went on, the sellers became more and more wary, and so the buying had to become more and more sophisticated. Agents found informers who not

only gave them information but gave them the necessary introductions to sellers. The sellers, to protect themselves, then made
it plain in the underworld that the penalty for informing was
death. The policy of *omerte,* silence to all outsiders, was a practical policy throughout the underworld which extended far beyond the Mafia. In the battle of wits, the informer became the
battleground. He is at the heart of all law-enforcement work
and, at the same time, the Achilles' heel of organized crime.

So, while the Bureau of Narcotics is a small, low-budgeted
outfit, everyone of its 297 agents, from Commissioner Henry L.
Giordano to the newest probationary recruit no more than a
month on the job, has done undercover work, posing as a heroin
merchant, infiltrating the underworld, developing and using informers, matching ingenuity with the experienced professionals
of the narcotics world. Together, they make up an elite corps of
men, specialists in dealing with only one aspect of law violations,
working an extraordinary number of hours every week to perform extraordinary feats of daring. Each man was chosen, tested
and approved by a supervisor of one of the seventeen districts of
the Bureau only after a full year's probationary work. Above
and beyond the basic requirements for federal law-enforcement
officers of four years of college or the equivalent work experience, above-average physical fitness, a high intelligence and an
impeccable background, the Bureau looks for men with a certain
"moxie," men who are "street smart," able to handle themselves
and maneuver in surprise situations. Each agent knows that his
fellow agents have the brains, ability and willingness to work the
long hours needed on the job. They depend upon one another as
they work on a case, and out of this dependence grows a sense of
camaraderie, an *esprit de corps* that is unmatched in the federal
civil service. The agent doing undercover work in the midst of
dangerous men knows he is covered by other agents doing surveillance work. A mistake by one agent could cost the life of
another.

Yet, while the men are bound by a certain dependence upon
one another, the Bureau of Narcotics also maintains a spirit of
competition among its agents. The undercover agent, although
backed up by other men, is out on his own, talking, negotiating,
dealing with men who might or might not sell him narcotics.

Within the Bureau, each agent makes his own reputation, like a gunslinger of the Old West, and he must constantly perform to maintain his reputation as the number-one, -two or -three undercover man of his particular district or group.

The satisfaction on the job is commensurate with the work involved; an agent goes out on a case, pits himself against a heroin merchant, and either outwits the man and makes an arrest or is himself outmaneuvered by those who slip away. The agent, young or old, experienced or new on the job, stays with his own case, making the decisions as he goes along, whether he has found a derelict pusher on the street or a mafioso of the caliber of Vito Genovese. Every day on the job is different from the day before. Every deal has its own variations, every man his own peculiarities, every case its own problems. The opportunity to come across a Mafia chieftain, even by chance, is always a possibility. The challenge is always there, enough to satisfy the Walter Mitty in every man. The narcotics agent's job offers him the rare opportunity in an increasingly bureaucratic and impersonal work world of being able to measure his own performance, ability and value as an individual: He either wins or loses each and every case he handles and he does so upon his own merits.

While it is possible for an agent to chance upon a Mafia chieftain or lieutenant or even an international supplier like Léon Levonian, it is not likely; such men do not talk narcotics with strangers. To gain admittance to such high levels of the business, a man needs references and recommendations from men willing to vouch for him. Of necessity, an agent must work for those references among those lower down in the hierarchy of the narcotics traffic. His career will depend to a great extent upon how many informers the agent has working for him plus the pressure and persuasion he can apply to each informer to gain his cooperation. From the addicts, the street pushers, the runners and such underlings whom he can "flip" into informers, the narcotics agent might work his way up to the insulated men who control the flow of narcotics through America.

John Pinto, a young but very tough agent, had one such informer, named Frankie, who was so trapped that he was obliged to phone in to Pinto regularly once a week. Frankie, with muscles instead of brains between his ears, had made two major mistakes. Not only had he sold heroin on two separate occasions to Pinto but he had confided that the heroin had been stolen from his boss, Tony Boccio, in East Harlem. Agent Pinto closed the vise from both directions. He threatened to send Frankie up the river for five years, the minimum sentence for a first offender, or, worse, he threatened to pass the word to Boccio that Frankie was a thief and an informer, leaving Frankie's punishment to the East Harlem mobster. Venom oozed from the hapless Frankie each time he was obliged to meet with John Pinto, but he talked.

They met usually on neutral ground in an all-night cafeteria on 42nd Street, where Pinto always took the precaution of having one or two other agents at a nearby table in case of trouble.

"Listen, I got the name for you of somebody really big this time," Frankie whispered, leaning across the Formica table, "but if I give you this name, I want for you to let me off the hook now. I can't keep coming to see you like this forever. Somebody see us like this, put two and two together and I'm a goner."

"What's the guy's name; we probably know about him already," Pinto said.

"You gonna let me off the hook, I tell you the name and we through, okay?"

"Not so quick, Frankie," Pinto explained patiently. "You know how you can get off the hook: Introduce me to some of the boys your way."

The informer shook his head. "I ain't never goin' introduce you to nobody. You want I should sign my death warrant?"

The stalemate between informer and agent continued. Frankie had been giving Pinto information for months in order to keep out of jail, but the names he brought forth always pertained to men outside of his own mob. From his point of view, it was the safest way to handle his problem.

"Like I told you, Frankie, you help me make a case on somebody big, not some shnook, and when I got him in the lockup, then maybe I'll let you off the hook." The agent paused and then said, "So, what's this guy's name and what does he do?"

"He's really big, I swear it, because he's the one who supplies

Boccio. I just found out last week because I was there when he took a hundred grand off Tony for junk."

"Did you see him deliver the junk?"

Frankie thought a while and then said, "Nah, I didn't see him deliver but I seen him take the dough."

"How did Tony pay him?"

"In cash," the informer exclaimed, "what do you think, he paid by check or something?"

"All right," said Pinto, becoming interested. "So, do you know when he's going to deliver? Or if he delivered already?"

"No, I don't know that."

"How much stuff is he getting?"

"I didn't hear that."

"But you're sure it was a hundred thou paid all at one time?"

"Yeah, that's right."

"Okay, Frankie, now tell me the guy's name."

Frankie grinned across the table. "You like it now, eh? We're going to call it quits between us, okay?"

"For crying out loud, Frankie, you ain't told me a damn thing yet," Pinto shot back at the grinning face. "I can't use what you told me for anything 'cause you told me zero right up to now. So, what's the guy's name?"

"Big Joe."

"Big Joe? That's all?"

"Yeah, that's the only name the guy was called. What you want, his whole pedigree? Can't you do nothin' yourself?"

Pinto tried to pump more information, but it seemed the well was dry on the subject. "Okay, Frankie, you can help yourself a long way if you come with me down to the office now."

Frankie was shocked. "Wha' for? I don't want to go down there, you know that."

"Well, if you don't know this Big Joe's name, you can look over some mug shots and maybe pick him out for me."

The reluctant informer was adamant and the two men argued at length until Frankie admitted that he could not pick out Big Joe's photo because he had never seen him. Pinto accused him of lying, making up the entire story, but Frankie insisted he had heard the story from a friend he trusted in the mob. He refused to give his friend's name but he swore on his mother's grave that his friend saw Tony Boccio hand over $100,000 to this Big Joe.

Pinto believed this final version of the story but he would not allow the informer to realize that. "Zero, Frankie, I don't believe that cock-and-bull story for a minute. We get crap like that all the time. I wouldn't even put it in a report, that's what I think of it," the agent said, lying. "You bring me that guy's name and then I can check it out, but you got to find out some more about him before you can sell that kind of story. You know, ask around."

"You're out of your mind. I ain't askin' no questions about anybody on a deal like that," Frankie insisted.

"All right, so what else is new?" Pinto said with a sigh. "Didn't you pick up anything at all?"

"Well, I can't go around being nosy," Frankie said petulantly. "What I hear, I hear, and that's all." He paused long enough for Pinto to realize that in his own slow way this man of muscle was trying to decide whether or not to disclose something else. Probably he could not figure out the ramifications of the information; if it led back to his own mob, he would not tell it, but if it led away from home ground, it was safe material with which to trade. The agent waited for the man to think it out, and the silence hung strangely over their table. Frankie was stymied by indecision.

Pinto tried sugar. "Look, Frankie, you're not really a bad guy; I could even get to like you. But I can't carry you forever. My boss is on my neck. You got to produce for us or else your case goes on the docket, but you give us something worthwhile and I'll see what I can do. But you got to give."

Frankie did not like any of it but he had little alternative. To escape the narcotics agent's clutches and that of his own mob, he would have to flee New York and run for the rest of his life. "You got me by the short hairs, you son of a bitch, so, okay, there was a guy I heard about last week who dropped a load in a stud game at Angie's and one of the boys told me about him. He was a little guy who's supposed to be an ex-fighter or something, and he deals in junk in Philadelphia."

"Did you catch this guy's name?"

"Yeah, I don't know him or anything but his name was Sicardo, Jimmy Sicardo, and he runs some kind of political or social club in the Little Italy section down in Philly."

"Anything else you know about him?"

"No, nothing else, some of the boys were talking and I couldn't get it straight whether he buys or sells up here in New York but he's a South Philly man, I know that."

"Who does he deal with up here?"

"I don't know that, I don't even know if he deals up here, I told you," Frankie exclaimed. "Oh, yeah." He remembered. "Somebody mentioned this guy Sicardo was a friend of a guy named Tee in Baltimore, but I never heard of this guy Tee."

Pinto pumped his reluctant informer just a bit before he threw up his hands in disgust. "Frankie, you got to tell me about deals you know about, what's going on up your way. This crap you're handing me isn't any good. You don't expect me to go chasing to Philadelphia after this character Jimmy whatever-his-name-is. If you want my help, you got to make a case here in New York for *me*. You get it?"

"Aw, I'm giving you what I can, what d'you want from me?" the informer whined.

"You know damn well what I want, so you do some thinking this week because your time may be running out," Pinto told him. "Take off now."

Frankie left the table in a slouch, but not before the agent called after him. "Don't forget to phone me next Thursday!" The federal agent walked out of the cafeteria a little while later, more pleased with the session with his informer than he had let on. He would apply the pressure and whittle away at poor Frankie until either by consent or mistake Frankie led him to his boss, Tony Boccio. Meanwhile, he would note for the record Boccio's connection with Big Joe, whoever Big Joe was. And, as for Jimmy Sicardo, agent Pinto himself would not go to Philadelphia, but he had a very good friend who worked there for the Bureau of Narcotics.

# 12

# Apartment in Kew Gardens

In that crowd of several thousand men, women and children, all of them waiting and expectant, there was no one more anxious that sunny spring morning in New York than the young, heavyset Armenian named Léon Levonian. Nevertheless, he stood there, well-dressed, expressionless and contained, watching his ship come in.

The mammoth French liner S.S. *Liberté,* guided by three small tugboats, rounded the edge of the pier on the North River and slipped into its berth. The decks and the dock were lined with smiling people. They waved from the ship and they waved from the pier. Levonian could not keep himself from scanning the far-off faces high up on the French liner. He hardly expected to spot his friend on the ship but he looked for him anyway.

He voiced some words of encouragement about the safe arrival to Trigano at his side, who was fidgety about the slow docking of the ship. Prepared for an hour or two more of waiting before they completed their business on the pier, Levonian felt absolutely confident. He had made his plans with the greatest of care, and each detail had been checked out by Dominique Benucci and Jean Paul Savelli. Everything had gone well up to this moment. And yet Levonian was aware of the tension welling up within him. The next hour or two was potentially the most crucial of all the periods of danger thus far since his meeting with Ahmet Baykal in Istanbul. Anything could go wrong in this business. The ship might have sunk during the crossing with his fortune aboard. But it hadn't. His friend might have gone to the authorities aboard the ship. But he doubted it. The customs officer might by chance search in the right spot. But he doubted that, too. The police might somehow have been tipped off about him. Even so, they could prove no connection between Léon Levonian and the twenty-five kilos of heroin hidden aboard that magnificent French liner docking in New York. He watched the first gangplank being lowered to the dock, the uniformed immigration and customs officials charging up onto the ship, and then the first of the passengers coming down to the pier, assembling for customs checks of their baggage in the alphabetical order of the letters hung from the high overheads of the closed pier.

Toros Malik came down the gangplank hesitantly, glancing about at the strangeness of this new land that was America. He was a young Armenian Frenchman headed for college study in Chicago, an intelligent lad not yet twenty and without a friend in this new country. He made his way through the crowd to the red signs of cabin class and the letter M and began to look for his luggage which the ship's stewards had brought from the ship to the pier. Levonian sighted him immediately, coming down the gangplank, before he even reached the cement pier. He pointed him out carefully to Trigano, for those two men had never met, and Levonian, instead of going forward to greet his young friend from Marseilles, held himself back and well hidden behind the mass of visitors on the pier.

They patiently watched the young college student open his suitcases for the obligatory customs search and they observed the officer go over the customs declaration. Malik's automobile, of course, would be declared on the list of items he was bringing into the country. It would be necessarily a long wait. Malik sat on one of his suitcases until the customs officer went about checking the baggage of the other passengers under the letter M and then, finally, as Levonian expected, the customs agent motioned to the French-speaking newcomer and Malik followed him to the elevator which would take them to the lower level of the pier where the automobile would be unloaded from the ship. Everything was routine.

They waited another ten minutes and then, with a final word of encouragement from Levonian, Trigano alone walked to the elevator which took him to the lower level of the pier. Levonian strolled casually back to the street entrance of the pier, glancing at the pretty girls on the way. When he had taken Trigano's big American car out of the parking lot nearby, he parked on the street, across from the pier entrance, and waited some more. Waiting was part of every business, but he was confident now. He knew exactly what would happen inside the pier and afterwards. Levonian had arranged it all. He had found Toros Malik, whose father bought grocery supplies from Levonian's brother, when he had learned that Toros was going to America to study business administration at the University of Chicago. There was always someone in France going to America on business or pleasure. He had had no trouble in convincing young Toros to take a car to America to be sold there for a five-hundred-dollar profit over what it would cost in France. He merely had promised Toros two hundred dollars of that profit. Toros, an Armenian with a good head for business, grasped the concept immediately. He understood the necessity of Levonian's using him to put his name on all the documents and to take the car over to America so that he, Levonian, could continue to send more cars with other tourists without arousing suspicion. Upon Levonian's instructions and with Levonian's cash, Toros had purchased a blue Simca sports model, and he agreed to allow his benefactor to use the car briefly so that it could be declared a used rather than a new vehicle in America. Levonian had road-tested the car. He had then concealed his cache of heroin, twenty-five kilos, in a natural hiding place built into the car, and then he had road-tested the car again. Fully satisfied, he had driven Toros all the way from Marseilles to Le Havre and had seen the sleek, low-slung sports car hoisted aboard the ship and lowered into a hold. Levonian had not once allowed young Toros to be alone with the car after the narcotics had been put inside. He was convinced that Toros suspected nothing of narcotics. Levonian had told him he would be met at the pier by a friend who would pay him the two hundred dollars immediately and then sell the car. When the ship had sailed, Levonian had returned to Paris for a night on the town and a flight early the next morning from Orly Airport to New York.

Now, waiting outside beneath the West Side Highway of the city which paid the highest prices in the world for heroin, Levonian could visualize in his mind's eye what was going on inside the pier. The customs agent, looking over the car, would sniff the factory smell of a new, unused article; he would read the odometer for the number of kilometers the car had been driven; he would inspect the car and see nothing suspicious, nothing removed and put back together again; he might even tap the fenders and the tires if he were suspicious and find they contained only air. Or he might just take one quick look at the almost new car, the honest face of the young student, and paste his little customs stamp on the car.

Levonian's smuggling scheme was neither complex nor completely original. It was simply a variation on the old false-bottomed trunks the Italian smugglers once gave to unsuspecting immigrants for supposed needy relatives in the United States or Canada. The trunks, brought in by the illiterate and poor immigrants, would no sooner pass customs than a cohort of the smugglers would claim it from the immigrant and carry it away from the dock. Levonian's variation was simply that he was bringing in not the few kilos of heroin a false-bottomed trunk would hold but a whole carload.

He checked his wristwatch and kept his eye on the pier entrance. By this time, he surmised, Trigano would have made his approach and welcomed Toros to America. He would have offered to help find gasoline needed for the new car, which he would duly admire, and he would have offered to drive the newcomer to the Henry Hudson Hotel. Everything would be done to help Toros get settled. All that Trigano would ask would be to have the car for the rest of the day to demonstrate it to a potential buyer.

At about the time Levonian expected it, as if on a predesigned schedule, the pale blue sports car came slowly out of the pier entrance. Trigano, at the wheel, waited long enough to be certain that Levonian had spotted the car before he crossed beneath the elevated highway to the northbound lane and headed uptown towards the Henry Hudson Hotel. The Simca rolled right by the Chrysler and Levonian shielded his face with one hand to be sure that Toros would not notice him. Toros was staring straight ahead. Levonian remembered to wait a bit to check that no other car was following; when reassured, he slid the big, unfamiliar American car from the curb and set out on the trail of the little blue valuable automobile.

He watched young Toros enter the hotel and come back out again to the car with a bellhop who helped him remove his bags. He saw Trigano smile and speak and shake hands and then drive off. Levonian followed the Simca crosstown towards the bridge which would take him to the apartment, watching the blue car ahead and glancing in his rear-view mirror to check on automobiles which might be trailing them.

On the other side of the bridge, Trigano sped along Queens Boulevard in time with the staggered lights until he reached a certain residential side street previously agreed upon. It was restricted to one-way traffic and lined with parked cars on both sides, with moving room for only one vehicle. Trigano slowed at the turn and then proceeded down the street, followed by Levonian in the big Chrysler. Levonian lagged as his partner raced through the street, turned at the far corner, and was away. He watched carefully to see if any car followed them or even hesitated at the turn. The street remained absolutely clear. He crawled at ten miles per hour the length of the long block with happiness swelling in his heart. If another car had tried to follow, Levonian was prepared to stall the Chrysler, blocking anyone, suspicious or not, from following the heroin the last mile or so to the apartment. But no one had followed because no one here in America knew that he, Léon Levonian, had brought twenty-five kilos of heroin all the way from Turkey to the Golden Market.

The little Simca car perched majestically in the spacious private garage which Trigano rented for his Chrysler. Levonian gazed at it in silent admiration. It was the same Oceane model he drove in Marseilles, a deluxe sports convertible which was both popular and expensive in France and virtually unknown in the United States. It had the same clean lines of the 1957 Thunderbird sans fins and would sell easily in the United States to anyone

who appreciated the beauty of a fine motorcar. Levonian anticipated getting all or almost all of his investment in the car back.
Trigano would return the car to Toros the following day with
instructions to sell the automobile in Chicago and then send the
money to Levonian in Marseilles. In that way, only Toros' name
would be associated with this particular vehicle and Toros himself would go on believing that Léon was still in Marseilles.

To Levonian, the particular beauty of this little convertible
was the deep well space for the convertible top between the back
seat and trunk of the car: Twelve inches wide, it stretched about
three feet long across the width of the car. In the bottom half of
this space, he had fitted a metal canister painted black and bolted
to the sides of the car so that it would not rattle. Inside the canister, he had packed his precious fifty-five pounds of pure heroin.
The canister appeared to be an integral part of the car to anyone
not thoroughly familiar with its specifications. A customs agent
looking down the well would see six or seven inches of space and
a metal partition. By removing the panel behind the back seat or
the panel in the front of the trunk space, he would see the same
black metal panel which had every appearance of being part of
the car. Levonian removed the canister from the car within three
minutes, and with a screwdriver he pried open the seams which
he had welded in Marseilles. Inside were fifty double clear
plastic bags, uniformly packed, each containing a half kilo of
white crystalline powder ten times more valuable than as much
pure gold.

They transferred the bags of heroin into two suitcases, disposed of the canister, cleaned up the convertible, locked the
garage and walked around the corner and down the block in
broad daylight, carrying a quarter of a million dollars' worth of
illicit narcotics to Trigano's apartment. It was all perfectly safe.
This was a quiet, residential neighborhood with a low incidence
of crime.

Pierre Trigano, who was not without certain skills, had
solved the problem of the stash quite beautifully. Levonian was
delighted when he first saw the layout of the apartment. Where
one hides one's supply of illicit narcotics is as important as the
buying and selling itself. Inventories waiting to be sold must be
stashed away in a "plant" which is safe both from police scrutiny

and from those who would hijack a load of narcotics whenever possible. At the same time, the plant must be accessible for ready use. The addict, who measures his horde in fractions of tea-spoonfuls, has all sorts of places available: the water tank of his toilet, the inside lining of an old suit jacket, a hollowed-out piece of furniture, a hole in the wall or in the floor. The street pushers and the sellers of ounces have more of a problem; but for men at the top—the wholesalers, distributors and suppliers—who deal in multiple-kilo quantities, the problem of where to stash and how to operate the plant becomes a true exercise in logistics, judgment and ingenuity.

Victor Dinella, who was probably the largest single whole-sale supplier of heroin in the United States, operating out of Montreal, used two plants. One was tantamount to a warehouse, secret and isolated, where he paid a "retired" boxer and part-time bank robber one hundred dollars a week just to "sit on the plant" and guard it with his life. Only Dinella himself or his chief lieutenant moved supplies from this plant to the working plant from which the Dinella organization sold merchandise to their customer. In this way, if the working plant was compromised in any way, Dinella stood to lose perhaps five or ten or even twenty kilos of heroin to the police or to burglars, while his permanent plant, with anything up to a hundred kilos of heroin, remained secure. Tony Boccio in East Harlem kept his big plant in a fashionable New Jersey suburb, and others of that ilk operated their stashes according to the same workable pattern, each with his own particular variations.

Although Trigano had arrived in New York four months before Levonian, they were newcomers to America, unfamiliar with their surroundings and unsure of their new associates. There was no one they could or would trust here with their valuable merchandise. Following the general instructions of their mentor in Marseilles, Trigano had found an apartment in an ordinary middle-class neighborhood of salaried workers in Kew Gardens. It was one of six apartments in a three-story walk-up building which looked like every other one on the block. The next-door neighbor was the landlady, an old Polish woman past seventy who minded her own business as long as the tenants paid the rent on the first of the month and did their own repairs. For

$125 a month, Trigano had rented a medium-sized living room, a dining alcove, two bedrooms (one larger than the other) and a small kitchen. He had explained to the landlady that his partner in his import-export business would be sharing the apartment when he visited America and that later his wife and little daughter would live there with him. The landlady had shrugged at the unnecessary explanation; in New York, as long as he paid his rent on time, he could do what he liked in *his* apartment.

Trigano had explained this to his Armenian friend upon his arrival. He also pointed out the one thing that made this ordinary apartment unique for their own purposes. In the front entrance hall there was a guest closet which had for some reason been built so that it contained, on the upper one-third of its right side, a cubbyhole about two feet high, two feet wide and three feet deep. The cubbyhole was useless, except perhaps for storage purposes, which was, of course, precisely what Trigano had in mind.

With the landlady's permission, Trigano had cedar-lined the hall closet, ostensibly for the protection of his expensive French clothes. In the renovation, the cubbyhole disappeared. Trigano's ingenious carpentry job defied Levonian's search for access to the cubbyhole even though he knew it was somewhere in the four-foot closet. What the Corsican had done was to notch the clothes bar at both ends so that only when it was twisted a half turn could the bar be pushed an inch into the left-side wall, thereby releasing the cedar paneling on the right-side wall. Then the upper third of that right-side wall could be lifted up to reveal the cubbyhole. With the clothes bar in place, interlocked with the panel, the right paneled wall was as solid as the closet itself. The separation crack of the panel was covered with a strip of molding which circled the three interior sides of the closet and supported a hat shelf. It was, all in all, a remarkable piece of work. Even before the arrival of the twenty-five kilos of heroin, Trigano had constructed an excellent stash for their future needs.

In their simple little apartment that night, the two young entrepreneurs from France rejoiced over their success: They had in their possession a fortune in white powdered gold and they were in the Golden Market. Neither of them ever in their lifetime had taken heroin internally; nor had they any desire for the supposed euphoric effects of this wonder drug. To them, heroin was as merchandise is to a businessman; it represented money, profits, riches, and all sorts of things that money, profits and riches can buy. Like misers handling gold, they separated the bags of heroin in groups of ten and counted them carefully. Five groups of ten equaled fifty bags of the purest heroin available in America. In each bag, packed so that the white powder lay flat not more than a half inch thick, was a half kilo of heroin, one and one-tenth pounds. The value of each bag was elastic, depending upon how and to whom you sold it. Here in New York, a man with a half kilo of pure heroin could make $5,000 or as much as $100,000, and here they were, Léon Levonian and his friend Pierre Trigano, in New York with fifty half-kilo bags of this heroin.

Levonian slit five of the bags at random with a razor, a small slice of less than an inch, and took from each of those bags just a few grains of heroin. The rest of the merchandise was carefully put away in the hall closet behind the new cedar lining. He placed the grains in five small bottles. These were his samples. Now he was ready to do business in America.

# 13

# Connection in Philadelphia

A man must have a connection. He who would sell heroin must find someone willing to buy; in order to buy, one must find someone able and willing to sell. The link that is needed is the connection.

James Sicardo, although often temporarily short of cash, was one of the best connections in all of South Philadelphia. He was the manager of a social key club in the Little Italy section of South Philadelphia where underworld figures in and about the fringes of the Mafia could gather in privacy. The club was important politically for its campaign contributions and the men it hired to help get out the vote on election days, but year around it served as a private clubhouse in which men could relax, drink, throw parties or talk business without fear. As manager of the club, Sicardo knew them all and served them as a fixer, an arranger, a connection for what needed to be done. This sideline brought him consistently more money than his club salary. Opportunities crossed his desk every week.

In his little office off the bar, Jimmy Sicardo gazed across his desk at a new prospect who had telephoned first and then had walked in on him.

"I wanna buy weight and I was told you could help me," the

prospect announced the moment he had seated himself across the desk.

He introduced himself as Mike Telano from the West Coast and explained that the heat was on in the West and so he was looking for the right connection in the East until it was safe for him to go back to his own territory. He did not say where on the West Coast. But he mentioned he had been traveling up the East Coast, Miami, Baltimore and one or two other cities, and he reeled off a few names, including that of Tee. One man had sent him to another until Tee had mentioned Sicardo in Philadelphia, so here he was.

The club manager approved of what he saw. More than the man's looks, the tone was right. He sounded like a rackets man, revealing in what he said just enough about himself to show who and what he was and yet not any more than was necessary. He looked tough: five feet nine, well over two hundred pounds, fat but solid, sallow complexion, heavy jowls, coarse black hair, not much forehead, bushy eyebrows, and the high gravel voice of a heavy drinker. Italian or perhaps even Sicilian. A sloppy dresser but expensive clothes. Money. Sicardo sized him up expertly because that was part of the business. He had noticed from the window of his office that Telano had arrived in a new Eldorado convertible that cost at least $8,500 and that he had a flunky waiting for him at the wheel of the car. That was class. It had the feel of money.

"Who do you know in Philadelphia?" Sicardo asked, wanting references.

"Nobody," Telano said, chewing gum. "I just got into town yesterday."

"Where're you staying?"

Telano named one of the big hotels in downtown Philadelphia.

"Well, I might be able to help you," the manager ventured cautiously. "But you got to tell me how much you want."

"How much can you get?"

"I don't know till I see," said Sicardo.

"You understand, I only want to buy stuff I can cut myself," Telano said. "I want it to be pure stuff right off the boat or pretty damn close to it. I'll pay good money for good stuff but I don't want no garbage, you understand."

"Yeah, I understand what you want," Sicardo said. "I'm not saying I can get it for you, but I can have a look around. I might know someone."

"Good enough," said the customer, getting up.

"You give me a ring at the hotel when you line something up, the sooner the better, or I'll call you here."

"Have you tried New York?" Sicardo asked.

"I don't like New York," he said flatly.

"Oh." The contact man got the impression that this heavyweight racketeer probably was wanted in New York or else he would have sought his narcotics contact there in the first place. He knew it was better not to ask certain questions at certain times: He would find out all he needed to know eventually.

Telano declined the offer of a drink at the horseshoe-shaped bar outside the office, and Sicardo watched the heavyweight Italian swagger down the stairs to the door of the club. He moved lightly for such a heavy man and Sicardo, himself a former welterweight fighter, guessed that his new customer could handle himself in the clinches. Beneath the loose-fitting clothing and layers of fat from high living and Italian pasta was plenty of muscle. Sicardo rushed back to the phone in his office, licking his lips in anticipation. His mind clicked off the names of several men he knew who had heroin to sell. The idea of a buyer who did not want to go to New York, knew no one in Philadelphia and was anxious to buy high-grade heroin in quantity whetted Jimmy Sicardo's appetite. This was opportunity. This, Jimmy Sicardo thought as he dialed, could be the start of something big.

That was precisely the thought and hope of the big Italian leaving the clubhouse as he stopped for a moment on the street to light a big cigar. He ambled around his Cadillac to the passenger side, patting the polished chassis with affection as he went, but once inside, he told the slender young man at the wheel, "Okay, let's get the hell out of here." The driver took off with a flourish, making the big car leap out of its parking spot. They turned the corner and cruised around the Little Italy section for a while and then headed towards the business section of The City of Brotherly Love.

"So, how'd it go?" the driver asked.

"No trouble at all," the big man said with a shrug, although he could still feel the flutterings of tension in his stomach. "He's a greedy bastard and I got the feeling he would've sold me junk on the spot if he had any. But he says he'll look around and then we'll get in touch. Give him a day or so, but I think we're in."

"Who would have thought it," the driver muttered, shaking his head. "But then you never can tell, eh."

The two men had spent almost the whole of the previous month searching Philadelphia for someone who could introduce them to Jimmy Sicardo. At the level at which they hoped to buy heroin it was considered absolutely essential to make an approach with either an introduction or references from men in the underworld who will vouch for you. But they had been able to find no one. So, Mike Telano had gone in cold, told his story, and, as far as he could tell, had been believed. Despite the business axiom, "If you don't know him, don't trust him, and if you do know him, don't trust him too much," Sicardo had trusted him. But, then again, Mike Telano was a very believable operator; he looked more like a hood than did Frank Costello, Tommy Luchese or Vito Genovese.

That is how and why, soon after the end of the Korean War, Michael J. Fulgoni had been hired as an agent of the Federal Bureau of Narcotics. Joe Lansky, Supervisor of the Philadelphia office at the time, had liked Mike's bulk and dark Italian looks. He had tutored and trained Mike himself and then thrown him against some of the top Italian racketeers of the Philadelphia-Camden area. Mike looked and acted the part of an Italian hoodlum so well he became known as one of the best undercover agents of the whole Bureau. Washington sent him on special assignments in California, Las Vegas, Texas, New York, around the country, and Mike had come to love the job for its excitement, freedom and challenge. Every day was different, every case was a new test of a man's ingenuity, every narcotics peddler a man to put behind bars. A graduate of the Rutgers Law School, and too poor to open a law office, with three years of service in the Army C.I.D. behind him, he had accepted the job because it then paid almost four thousand dollars a year. Mike dreamed of someday opening a law office, keeping regular hours and having clients come to him. But he could not give up the everyday challenge and personal satisfaction of his "temporary" job as a federal narcotics agent. Of course, he was one of the lucky ones, skillful and successful at his work, with an understanding and capable wife at home. She could cope with a life in which her husband worked twelve to sixteen hours a day, ate dinner at home no more than once or twice a week and sometimes on a special case dropped out of sight for three or six months. Mike was a happy man, too. When out on a case, he could give his full attention to the job without worrying about his wife, children and home. He had been fortunate in choosing a wife after he had chosen his career so that when she had accepted him, she took him with his job. A good many other wives, unable or unwilling to share their husbands with the demands of his job, forced them to choose. Some very good agents chose their wives and gave up the Bureau of Narcotics, and some selected their jobs over their wives. Those unable to make a choice lived in the limbo of ambivalence, and they were not very good agents or particularly good husbands.

In laying the necessary foundation for his attempt upon Sicardo, Mike had taken on the fictitious name of Telano. His true name, Fulgoni, was too well known in criminal circles throughout the Philadelphia area; but the name was known. Most of those who knew Mike Fulgoni by both name and sight were behind bars. Physical descriptions good enough for identification are next to impossible to transmit on the word-of-mouth grapevine of the underworld. The identity of Mike Telano had been carefully constructed before his first meeting with Sicardo. Mike Telano had a false driver's license, California registration plates on his Cadillac (which the Bureau had seized and confiscated from a man foolish enough to use it for transporting illicit drugs), a false FBI "rap" card sent to the local and state police files, and a false registration card stating that Mr. Michael Telano was registered in a single room at a downtown hotel (where the manager was a personal friend of agent Fulgoni's).

Mike's partner agent, Alan Weiner, who served as his front

man in their undercover roles, also sent in his fingerprints and imagined criminal record to the FBI in Washington so that an arrest sheet could be circulated that one John Goldman (alias Johnny Gold, Goldie) had been arrested as a juvenile offender, a numbers runner and was suspected of trafficking in narcotics in the Los Angeles and San Francisco areas. In reality, Alan Weiner was one of the Bureau's most promising young agents, a product of New York's Lower East Side who had been a teen-age gambler and numbers runner before he moved "uptown" to Greenwich Village, attended New York University, studied business administration, decided he did not like desk work and joined the Bureau of Narcotics for the sheer adventure of the job.

In appearance and personality, he was a stark contrast to his elder partner. Mike Fulgoni was heavy-set, gruff, direct and the model of a tough guy; Alan Weiner was tall, slender and smooth-faced and seemed younger than his 28 years. He was a sharp and impeccable dresser, a glib talker, unmarried and attractive to the girls. The two men complemented each other; what one lacked, the other possessed in abundance. They made a good team by Bureau standards and, besides, they liked one another.

In his office, Mike wrote his report on the start of the Sicardo case and worked on three other suspects in cases pending at the time. When he went out to meet the club manager, he slipped into the role and character of Mike Telano, West Coast hood and experienced narcotics dealer. His voice slid down a tone to almost a snarl, the gutter words of the street came easily to his lips, the natural suspicions of a man living outside the law governed his every response. For an experienced agent and undercover man this was not too difficult.

On their second meeting, Mike bought drinks and dinner for Sicardo in an out-of-the-way roadhouse and they swapped stories of their past exploits. He soon discovered that the man was a braggart, who dropped names like a middle-class status seeker as he discussed the rackets current in the city. Mike paid the bills and tipped heavily, each time flashing a huge roll of bills he carried, secured only by a rubber band, in his side pocket. He explained that he had the customers on the West Coast but he needed a connection in the East who could supply good French heroin. Sicardo said he was looking for the right connection.

At the third meeting, Sicardo accepted an order for a quarter of a kilo of heroin, and when his new friend refused to give any money in advance, Sicardo asked to borrow $350 against the coming purchase. Telano sympathized with his friend's embarrassment at being short of cash and whipped out his flash roll. He peeled off the top three hundred-dollar bills and one fifty. Sicardo was visibly impressed at the size of the bankroll. He had no way of knowing that the inner core of this "Michigan bankroll" was composed of a hundred singles. Make Telano had already established himself as a bigger, tougher man than Sicardo himself.

Later, agent Fulgoni was obliged to justify to his boss, the supervisor of the Philadelphia office, his handing out $350 of the Bureau's money with nothing but promises in return. He reviewed his conversations and negotiations with Sicardo and his own personal "feel" of the case. It was about to take off, Mike felt; of course, in dealing with another person, nothing is absolutely sure. There was the possibility that the club manager had uncovered the agent's true identity and had decided to "borrow" $350 from the government before breaking off relations, just for the sheer amusement of the ploy. There is no law against borrowing money. But it would have been a bold risk. Fulgoni doubted that Sicardo had that kind of nerve. As he reviewed the case, a telephone call was transferred to him in Supervisor Lansky's office. It did not resolve all their doubts, but it indicated that Jimmy Sicardo was not quite as naive and trusting as Fulgoni had thought.

The call came from the agent's friend at the downtown hotel where he was supposed to be registered; a plainclothes sergeant from the Pennsylvania state police had been around inquiring for Mike Telano.

This new development was not difficult to interpret; outside of the Bureau's office and the downtown hotel manager, Mike Telano had met only one man in Philadelphia.

Agent Fulgoni telephoned two friends at the state-police barracks and requested that any inquiries concerning one Mike Telano be referred to the Bureau of Narcotics. Then he sat back and waited.

Two days later, the police sergeant walked into the Bureau

office. Fulgoni was summoned into the supervisor's office. Lansky introduced them. "This is the agent handling our investigation of Telano. Tell him what you want Telano for." The sergeant repeated the story he had outlined to the supervisor. He had information that a big-time racketeer from the West Coast named Mike Telano was in town and mixed up in something big which the grand jury was now investigating. He wanted all the information the Bureau had on Telano and where and how he could be found.

"What kind of grand-jury investigation?" asked Fulgoni. The sergeant refused to divulge that secret information. Fulgoni refused to disclose any information on Telano, insisting that the Bureau also was investigating the racketeer. The sergeant threatened to subpoena the federal agent before the grand jury and force the information out of him. Mike egged him on, refusing cooperation until the sergeant explained why he wanted Telano. Finally, after a toe-to-toe high-volume argument, when the sergeant had fully committed himself to his lie, Fulgoni sprung his prepared trap. "Okay, Sergeant, if you really want this Telano so bad, we'll give him to you 'cause you're looking right at him. I'm the only Telano in Philadelphia!"

The sergeant staggered back in surprise, speechless.

"Now, Sergeant, you are in this thing up to your eyeballs," Fulgoni shouted, poking his stubby index finger at the sergeant's chest. "You know what you've done? You've stumbled into my biggest undercover case and I'm going to hold you responsible for my safety from now on. If I am uncovered, you're the guy we're going to blame and I can promise you now, if that happens, I'm going to bring you up on charges."

He allowed that to sink in and when the sergeant tried to explain that he had no idea that narcotics were involved, Fulgoni brushed aside his excuses. "We want you to do a little work for us now and you better be good because you're part of this case now."

The sergeant admitted that he was doing a favor for Sicardo but he pleaded that he had no idea narcotics were involved. Fulgoni handled him brutally. "If you had any brains, you would have found this rap sheet down at your place." Fulgoni thrust the FBI card at the sergeant. "Now, we want you to call

Sicardo and read this sheet to him and tell him you really want to get this Telano because he's wanted real bad on the West Coast. It would be a feather in your cap if you find him, see, and if Sicardo will help you, then you will owe him a favor. I want to see if he'll cooperate with you on this. And you better be good at it."

The sergeant, briefed by Fulgoni, telephoned the club. "Jimmy, this guy Telano's wanted in Frisco. He's got a record long as your arm, robbery, assault with a deadly weapon, manslaughter, questioned on a gang killing, gambling, narcotics. He's put in time in the joint." The cooperative sergeant was good. "Listen, Jimmy, they want this guy bad in Frisco and he's checked out of that hotel you told me about. You could do me a good turn if you can help me find him, understand? Do you have any idea where he might be?"

There was a pause at the other end of the line and then Sicardo came through. "No, if he checked out of that hotel, he's probably left town."

Fulgoni, who had an appointment with Sicardo for the following evening, prompted, and the sergeant asked: "Do you expect to see him?"

"No, I don't even know the guy, I just heard he was around town, that's all," Sicardo lied. "But if I hear anything, I'll let you know."

When the chastised state policeman left the office, Fulgoni and Supervisor Lansky grinned at each other. The club manager had chosen sides and Mike Telano, who had approached him cold, now had all the references and recommendations he needed to do business.

A week and two days afterwards, in an alley three blocks from the clubhouse, Sicardo delivered a quarter of a kilo of heroin, and Mike Telano flashed his roll again. He paid $5,150 to the little club manager while three other federal agents observed the transaction from their various hiding places.

A single illicit sale of narcotics, even when corroborated by three or more Treasury agents who were eyewitnesses to the transaction, is not always sufficient evidence upon which to secure a jury conviction. In court, the suspect appears neatly attired, a different aura about him, and pleads he was entrapped by the arresting officer. The Bureau of Narcotics, which trains its agents in the law of evidence, therefore follows the policy of making two or three buys so that the suspect cannot afterwards claim in court that he was merely doing a favor for a supposed friend on three separate occasions.

Agent Fulgoni made his second buy from Sicardo, ten ounces of heroin, a week after the first buy. He had even convinced Sicardo to introduce him to the man supplying the drugs, a small-time hood named John Sudora. Then he complained to Sicardo that the heroin was of poor quality. After the second purchase, he refused to do further business unless the club manager could find a better-quality merchandise. Their friendship continued, however. Sicardo promised to find a better "connection" for his customer. They talked on the phone at least once a week, and somewhat less frequently they met to drink or dine together. Sicardo was introduced to Telano's partner, "Johnny Gold," a slim, dapper, fast-talking Jewish boy in his mid-twenties whom Sicardo accepted as the usual front man a racketeer like Telano would use for all the more menial aspects of his various enterprises. Johnny Gold fit the pattern, and he was no more suspected by Sicardo of being a federal agent than was tough, gruff Mike Telano. Jimmy trusted them completely. He even introduced them to another seller, Ray Malti, who sold Telano six ounces of heroin he claimed his partner stole from a stash somewhere.

Months went by, and the agents kept their case on Sicardo open. It seemed to them that Sicardo was trying to control the situation by dealing only with sellers lower in the underworld hierarchy than himself. It was equally apparent that Sicardo, as manager of a club frequented by some of the top racketeers of Philadelphia, could, if he so desired, put Telano and Gold in touch with the men much higher up.

The agents pushed and pressed Sicardo at every opportunity. They wanted a connection who could sell them uncut and unadulterated heroin in kilo lots. They promised to pay well for the right stuff. They threatened to move on and out of Philadelphia if he could not come through for them. "Look, Jimmy boy, I don't want to deal with punks," Telano told him. "I want somebody who can supply me with weight and on a regular basis. I'm gonna lose my customers if I can't come up with the right stuff."

It was, after all, nine full months from the time of their first meeting that Sicardo made his own proposition to Telano on supplying the right connection. By this time Telano and his partner had ostensibly established themselves in a New Jersey motel on the Black Horse Pike, a well-traveled highway which connected Philadelphia with Atlantic City. Jimmy Gibbons, the Negro proprietor, was a middle-aged drug addict with a long police record who had served time for, among other offenses, receiving stolen property, running a house of prostitution and possession of narcotics. Despite the one cabin in the motel he used for "entertaining" traveling men, Gibbons was suffering some lean years; all his profits were going out for marijuana. He had readily accepted the Mike Telano who had burst in on him as a mafioso from the West Coast who promised big times once he started operations. Gibbons, a big, fat and flabby Negro who looked as though he might weigh three hundred pounds, was happy to provide a free room for two Mafia gentlemen. He even agreed to say for appearances' sake that Mr. Telano was a half-owner in the motel. Gibbie was anxious to make the "big time" at last. To make certain of his continued cooperation for the future, Mr. Telano on three separate occasions purchased several bags of marijuana from the proprietor.

Gibbie, who now served willingly as a flunky, relayed the message that Mr. Sicardo had telephoned, and that brought about the crucial meeting in Sicardo's club office. "I got you a New York connection that's really big," Sicardo announced. "This is the guy who can supply you with all you want, but I want my cut before you meet him. Two G's."

"You're out of your blinking mind, two thousand bucks just for an introduction!" Telano retorted, knowing full well what the Bureau's reaction would be to this expenditure.

"It's a one-time cut for me and then I step out," Sicardo explained. "I swear to you this guy is in with a mob in New York which can get you all the junk you want."

They negotiated at length but Sicardo was adamant; two thousand dollars or no deal.

"Okay, we'll pay the two thousand dollars, but only after this big connection of yours comes through," the federal agent agreed. "Remember, you don't get a dime until after we make the buy, when we got the stuff in our hands."

Sicardo agreed to that and with a smile.

"I'll be in touch with you at the motel," he said.

Agent Fulgoni's junior partner was obliged to sleep at the motel for two nights before Sicardo's telephone call came through. Fulgoni himself tried to lay plans for the future, consoling himself with the thought that the Bureau would not have to pay out the two thousand dollars, which rankled, until after it could assess the value of the narcotics dealer to whom Sicardo would lead them. The long investigation and undercover work was possibly about to bear fruit but only at a considerable outlay of money. But then, as everyone in the Bureau realized, heroin is an expensive commodity and you have to pay for what you get.

Unable to know in advance whom he would meet, agent Fulgoni went to the rendezvous armed with a .38 Smith and Wesson in his waistband. Three agents were posted outside the club to cover him in the event he had to signal trouble from inside the club. How the agents outside would manage to break through the heavy locked door was a logistical problem they never did solve. But Sicardo arrived alone and Mike Telano met him outside the club at 2 P.M. Sicardo unlocked the front door and they went upstairs to the bar together. Officially, the club was closed to guests until late in the afternoon, and Sicardo went behind the bar to serve drinks while they waited. He was quite nervous.

"Mike, you got to be very careful what you say to this guy from New York because he's really very big in the business and he don't like no fooling around. You know what I mean? He likes to run things his way."

"Don't worry about a thing, I'll be careful what I say." As an agent completely alert to the implications of what was said and not said, Fulgoni had two intermingled impressions. Sicardo was completely convinced that the man in front of him was a tough, short-tempered hoodlum from the West Coast; and in bringing in this new connection Sicardo was venturing into deep water and was afraid.

With one elbow on the bar, Fulgoni faced the door leading into the big, empty clubroom. He heard the man mounting the steps before he entered the room. His hand dropped to his lap. When the connection came through the door, Fulgoni recognized him immediately. He was fairly certain that the man did not recognize him.

He approached the agent casually, not quickening his pace, a man about fifty-five years old, a heavyweight about the same size as Fulgoni and only a few pounds lighter. Yet his face had a lean look, hard and bereft of expression, a thin aquiline nose, thin lips and cold gray eyes. There was no mistaking him. This was Nicolas Golino, listed by the Pennsylvania state police as one of the top ten mobsters in the Philadelphia-South New Jersey area. He was suspected to be a member of the policy-making council of the local Mafia, involved in a struggle with two other men for the top position, vacated several months before by the death of a racketeer for whom Golino had been chief lieutenant. The state police believed Golino had a finger in every racket within his area of jurisdiction, but they could prove nothing against him; the Bureau had had nothing on him concerning narcotics. In his younger days, before the rackets, he had been a bodyguard and a gunman, which had certain implications, and yet his personal police record was clean. He had been brought in for questioning on numerous occasions over the years, but never charged with a crime. Fulgoni recollected quite well the police dossier on Nick Golino. He was a cold, brutal mobster and an efficient rackets man, and very dangerous.

"Mike," cried out Sicardo, with false bravado, "I'd like for you to meet my friend, Charley, from New York. Charley, this here's Mike Telano who's in town from the West Coast, like I told you about."

Golino seated himself one bar stool away from Fulgoni and tried to stare his way through him. His gray eyes, unblinking, were like stones. They talked through the preliminaries until Golino, sipping at a bourbon, broached the subject. "Jimmy boy tells me you are interested in buying wholesale."

Fulgoni, as Telano, explained his situation and his attempts at finding the right connection for his customers on the West Coast. "I've been trying to do business here for months, but all I've been getting lately is a runaround and a whole lot of horseshit, promises, and no horse."

Golino listened at length without saying much, keeping his own judgments to himself. When Fulgoni completed his sales pitch and lapsed into silence, Golino sat for a moment and then swung around to Sicardo who was still behind the bar. He posed just a single question but it went to the heart of the matter. "Jimmy boy, how long you know this guy?"

In the moment that intervened between question and answer, Fulgoni could feel the flutter in the pit of his stomach. Sicardo now had to choose sides. If he admitted to how little he knew, he would lose that two thousand dollars, because Golino would either start negotiations from the beginning or walk out; if he lied for the two thousand dollars, he would be risking the wrath of a dangerous man.

"Hell, I know this guy twenty years," bragged Sicardo.

"You're sure?"

"Sure, I'm sure."

Golino turned back to Fulgoni. "Kid, your troubles are over. I can get you anything you want, from half a kilo to a ton, anything you want."

Fulgoni stifled a sigh of relief. He had crossed the first bridge and now he was on the safe side. His thoughts did not show upon his face. Golino, in his own way and with his soft voice, was trying to impress him, and the agent, of course, adopted the attitude of distrust traditionally felt by a buyer of unknown merchandise. "I want the high-grade stuff, you know, uncut," he told the racketeer.

"I'll guarantee you'll get pure stuff, just like right off the boat." The voice was calm, matter-of-fact, like that of a businessman who had been selling all his life. "I can get you a good price, too, if you buy wholesale. You know what it's selling for now, don'tcha?"

"Yeah, I know, but I'm more interested in the purity than in the price 'cause I cut it myself."

"It'll be good stuff, I told you, and I can give it to you for twenty thousand bucks a kilo, which is two or three thou under what you would pay anywhere else," Golino said with assurance, adding, "so how many kilos you want?"

Fulgoni rubbed the stubble on his chin, thinking. He recognized the hoodlum's need to establish his superior position and he knew full well the Bureau's budget. "Well, I like to see how good the stuff is before I buy weight so maybe I should try a sample first, eh? How much for half a kilo?"

"I thought you wanted to buy weight?" Golino said, with a bit of needle in his voice.

"Ah, I want to see what kind of stuff you deliver first," Fulgoni repeated.

"All right, I can get you half a kee at the same price, if you're gonna buy weight later, ten thousand for half a kilo."

"When can I get it?"

"I can get you delivery tomorrow." Golino stared at him, as if to say, "Put up or shut up."

With a pause for thought, Fulgoni countered, "Tomorrow's too fast. First I got to get things lined up. How about next Monday?"

Golino agreed to the date five days off and announced peremptorily that the delivery would be made in New York and only according to his own plan. Telano and his partner would meet him and Sicardo at the bar of the Hotel Lexington at 6 P.M. that Monday. They would bring the money with them and they would go by car. They would leave their car in the parking lot across from the 48th Street entrance of the hotel. While they were all together at the bar, someone else would put the heroin in the car. Then, either of them could go out and check the stuff while the other one remained with him at the bar. When they were satisfied with the merchandise, the money would be paid to Sicardo who, in turn, would pay him.

Fulgoni accepted these instructions, recognizing the professionalism. The two buyers would be separated and unable to run off with the heroin without paying; neither would see the man actually delivering the goods; neither Golino nor Sicardo would be seen handling the heroin and Golino himself would not even have touched the money in the presence of the new customers. It was good, standard business procedure.

The four men shook hands in the empty clubhouse; they had a deal. Each in his own way was quite satisfied with what he thought would happen on the following Monday and they were all wrong.

# 14

# Five Steps Down

The correct and proper way to buy or sell narcotics, or any other illicit commodity, is to know the man with whom you are doing business. This is not always possible. So every businessman, whether the enterprise be legal or extralegal, must be willing under the proper circumstances to take certain risks in order to find new customers and to expand his business. Greed and carelessness overcame Jimmy Sicardo's natural caution. But Léon Levonian, under the tutelage of Dominique Benucci, had had his American customer come to him for a proper and correct introduction.

At the prospect of a new source of supply, Joseph J. Biani had flown to Paris and on down to Marseilles without hesitation. His crime was that of conspiracy, which no customs agent can detect, for Biani never personally handled drugs. He was too big for that. He was the head of a Mafia family in New York which, while not as large and as diverse as some, was as efficient as any. He was listed in the Who's Who of narcotics, a brown leather-covered book known as the National List of Major Narcotics Traffickers, which contains 437 names; and yet neither he nor any other member of his syndicate was under current investigation by the Bureau of Narcotics. His criminal record dating back to 1932 included arrests for robbery, concealed weapons, receiving stolen goods, extortion and counterfeiting OPA stamps. After the end of the Second World War, Biani had concentrated on narcotics and was duly listed as a major suspect in the Bureau's special file, but then he had dropped out of sight and suspicion. He might have been retired, or deceased for all the Bureau of Narcotics knew. Actually, he was operative and living in luxury on a $250,000 estate near Alexandria, Virginia, not far from the nation's capital but well out of the mainstream of narcotics traffic. He had so organized his affairs that he himself only made arrangements and decisions. He did not handle the merchandise; he did not expose himself to police scrutiny. He might trade or lend or borrow merchandise but only with trusted men of his own rank in the business. If Tony Boccio were short one month, for example, Joe Biani might lend him one, five or ten kilos of heroin on his word alone. He would expect the same favor in return whenever needed. It was an honor credit system of a sort. One did not share customers or lend money without interest, but where two businessmen could cooperate for their mutual benefit, they did so. These mutual benefit associations are the heart of so-called organized crime, and the Mafia is the most successful of all such associations or fraternities. Its members have, in addition to their parallel ventures in crime, a common background and heritage of nationality, race, and blood relationships that go back through generations of intermarriages, with family ties in the United States and in the old country, Sicily.

For the same reason that heroin merchants guard and keep secret the identity of their customers, Biani handled the negotiations for the buying of heroin himself. It provided him with control over the affairs of his own syndicate in the United States.

He traveled in style and stayed at the luxury hotels in each of the cities he visited. In Marseilles, he was the guest of Dominique Benucci, an old friend and business associate, who, in the midst of wining, dining and providing entertainment for the visiting American, introduced him to his new protégé, the young Armenian Léon Levonian. Benucci proposed at the proper moment an enticing offer: This young man could and would deliver in New York an unlimited supply of the finest heroin available at $12,500 per kilo.

Without questions and without any hesitation, Biani accepted the proposition. He had been paying from sixteen to eighteen thousand dollars per kilo in Canada, which he knew full well was the same heroin supplied by Benucci.

Biani agreed to pay cash on delivery if he could buy his heroin from Levonian on the installment plan. He would take a minimum of five kilos per week, so that he could sell one batch in order to pay for the next. Levonian agreed to bring the heroin to the United States at solely his own risk, without any advance payment, and to make Biani his exclusive customer as long as he took five kilos per week. And all three agreed that it was in their best interests to keep this arrangement a secret from any other business associates.

Levonian's operation in the United States was to be a new branch of the business. Benucci would continue to supply his regular customer, Vic Dinella, in Montreal, as before, and Biani would continue to buy from Dinella as before, either by increasing his sales or reducing gradually his purchases from Canada.

The contract, although not inscribed on paper or enforceable in any court of law, was most carefully drawn. As in all well-prepared business agreements, each of the participants was satisfied that he was getting what he wanted and at a fair exchange. Biani, the purchaser, was delighted with a saving on each kilogram of heroin of from four to six thousand dollars under the current market price in Canada. Levonian, the supplier, was assured of the price he wanted, ten thousand dollars per kilo. And Dominique Benucci, the financier and middleman, was satisfied with a clear profit of $2,500 on each and every kilogram Levonian sold in America, without investing any money or taking any risk himself. Implicit in the agreement, and perhaps of overriding importance, was the factor of safety for each man involved. To their minds it was the best of all conspiracies: small, tight and foolproof.

Before departing for America, Léon Levonian had driven in his little sports car, along with a young female companion, to Geneva for business and pleasure. One was a cover for the other. There, in the banking capital of the world, he had met with his Turkish colleague, Ahmet Baykal, paid the remainder of his bill and, at the same time, arranged procedures to be followed for future shipments of merchandise. He also made certain necessary banking arrangements in the Swiss city, and then, since business affairs do not consume all the hours of the day, he enjoyed himself.

In America, once the merchandise was secured, Levonian began to enjoy himself once again. He had a true zest for living. Soon he was fascinated with the island of Manhattan, particularly the center and heart of the city, where he marveled at the variety of shops, the international choice of restaurants, the galaxy of attractive, well-dressed women promenading along Fifth Avenue. Mid-afternoon at Rockefeller Center, when the sidewalks were not too crowded, was a spectacle. To a European like Léon Levonian, all this represented wealth and the good things money could buy and a way of life he greatly craved.

Although Levonian and his friend Trigano shared the experience of their new life in America together, living in the same apartment, eating and drinking together more often than not, their attitude toward almost everything was completely different. The Corsican was overwhelmed with the strangeness of a foreign country, the different and difficult language, the speed of routine living and, above all, the danger he sensed all around him. He missed the familiarity of Marseilles and he longed for his wife and daughter. Levonian, on the other hand, plunged into his new life with the zest of a teen-ager, sublimely confident of success which he attributed to his own shrewd know-how. He enrolled in the Berlitz School of Languages at Rockefeller Center for daily instruction in English. He joined a social club for French-speaking people and delighted everyone with his droll sense of humor. He sampled a different restaurant each night, for he loved to eat well. He tried a succession of movie theaters. He opened an account at the New York branch of his Swiss bank and propositioned the secretary of the official who handled his account. And when Trigano introduced him to the Perera & Co. office at Rockefeller Center, where he gave Levonian a power of attorney to make deposits to the Savelli Swiss bank account, the Armenian posed as a former prizefighter, an investment broker and a mink farmer, all in one, and tried to date the assistant cashier. When she refused, he asked if she had any friends. By the end of his first month in America, Léon Levonian had a mistress. He swore to marry her, too, as he had promised the girl in Marseilles and the girl in Beirut. Promises came easy to him.

When he felt properly attuned to his new environment and ready to conduct business, Levonian lifted the telephone and followed instructions given him in Marseilles. He was promptly invited to dinner at one of New York's finer restaurants off Park Avenue. The service was impeccable, the food superb, the wine list excellent and the surroundings suitably quiet and affluent. Levonian's affable host was Big Joe Biani, returning the hospitality extended to him in Marseilles. They conversed on social and general business affairs through the dinner, as would insurance agents, stockbrokers or any merchants, for the heroin market varies from week to week or month to month according to supply and demand and to the activities and personalities of the traders. A single arrest can put a sizable dent in the supply available; a death or retirement of a particular supplier or customer can change the alignment of a whole series of purchases and sales. Their business gossip might have sounded boring to an outsider, for the product was never mentioned, but to the men involved such talk was of sparkling interest. They consumed the courses of their meal with the delicacy of good manners. Not once did the sordid world of heroin addiction intrude upon their thoughts, their conversation or their concern.

By the time the espresso, brandy and cigars were brought to the table, the two men were satisfactorily attuned to one another. Quite naturally the conversation turned to the practicalities of business. Between two knowledgeable and capable men of affairs, negotiations can be conducted swiftly in a sort of shorthand language.

The price was reconfirmed at twelve and a half.

Cash on delivery.

Quantity, anything from five to twenty-five.

An offer on all twenty-five, paid half on delivery and half on consignment, was rejected.

Ten kees at twelve and a half each, cash at delivery in one week, agreed upon.

Place, time and method of delivery, agreed upon.

Social conversation, a handshake at the door, and a safe parting.

At mid-morning the next day, Levonian and Trigano made a practice run in the Chrysler, across the Queensboro bridge, down Second Avenue, left on Houston Street and on down to Mott Street on the Lower East Side. The place of delivery appeared to be an empty, derelict building in the center of the block between Mott and Elizabeth streets, a deserted store front on the ground floor and three stories of grimy, shadeless windows above. They circled the block twice before Levonian left the car to inspect the premises. As he had been told, five steps led down from the street to a green door at the basement level. The stairwell was guarded by a waist-high iron picket fence, and the basement door was secured with an oversized brass padlock. He tried to rattle the door but it did not give a fraction of an inch. The whole building gave him the feeling of long, long disuse. But he knew that was just appearance. That door was solid, bolted from the inside.

The two men stayed in the city that day so that Levonian could go to his English lesson at Berlitz and Trigano could attend to his collection for that week. The arrangement was simple and effective. Levonian watched it from a discreet distance and it never varied. Between 5 and 5:40 P.M., Trigano would pick up the French newspaper reserved for him daily at a French book shop on Rockefeller Plaza. He would stop outside the door of the shop, tuck the newspaper under his left arm, light up a cigarette and wait. The courier, a different one almost every time, would make his approach, reciting almost the same words each time in varying degrees of bad Italian.

"Are you Pierre Trigano?"

"Yes, that's me."

"Can you show me some proof?"

Trigano would offer his passport and the courier would inspect the name and the photograph carefully and then, satisfied, he would hand back the passport, and say, "I have a package for you."

"Good, I was expecting one."

A long manila envelope, sealed with three bands of Scotch tape, would be handed over. Trigano would glance at the plastic tape for certain markings beneath it which told him the package had not been opened and resealed. Without those markings, he would reject the offer. With them, he would thank the nameless courier and they would part, two ordinary men in a New York crowd.

The procedure went this day as before, and Levonian followed his friend as he walked the half block through the plaza, around the skating rink, and to the money-exchange office of Perera & Co. There, in the privacy of a cubicle, the Corsican would extract the money, count it, deduct his 2.5 percent, and deposit the principal to his Swiss bank account #67,252NT. The account was registered under a fictitious name, Lucien Suchen, but even that name did not appear on the deposit slip: only the number of the account. A duplicate deposit slip was Trigano's receipt.

The sums ranged from ten to twenty to thirty and occasionally to forty thousand dollars. The collections were made usually once a week, sometimes twice, occasionally three times a week, whenever a phone call came with the signal. They knew that the money was paid by Vic Dinella in Montreal for heroin delivered by one of Savelli's seaman couriers, with Dominique Benucci masterminding the entire operation. But that is all the two men knew. Benucci and Savelli maintained a steady supply line of heroin to the Canadian syndicate which distributed to several Mafia families in New York, Chicago and Detroit. Because it was considered too dangerous to attempt to bring heroin into New York Harbor on a regular basis, the Dinella operation had been established in Montreal. It was simple for Dinella to dispatch the heroin across the loosely protected Canadian-United States border. He paid couriers to drive it across as motoring tourists visiting New York or Detroit. For Chicago, the courier operated his own private airplane. How much heroin traveled from Marseilles to Montreal and into the United States? That was beyond what either Levonian or Trigano needed to know for the success of the operation. Certainly, Levonian's other twenty-five kilos of heroin, which he had supplied to Benucci, had been delivered by some seaman to Montreal. But neither Levonian nor Trigano could correlate the money received outside the French book store with the amount of heroin delivered to Montreal. The Montreal organization maintained a floating account in the numbered Swiss bank account so that as long as the total deposits were maintained at a prearranged amount, usually

$100,000, the heroin was delivered in ten-kilo lots according to the schedule of freighters plying the sea-lanes between the ports of France and those of eastern Canada, and payment was made from the Swiss bank account.

Levonian's primary concern was the first exchange of ten kilos of heroin for Biani's money. For Levonian, this would be the climax of his long venture which had begun months before in Istanbul, nine thousand miles away. The heroin itself would, of course, continue its journey on to the consumer, but this was of no concern to the Armenian.

To make money, one must either work hard or take a risk (whether that risk involves capital, creativity or crime), and since the essence of crime is to make "easy" money, the criminal must be prepared to take certain risks. Over and above vulnerability to the police when handling illicit narcotics, the greatest danger in trafficking in narcotics hovers over the situation in which an enormously valuable amount of heroin is brought together in the same place with a tremendous amount of money. That is the point of temptation. Conspiratorial secrecy guards against a third party robbing either the money or the narcotics. But what is to prevent one of the conspirators from robbing the other?

Levonian, recognizing and accepting the irreducible risk, planned as many precautions as were possible. On the assigned Thursday he set off with his friend and ten kilos of his precious heroin, packed in twenty half-kilo plastic bags and wrapped into one compact package. They drove in accordance with all the traffic laws of New York, except that the automobile and Trigano's driver's license were registered to a nonexistent address in Yonkers. The appointment was set for 3 P.M. While addicts and street pushers might scurry about their meetings under the false cover of night, the dark of night is also the time when the narcotics police are out at work. The big business, however, is transacted as often as not during the innocence of the daylight hours in New York.

Houston Street is a major cross street of the Lower East Side, traversing Manhattan Island east and west, with traffic flowing in both directions, busy, impersonal and typical. Levonian approached the rendezvous alone and on foot, having left the car and the heroin two blocks to the north. On Houston Street, he walked the length of the block and back again to the tenement building. Being on strange ground, he could not appraise the terrain as well as he could his own home ground, but intuitively he felt that the man lounging in front of the tenement was neither a loiterer nor a plainclothes detective. Young, dark, overweight, tough, Italian, he had the look of a muscle man or a gunman. Levonian decided he was protection for Biani. Nothing had been said of such an arrangement, but the Armenian could not blame Biani for protecting the amount of money he would be carrying. For a moment, Levonian caught the man's eye. The man stared contemptuously. Nor did he move as Levonian walked past him to the steps leading to the basement's green door.

The brass padlock was gone, Levonian noticed immediately. He walked down the steps casually, without looking back at the guard above, and pushed on the door. It did not budge, locked from the inside. Taking a deep breath, he rapped soundly on the wood. He heard the bolt being slid back and the door opened almost immediately, revealing to him a man he had never before seen, a six-footer with a big, prominent nose.

"François?"

"Yes."

"Come in."

No sooner had he entered than the door was slammed shut and rebolted. He found himself suddenly wrapped in darkness. For a moment the thought struck him: an attack could come now when he was helpless in the dark. But then he heard one or two steps and a rap on another door. Again, he could hear the sound of a bolt being moved, and at the other end of a short corridor, another door opened. Biani greeted him heartily in French, using his fictitious name. The young Armenian looked about him. The basement room was so large and dark that he could not be sure where the walls were. In the center of the room stood a large round poker table covered in green felt and lighted brilliantly by an overhanging bulb and green shade. Beyond the table, there were two or three men seated in the dark. Levonian could barely make out their forms. He listened patiently as Biani explained the safety features of the windowless basement which was used for a high-stakes poker game. As Biani talked, Levonian noticed himself being inspected. The Mafia boss obviously was wondering where upon his person this French Armenian could possibly have hidden twenty-odd pounds of heroin. Finally, the question burst out. "Where in hell have you got the stuff?"

"I don't got it," he replied, smoothly if ungrammatically. "My partner got it outside."

Biani's eyes narrowed to slits. "Your partner? You didn't say anything about a partner."

Levonian had his explanation ready. "Everything's going to be all right. My partner is nervous and he likes to stay back out of sight. He worries all the time, and he wanted for me to come in and see the way this was all set up.

"He's in the car outside, riding around, and he wants for me to pick up the money, count it, and then give it to him in the car and then he will give me the ten kilos for you. And I will stay with you, of course, while you look it over and you are satisfied."

"Well, this is a switch," Biani muttered, half aloud. "Why didn't you tell me about this partner of yours?" he asked finally. "I thought this heroin was all yours 'cause you told me you brought it all the way from you know where."

"Yes, it is mine but I have this partner who is a good friend," said Levonian. "It is only a precaution."

"Yeah? So what if this partner of yours takes off with the money and doesn't give you the stuff?"

Levonian reassured his customer. "I know him for years, and I know his family, his mother and his father and his daughter. He is like a brother to me."

"I thought you trusted me completely," Biani replied. "We were going to do so much business together, this is no way to start."

"It is perfectly safe for both of us," insisted Levonian, who was concerned really for his own safety. "You can come with me to the car and see it all. There will be no foolery."

"Well, I want to meet this partner of yours," Biani said. "I like to know a man I do business with."

"Of course, this is only for the first time," said the Armenian. "I will have my friend meet you, if you like, or, he can make the delivery the next time. We are partners like brothers."

Levonian looked at his Swiss watch pointedly and added, "But we must hurry because he will be coming by here in another ten minutes."

Biani did not consult the men hidden in the shadows in the back of the room. He came to his decision himself, Levonian noted, as he watched Biani throw a small airline bag onto the poker table and say, "Okay, count it."

Levonian sat down at the table and, containing his emotions with just a lick of his lips, he unzipped the travel bag and gazed inside at his spoils. The money was arranged in bundles, each of them secured with a rubber band with a slip of paper denoting the amount, $1,000, $5,000, $10,000. The bills were of all denominations and of varying ages, some new, some old. He looked through one bundle, inspecting the bills. Then swiftly he added up the sum noted on each bundle and announced his satisfaction. He was indeed pleased, and he dared not actually count every bill for fear that the Mafia chief might take it as an insult. He did not know the man *that* well and everything seemed to be going his way.

Accompanied by Biani, Levonian reached the curb in front of the basement in time to observe his partner's convertible rounding the corner at no more than five miles an hour. The car crawled, according to plan, so that the inside lane ahead of him was fairly clear of other traffic. In plenty of time, Levonian led Biani to a street lamp at the curb. Then he walked out into the street between two parked cars which were to the right of the street lamp.

If he had stood to the left of the street lamp, it would have been a signal for Trigano to drive by without stopping. It would have meant that something had gone wrong inside and that the heroin should not be delivered.

Levonian's position, however, was plain to see: at the right of the street lamp. Trigano stopped for only a moment. The airline satchel was dumped into the car; a small package wrapped in plain brown paper was passed through the open window. The car sped off. The transaction was complete.

Levonian immediately placed the merchandise in his customer's hands. Biani had affixed himself within grasping range throughout the transfer, and now the tall, lean Italian led the way back into the basement room. Levonian smiled and made small talk as he watched Biani put samples from each of the twenty bags of heroin to the melting-point test to determine the percentage of purity of the heroin. The Armenian merchant exuded confidence. According to his own sense of values, he considered himself a man of honor: He was not a thief, he gave full value for money received.

When Biani was satisfied, as a sign of good faith, he introduced Levonian as his Marseilles friend "François" to his colleagues in the back of the room. The first was Biani's partner, Frank Merlotti, a coarse man in his mid-fifties who had seen better days. He might have been the same age as Biani, but while Biani was slim, well attired and tall, Merlotti was no more than five foot six, with an unconcealable beer belly jutting over his belt; the few remaining strands of hair on his head he wore combed sideways over a knobby, oft-injured pate. He had a mean look. The other man was the six-footer with the prominent nose, still in his twenties, who had opened the doors to the basement for Levonian. He was introduced only as Tony. His part in the organization was not explained. Nor did Levonian think it wise to inquire.

When Levonian took his leave, politely declining an invitation to join the others in a drink, he passed the bodyguard still posted at the tenement steps, glanced at the shabbily dressed passersby in the street, and made his way uptown by taxicab. From there he took a subway to Kew Gardens and another taxicab to the apartment.

Trigano had promised to wait and not to touch the money until he arrived so that together they could both enjoy the pleasure of handling and counting one hundred and twenty-five thousand American dollars. No one at this point in his life could have convinced Léon Levonian that crime does not pay. He knew better, and besides, the profits were so high.

# 15

# Midtown Rendezvous

The stupid and dangerous way of transacting a heroin deal is to buy from or sell to someone whom you do not know personally or can trust completely. However, when one wants to buy or sell desperately enough, he must take certain risks.

James Sicardo began to worry for all the wrong reasons when his customers, Telano and Gold, were more than fifteen minutes late for their six o'clock appointment at the Hotel Lexington in New York. Since ten minutes before the hour, Sicardo had been walking up and down Lexington Avenue between 49th and 48th streets, first on one side of the street and then on the other. In his topcoat pocket he carried a little more than one pound of heroin, half a kilo, worth ten thousand dollars when he sold it and five to twenty years in jail if he were caught with it.

With his coat collar turned up against a light drizzle and a chill in the air, Sicardo, with increasing impatience, inspected the flow of traffic, looking for Telano's flashy Eldorado, a hardtop Cadillac convertible with a black vinyl roof, silver body and gold-spoked wheels. He wanted to intercept the car before it was parked across the street from the hotel so that he could get rid of the heroin in his pocket. He was tense, even though he knew he was as inconspicuous as any other forty-year-old man on a street in New York. He realized no one could stop and search him on the street without cause: That would be unlawful search and seizure, even if the search produced the heroin in his pocket. Nevertheless, he was nervous.

Of course, he was totally unaware of two other equally inconspicuous men pacing Lexington Avenue. They were agents of the Federal Bureau of Narcotics. Nor did he notice two other agents seated in an unmarked car parked at the corner of 48th Street. Nor did he have any reason to suspect the driver of a taxicab parked across the street from the hotel entrance who turned away customers on the excuse his cab was out of order. Sicardo was concentrating upon the Cadillac carrying his two customers.

Fully twenty minutes past the hour, Sicardo spotted the Cadillac he wanted. He rushed to the car as it stopped for traffic just past 49th Street. "My God, you're late," he shouted through the window, and then he noticed that the man he knew as Johnny Gold was at the wheel, alone in the car. Sicardo opened the door and slipped into the front seat. "Where's Mike?" he demanded.

"You don't know the trouble we had," exclaimed Alan Weiner in a tone of utter exasperation. "I'm lucky to get here myself. I never thought I'd make it, but I didn't want to stand you guys up . . . you have no idea the trouble . . ." The federal agent talked on and on as he maneuvered the car around the corner and toward the parking lot on 48th Street. Still he did not give out too much information, waiting for Sicardo to interrupt.

"All right, all right, so what happened to Mike?"

"He had a heart attack!" exclaimed Weiner.

"Is he dead?"

"No, he's in Trenton Hospital," said Weiner. "We was on our way here, just past Trenton when all of a sudden he grabs at his chest and passes out cold, so I had to double back and take him into the hospital. He looked just awful, but at the hospital they said he would be all right. So, when they said that, I came on here."

"You got the money?" demanded Sicardo in a tone of utter fear.

"No, Mike's got it on him."

"Why didn't you take it off him," Sicardo cried amidst curses and accusations that Weiner had "fouled up" the whole deal.

"I couldn't get the money after I checked him into the hospital," said Weiner. "How'd it look if I took money off a guy brought into the hospital with a heart attack?"

They argued as Weiner drove into the lot across from the hotel entrance and parked his car. "What in hell am I gonna do with the junk?" Sicardo complained, "I don't want to walk around town with junk in my pocket."

Weiner, trying to calm the irascible club manager, insisted that Telano would be better and out of the hopsital in a day or two and that they still wanted to buy, that he could take the junk now and pay for it later. That decision, said Sicardo, was up to "Charley," and "Charley" was now waiting for them in the bar, but he himself did not intend to walk into the hotel with the heroin in his coat pocket. He wanted to leave it in the car until "Charley" decided what to do.

Agent Ted Harnett, at the wheel of the taxicab outside the parking lot, reported the scene on the car radio: "Weiner is getting out of the car . . . he is opening the trunk . . . going around to the right side door. The door is opening a little bit. . . . Suspect passing out a small package. . . . I think it is brown paper bag . . . Weiner put it in the trunk . . . getting back into driver's seat. . . . Now they're both getting out of the car and walking this way, toward the hotel." It was all evidence, this surveillance, to be used in court later, possibly.

In the radio room of the Bureau's New York office at 90 Church Street, the transaction in the parking lot was recognized agonizingly as the point of no return. Weiner had taken possession of the heroin. As a government agent he could not return it. If Golino demanded it back, Weiner would have no choice but to arrest him and Sicardo, and that would bring the case to an abortive end, shutting out any possibility of discovering the source of the illicit drugs.

The whereabouts of the heroin was Golino's first concern when Weiner and Sicardo joined him in a dimly lighted booth of the Lexington Bar. His eyes narrowed to slits as Sicardo spewed out the news that Telano was in the Trenton Hospital with a heart attack. "Where's the stuff?" the experienced racketeer demanded.

"I put it in his car," replied Sicardo, pointing to Weiner. Golino sighed with relief; he didn't like any direct contact with heroin any more than did Sicardo. He listened in cold, ominous silence as Weiner launched into a detailed description of how his partner had been stricken on the way to New York and had had to be taken to the hospital at Trenton, New Jersey. At the end of Weiner's explanation, Golino struck directly at the vital point. "That was God damn stupid of you, letting the guy go into the hospital with that much cash on him. Somebody could steal it from him in the hospital. Then where would you be, eh? Or suppose the guy dies there, then how are you going to get the money?"

Weiner reassured him that Telano had rallied at the hospital, regained consciousness, and had told him to keep this appointment. "I was so late then that I rushed right out and I forgot the money," Weiner said. "But Mike's going to be all right and I know we got these customers all set up on the West Coast, ready for the junk, so I thought, driving up here, you could give me the stuff on consignment and then we could pay you tomorrow or the next day, when Mike gets out of the hospital."

Golino shook his head slowly from side to side, his thin lips pressed tightly together. "I don't think I can do that without money on the line," he said, almost wistfully. "I got my other partners here in New York to answer to, and, you see, I just don't know you good enough to trust you with that much junk. It's nothin' personal, you understand, it's just that this is our first go-around. So, maybe it would be best if you give the stuff back to Jimmy here, and then when Telano gets better, we can try again."

With his reputation as a glib talker at stake, the government agent invited the two racketeers to dinner and further discussion. Over an excellent meal at Christo's Restaurant, a short walk from the hotel, the men discussed their dilemma which centered more and more upon the money involved. "If he dies, how am I going to get paid?" That was Golino's chief concern.

Weiner leaned across the table and in his best confidence

manner explained, "Believe me, you got nothing to worry about. If he dies, I take over. I'm the delivery man. I know the customers. If he dies, I'll sell the stuff and pay you myself. But, to tell you the truth, I don't think that old son of a bitch is going to die. He looked a whole lot better even when I left him."

Golino thought all this over and finally suggested that they telephone the hospital and check up on Telano's condition. "I want to be sure the guy's still alive," he said.

Weiner went to a telephone booth near their table and dialed Information for the phone number of the hospital. Then he dialed and deposited the correct amount of change.

"Trenton Hospital," the sweet voice of a receptionist sang out at the other end.

"I want to talk to one of your patients, Michael J. Telano, who was brought in today, a heart patient," Weiner shouted into the phone. A few moments later, he cried out, "Hello, Mike, how're you feeling? I'm here with Charley and Jimmy now, in a restaurant, and they're kind of worried. Yeah, about the money . . . you know, about how they're going to get paid for the merchandise we are buying." Weiner talked on as both Golino and Sicardo rose from the table and approached the telephone booth. "Yeah, Mike, that's a good idea, he said, reciting the phone number in the booth and then hanging up.

Turning to Golino, he explained, "Mike said he'd call back from a booth in the hall. He don't want to talk in his room 'cause there's another guy in there with him."

Golino took the return call and solicitously asked about Mike's health and went on to explain the problem of his New York partners and the need for them to be assured that they would be paid.

Fulgoni's response was pure, ill-tempered rage. His voice came through the telephone receiver like that of a wild, croaking boar. "I don't give a * * * what you do with your * * * junk, you can shove it for all I care. Here I am half dead and you guys worrying about a few grand like you don't trust me. If you don't want to sell, just say so, and that's that. But I'm gonna be getting out of here tomorrow or maybe the next day and I'll remember what you decided. Either we trust each other and we do business or I'll just have to find me another connection. I trust Johnny there to handle the junk for me. But if you don't trust me and my partner, then you take your horse back and let's forget the whole damn thing."

"I trust you, I trust you," placated Golino, again explaining the normal doubts of his own partners in New York.

"Well, that's up to you, either you trust us for a day or two and we'll pay you when I get out of here, or you don't and that's that." Fulgoni let loose with a fit of coughing into the phone.

Golino, after a moment's pause, said almost plaintively, "Well, I'll have to talk it over with Johnny here before I decide."

"Yeah, you do what you like," Fulgoni rasped and slammed down the phone before Golino could reply.

Then, with a sigh, he commented, "Well, that's the best I could do. I just hope Alan can come through." He leaned back in his swivel chair and stared at the silent black telephone, the silent radio equipment and the smiling faces of two fellow agents in the Bureau's radio room, a small, glassed-in cubicle near the supervisor's office. Aside from an attack of nerves which knotted his stomach, the government agent was in perfect health, carrying out a deception made necessary by the Deputy Commissioner's decision earlier that morning not to advance any more money to buy heroin in the Sicardo case.

The Deputy Commissioner had balked at the idea of spending twelve thousand dollars more of the Bureau's money on the case. Fulgoni already had made three buys from Sicardo and the Deputy Commissioner considered it unlikely that either Sicardo or Golino would lead the agents to their sources in New York. He had ordered the agents to effect the arrest of Sicardo and Golino when the half kilo of heroin was delivered, despite Fulgoni's pleas that they had at that time only an imperfect case of conspiracy against Golino, who, cautiously, had never actually handled any narcotics.

Fulgoni's aim, of course, was to extend his investigation as far as he could, tracing the traffic in heroin up the line to each supplier and, if possible, to the ultimate point—locating the stash, which is every agent's dream.

Bureau headquarters in Washington, however, views each case as part of its overall effort and weighs the expenditures for one case against the needs of all other cases then in progress. The

Bureau is necessarily tightfisted. Its special fund earmarked for "purchases of evidence," a kitty of $300,000, must be made to cover all the heroin buys made by agents in its sixteen regional offices over the entire year. And so, while Fulgoni was optimistic and eager to try to find Golino's source of supply in New York, the more experienced and presumably wiser heads in Washington viewed the odds as exorbitant. The Deputy Commissioner refused to advance any more money on such a slim chance.

Conferences, plans, alternate plans and telephone messages on the tie-line between Washington and New York occupied most of that morning before a compromise was reached: Fulgoni could keep his case open if he could get the heroin without paying out any money.

Fulgoni had devised the heart-attack ploy with Weiner and the supervisor of the New York office; Weiner, the glib talker, was given the task not only of conning two experienced heroin dealers out of their merchandise but also of somehow forcing them to lead the surveillance agents back to their source of supply somewhere in New York.

In the restaurant, Weiner talked on and Golino slowly came around. Sicardo, with his two-thousand-dollar fee at stake, vouched for the two men he knew as Telano and Gold as reputable, trustworthy dealers, reminding Golino that they were not likely to run out on them since they owned part of the motel on the outskirts of Philadelphia. He put forth his opinion with caution, not because of any doubt of Gold or Telano, but out of fear of the quiet-spoken Golino. "Okay, I'll go along with you guys but I have to speak with my partners before I give you a final okay," Golino announced.

Weiner blithely suggested that Golino take him along so that he personally could explain the situation to the partners.

"That's impossible," retorted Golino, "my partners don't want to meet anyone. I have to see them alone."

Hardly expecting an affirmative answer, Weiner agreed to wait for Golino but asked only that he be taken to the same neighborhood so he would not lose too much time in getting back to Philadelphia.

Golino made a phone call while Weiner paid the bill, and then the three men took a taxi crosstown to the Hotel Forrest on

West 49th Street between Broadway and Eighth Avenue. During the ride, Weiner neither asked nor looked out the window to see where he was going. It did not matter. He knew full well, without having to check behind him, that the taxi was being followed by the team of narcotics agents who had the restaurant under surveillance during the hour-long dinner. Heavy evening traffic in midtown New York effectively camouflaged the procession behind Golino's taxicab: agents Harold Cooper and Danny Monahan in another cab, agents Leonard Shuster and John Connelly in a radio car, agents Bob Courtney and John Riley in a black Ford. The Bureau's own taxicab remained at the parking lot. Agent Ted Harnett's job was to keep an eye on the evidence in the trunk of Fulgoni's Cadillac to be sure no one stole it.

When Golino, Sicardo and Weiner alighted from their cab on 49th Street, about midway between Broadway and Eighth Avenue, the surveillance teams deployed themselves quickly. The agents' cab drove past Golino and the two agents got out on the street at the far corner. The second car dropped one agent at the corner of Broadway and the third car was parked at the curb about a half block from the Hotel Forrest. Both ends of West 49th Street were covered.

Golino, taking his own precautions, instructed Sicardo to wait with Weiner outside the hotel and strode off. Agent John Riley, whose tall skinny body made him look as emaciated as a junkie, fell in behind Golino at Broadway and ambled along after him. Golino, confident that he would not reveal his partner to his buyer, entered Paddock's Bar on 50th Street, oblivious to the action around him. Agent Riley walked past the bar, stopped and then doubled back. But he did not go in. Agent Hal Cooper, a husky all-American type, took over. He walked in a few minutes later, looked around and then elbowed his way into a place at the bar alongside the man from Philadelphia.

The two men drank whiskey side by side, Golino facing the door, expectant, Cooper gazing into the bar mirror, nonchalant; and no one seeing these two men there together could have said with any certainty which was the crook out on a ten-thousand-dollar deal and which was the police officer working for civil service pay.

When the so-called partner walked in and joined Golino at

the bar, Cooper appraised the man with a glance and then turned his back on the two conspirators. Now he had no need to see them, so long as he could hear what they said. His professional eye already had taken in the new man's bald dome, thin features and heavy stomach so that although he could not identify Frank Merlotti by name, he would be able to pick him out of a lineup at any time within the next year.

Oblivious of the others at the bar, neither Golino nor his connection bothered to lower their voices.

"I don't have the money," Golino explained. "One of them got sick and his partner had to come alone."

"So, where's the package now?"

"In the trunk of their car on the East Side. Don't worry, they're good for the money."

"I don't know . . ."

"Listen, they're supposed to give me the money tomorrow," said Golino, exaggerating slightly. "You come down [to Philadelphia] on Wednesday and you'll get your money."

"Are you sure?"

"Yeah, I know them. I tell you they're good for the money. You come down on Wednesday as my guest. I'll show you around town a little and you'll have a ball."

"Agh, I don't want to hang around there."

"Okay, you won't have to wait. Once you get the cash, you can do as you please."

"As long as you're damn sure. I'll give you a ring and maybe I'll send one of my boys down for it."

Agent Cooper followed the conversation only until he had overheard the important elements; then he quit the bar ahead of the two men. Outside, on Broadway, he outlined the situation to the other agents and they planned the logistics of following Golino, his connection in the bar, and Sicardo, whichever way the three split up, and then the agents waited. One man took time out to radio the New York office that, according to plan, there would be no need for an arrest this night; Golino would give the half kilo of heroin to Weiner on consignment; he also had led the agents to his connection in New York.

Mike Fulgoni in the radio room heaved a great sigh of relief. The tingle of success is so sweet. He knew he would get Nick

Golino now, unless he himself made an egregious error. The first sale was always the hardest.

Golino remained in Paddock's Bar longer than expected, and so Hal Cooper went back inside, this time along with Bob Courtney, the senior agent on the surveillance team. They took positions further down the bar, from where they could observe the two suspects without themselves arousing any suspicions. Agent Courtney did not recognize the man with Golino, any more than did Cooper. But it was apparent that neither of the two men was aware that they were under observation.

Golino left the bar first, and walked rapidly down the block and up 49th Street to inform Weiner that he could have the heroin. "I'm taking a chance on you guys 'cause I think you're okay, but the money better be paid by Wednesday like I promised my partners, not a day later, and don't you forget it."

Weiner, the last agent on the case to know of his own success, pledged with all the sincerity he could muster that the money would be paid. "Charley," he told Nicolas Golino with a straight face, "Telano's going to appreciate this favor and you'll find that we're goin' to be good customers."

A happy Sicardo clapped Weiner on the back. "This is going to be a great thing as long as we work together and trust one another. No secrets. I want you to know that I told Charley here about my commission of two grand, so there are no secrets, eh, between us. You'll have that two thousand dollars with you on Wednesday, right?"

"Right."

The ever-practical Golino summed it up before they parted: "Don't forget, we'll see you at Jimmy's club on Wednesday at one o'clock with the full amount, twelve thousand dollars."

"Right."

Weiner took a taxi back to the parking lot on the East Side and delivered the half kilo of heroin to the Bureau's office at 90 Church Street. There it was tested for a positive reaction, weighed, sealed, initialed in the presence of two government agents and locked away in a safe as evidence.

Golino and Sicardo were followed to three different night spots in the Broadway area before they picked up their car and headed back to Philadelphia.

Golino's connection left the bar and went directly home. Three agents, one in a taxi and two in a radio car, trailed him back across town and observed him enter a tall, luxury apartment building on 63rd Street at Second Avenue. The two agents in the radio car staked out the building for six hours, not daring to make inquiries which might get back to the suspect; at 3 A.M. they decided that the apartment building was indeed his home or his home away from home, and they called it a night.

Two days later, Mike Fulgoni played out the last scene of this particular charade. Weiner showed up at the club on time but alone and without the money. Telano was out of the hospital, resting at the motel; he had the money, but he wanted both Charley and Jimmy to come to see him and then he would pay them. Weiner stuck to that story until Jimmy relayed it to Golino and all three men drove out to the motel.

They found Fulgoni propped up in bed wearing outrageously gaudy flowered pajamas, three pillows stacked behind his head, and an array of medicine bottles on the small night table by his side. It was a proper sick room. The sick man wheezed and coughed as he replied to Golino's solicitous inquiries. He described his close call with death and he told them that lying in bed he had had time to think and there were certain things about their deal which he did not like. Golino listened without committing himself, but Sicardo began to fidget with anxiety. "You got the money, ain't you?" he asked.

"Sure, I got the money," Fulgoni shot back at Sicardo. His rage suddenly filled the room. Lifting himself from the pillows, he shouted at the little club manager. "You are a double-crossing * * * bastard, a liar and a cheat and chiseler. You think you're dealing with a couple of fools? You thought you could pull a fast one on us, didn't you? You told me this guy's a big wheel from New York. He ain't even from New York. I checked around and I know who he is. He's Nick Golino and he's from right here in Philadelphia, buying junk from New York and selling it to us at a profit."

Golino interrupted. "Now don't get yourself in an uproar, take it easy." When he had eased Fulgoni back onto his pillows, Golino admitted his identity, but he assured the man in bed that he was the Philadelphia connection for his New York partners long before this deal. "You're getting a fair shake on that junk, and you know it."

"Okay, maybe you're right on that," Fulgoni said. "You're okay, Nick, but that son of a bitch is a cheap chiseler." Turning once again upon Sicardo, Fulgoni lashed out. "I ain't giving you no two thousand! You didn't get me a New York connection. I owe Nick here ten grand and I'm going to pay that, but no two thousand."

Sicardo screamed back that a promise was a promise, he had supplied the connection, they had got their stuff, and he was owed two thousand dollars. The argument went on amidst swears and curses, accusations and denials, until Fulgoni, at the height of one of his harangues, clutched at his chest, coughed, fell back on his pillows, and rasped to Weiner, "Quick, Johnny, get me the pills."

Weiner grabbed the bottle in front, marked "H T Nitroglycerin 1/150 grams," and shook out two pills. Fulgoni popped the placebo tablets into his mouth and lay there as if waiting for relief. No one spoke.

Golino picked up the bottle of nitroglycerin pills and nodded his head. "These are very good for heart cases, I know, but you mustn't get so excited, Mike," he said.

Fulgoni, taking in big gulps of air, remained silent as long as he thought he could hold the men enthralled, and then he announced, as if after due deliberation, "All right, Jimmy, I'll give you one thousand bucks and that's that!"

Little Jimmy Sicardo, who had a fiery temper of his own, renewed the argument and Fulgoni once again allowed his feigned wrath to rise. Golino broke in with a command which settled the dispute. "Take it and shut up," he told Sicardo. "Mike here has got to take it easy with his ticker. We'll all make plenty of money, so let's not fight when we just got started." Sicardo subsided to the voice of authority, but he was unhappy. Golino then turned to Fulgoni. "You better pay us now, I gotta get back to town."

Fulgoni treated himself to two more pills and then counted out ten thousand dollars for Golino and one thousand dollars for Sicardo in Federal Reserve notes, the serial numbers of which were recorded in the Philadelphia office. He told Golino he would be ready to place another order in a week or ten days. The Philadelphia racketeer responded that Mike should take it easy for at least a week and then they could all go into New York for a few days' relaxation and business.

When they had left, Fulgoni knew he had not only saved the government one thousand dollars with his act but had also won Golino's respect. He had shown that he was not the kind of man to throw one thousand dollars around. He had acted as any good racketeer would in conning Sicardo out of some money.

On the half-hour drive back to Philadelphia, Golino remarked to Weiner, "You guys have a good setup at that motel. What you should do is buy two or three kilos at a time, then we wouldn't have to make so many trips to New York, and you can stash it right there in the motel."

"Yeah, that's a good idea," said Weiner. "I'll tell Mike."

# 16

# A House in the Suburbs

The ten kilos of heroin which Léon Levonian had brought into New York City continued on their journey, now backtracking out and away from the narcotics capital of the United States. Any number of men would, if they could, commit murder to get their hands on twenty-two pounds of pure heroin. That was enough to establish an independent business. New York, a city of opportunity, was considered too dangerous a place in which to stash away any more heroin than was absolutely necessary for the day's business at hand. Too many things could happen. There were too many federal narcotics agents, too many city detectives concentrating on narcotics, too many informers, too many men on the lookout always for a dream treasure of narcotics.

When Biani and his partner Merlotti had escorted "François" from their basement to the neutral territory of Houston Street, Tony the Nose tucked the package of heroin under his arm and beneath his coat and quit the basement by way of an escape hatch in the back which led him out to an alley, not far from where his automobile had been parked. It was a plain car, a Plymouth sedan three years old, but equal to the task for which it was ordinarily used, and as a vehicle it drew no undue attention to itself. Tony was saving his money towards the purchase of a new, bigger car, in keeping with his rising status, one which he had no intention of risking in the traffic of illicit drugs.

He was a well-built six-footer and not a likely candidate for a chance mugging in an alley, but he was as aware of that risk as he was of the possibility of being picked up by the police. These were the hazards for which he was paid a salary of two hundred dollars a week.

Tony Martino, in the parlance of the street, was a punk, a cog in the wheel, a workhorse, the one who took the greatest risk the most number of times for the least amount of money. Yet any number of men, young and old, would gladly have taken over his job, if given the chance, simply because he was an accepted member of an organization, a part of organized crime, albeit on the lowest rung of the ladder, and everyone knows that it is far better to be a punk in an organization than a punk out on your own. Tony Martino was the delivery man for the Biani organization. As a way of earning a living, it was better than rolling drunks, holding up liquor stores or burglarizing apartments for fences who reaped the profits. He had a steady income, a steady job, and he was only twenty-six years old with, as his father had told him, plenty of time to learn. Meanwhile, he did as he was told. He made the pick-ups and the deliveries as instructed. He never handled the money, other than that which was paid to him, and he never cheated on his bosses, either Biani or Merlotti. His wife, yes, but his employers, no.

To his parents, he was still Antonio, their only son, a good, dutiful boy raised in the strict tradition of the old country. He loved his mother and emulated his father who, now in his sixties, was semi-retired from the rackets. Enrico Martino had been an important bootlegger in Kansas City in the 1920's and early '30's, and he still had good contacts with the old-timers who knew and trusted him. He had served two terms in prison, one for operating an illicit still and the other for distributing bootleg whiskey. After the second two-year term, he had moved to New York and then out to Long Island. The people in town knew him only as an old Italian tailor, deft with his fingers, who labored all day at the sewing machine, saved his money and managed to buy two 2-family houses; he lived in one with his wife and the other he gave to his son, drawing rental income from both houses. He lived modestly in Valley Stream, Long Island, and kept to himself. What his neighbors could not see, they could not know. In the attic of his own home, he minded the heroin supplies of the Biani syndicate; and as an old bootlegger, it was no trouble at all to learn how to mix milk sugar with the narcotic drug to produce whatever strength the organization desired. His modest and plain home served as an ideal stash for a New York City outfit. It was out of the way and unnoticeable, in a quiet community with a very small police department. It had been only a matter of time before old Rico introduced his son Antonio to Big Joe as a good boy who could be trusted to deliver the merchandise from the stash to the customer.

When Tony brought home Levonian's ten kilos of pure heroin, he embraced his mother and went directly to the attic where he tucked the package away and relocked the attic door. That night, he knew, he would join his father in "whacking up" the new merchandise. When he came downstairs from the attic, his mother had hot coffee waiting for him on the kitchen table.

In preparing Levonian's ten kilos of heroin for resale in America, Tony served his father as a general helper. He fetched, moved and arranged supplies and equipment as needed so that the old man could concentrate upon the task at hand. They worked in the attic on an old square table covered with heavy, nonporous oilcloth upon which were set the scales, a hot plate, a flask with a special melting-point thermometer, cans of milk sugar and the twenty glassine bags of heroin.

First, the merchandise was weighed and then its purity was tested by measuring its melting point. When old Enrico had checked and rechecked that he had ten kilograms of heroin with a purity of 88 percent, he then set about adulterating the product.

The process is simple: Just add milk sugar, which resembles heroin in appearance, and then add a touch of quinine to replace the bitter taste lost in the process of dilution. The vital question for anyone diluting pure heroin is, How much should you cut it?

The more you cut it, the more money you will make. You can cut heroin of 88 percent purity sixteen times to produce sixteen kilos of heroin of 5.5 percent strength that would sell for a fortune, something like a quarter of a million dollars. But there is a rub: You would then have to sell that 5.5 percent heroin to the addicts on the street. And that is risky business. Even if you cut the junk only eight times for half the profit, you would have to sell to the untrustworthy pushers on the street. And that is risky business.

That, as a matter of fact, is the business the Mafia reputedly quit back in 1957. The "law" was passed and the "word" handed down at the now famous Apalachin meeting of Mafia chieftains: The *capo dons* were to survey their territories, and each and every member was to be given six months in which to get rid of his heroin inventory and then to get out and stay out of the junk business.

It had been debated for all of the previous year, and there had been considerable opposition from the younger men who thought they had not yet reaped the profits to which they were entitled. But the Apalachin meeting decided the matter. Two reasons lay behind the decision: The then new Narcotics Control Act of 1956 provided very stiff penalties, which, in the opinion of the top bosses, outweighed the profits (five to twenty years for the first offense, ten to forty years for subsequent convictions, without benefit of probation or parole); and the public's growing awareness of heroin addiction, combined with headline stories of narcotics arrests of men with Italian names, was casting disgrace upon the Italian community as a whole in America.

Immediately after the six-month clearing-up period expired, the Mafia "law" was enforced. Several rebellious Young Turks who could not or chose not to forsake the profits in narcotics were made to serve as examples to the others. Tony De Marco, for one, was clubbed with a hammer, stabbed fifty-seven times, mutilated and left to die in an abandoned car. Others got the message. Narcotics sales at the street level were left to others, primarily the Negroes and Puerto Ricans in the business. But as time went on, the Mafia law was amended to permit members, particularly the top members, to import heroin from France and to sell it only once on the much safer wholesale level. After all, it was thought, it was only the Sicilians who did have the proper contacts with their Corsican cousins in France.

And so, when Enrico Martino cut Levonian's heroin for his organization, he whacked it only once. From each half-kilo bag, he extracted two ounces of heroin. He replaced it with two ounces of milk sugar, an extract of milk sold in one-pound tins at any drugstore. When he was through, the ten kilos of pure heroin supplied by Levonian produced eleven kilos and five ounces. The purity was reduced only to 77 percent, which most of Biani's customers would consider pure heroin indeed, top grade. Meanwhile, what Biani had bought for $125,000 would bring in, at a minimum, a quick and easy $200,000, a profit of $75,000 for precious little work and a great deal of know-how.

As a matter of course, the eleven kilos of new heroin were repackaged in half-kilo lots in new, unused double glassine bags, folded down at the top, stapled shut and inserted into ordinary brown paper bags which also were folded shut and secured with wire. The finished product looked as innocent as would any twenty-two grocer's bags containing a pound of coffee each. Biani would sell them as pure, unadulterated half kilos of heroin because few of his buyers, if any, would differentiate between purities of 88 or 77 percent.

The first delivery of the heroin brought all the way from Turkey by Léon Levonian was made, several days after the cutting, to Louis Pacinello, a distributor who lived in Tenafly, New Jersey, and supplied an area on the West Side of Manhattan a mile or so north of Columbus Circle. Pacinello, a thug who had served time for assault, for robbery, and once for possession and sale of narcotics, waited for Tony Martino at a prearranged meeting place where the police would hardly expect to find him: an ice-cream parlor off Sunset Highway in Queens. He drank coffee, black, until Tony joined him at the counter. Their conversation was most general, for each man knew what he was there for.

"You're coming up in the world, eh?" Tony commented.

"Yeah, things are looking up these days."

A meaningless exchange to anyone overhearing them, but Tony had been delivering to Pacinello for almost a year, usually a half or a full kilo, and this order was for three kilos.

When they had finished their coffee, the two men strolled out to the parking lot, where Tony had parked his Plymouth alongside Pacinello's Cadillac. Having looked about to be certain that they were not observed, Tony unlocked his car, took out the package and simply handed it to the purchaser. Pacinello tripped a series of electrical connections inside his car, and the backrest of the rear seat flew open. He deposited his merchandise and snapped the seat shut again. The use of solenoids to trip hiding places in cars, popular in the underworld in the 1930's, was considered out of fashion in the '60's, since the police and federal agents knew all about them. Yet, Pacinello delighted in his own car safe in which the lock on the rear backrest was tripped only when the heat control was put at full blast and the ignition key turned to the left.

The two men talked and swapped jokes in the dark of the parking lot, behaving in the perfectly ordinary fashion of two friends meeting in a public place, and then they parted, each in his own automobile, each going his own way. Delivery of narcotics at the wholesale level is as simple as that. So long as the men were not recognized for what they were, they acted in almost perfect safety.

There were many different means of delivering narcotics. Tony had delivered to Pacinello before, without leaving his own car, on a public street in New York. He simply met him on a prearranged street at an agreed-upon time, passed the package through his window into Pacinello's car and drove away. That transaction never took more than a few seconds. It had the disadvantage of arousing the momentary suspicion of anyone observing a package being passed from one car to another. Meeting in a parking lot took more time but was less suspicious, although any method worked so long as it went unobserved by a policeman alert to the flow of traffic in narcotics.

Tony Martino also delivered to customers he never met, simply by getting a key and instructions from Frank Merlotti, then depositing the purchased narcotics in the trunk of a car parked on some side street and going on his way.

The money was always paid to Merlotti, either before or after or perhaps at the time of delivery. That was not the concern of Tony Martino. He made deliveries and took orders from the short fat man who ran the operation for Big Joe. Tony realized that he himself was only a cog in the wheel, yet he was not dissatisfied. The nerve center of the operation was Merlotti's apartment on East 63rd Street, safe in the luxury of New York's affluent. After all, the Rockefellers, the Nixons and the Harrimans lived not more than a mile away. Tony had been up to the apartment, but never when carrying narcotics. The apartment was the base of the operation and its managers wanted to keep it clean.

# 17

# East Side Address

Frank Merlotti lived comfortably elbow to elbow with two million other New Yorkers on the island of Manhattan, protected by the anonymity of sheer numbers and the solid, soundproof door of his apartment. His door, marked 7-K, was the same size, shape and color as every other apartment door in the sixteen-story building. His large living room, dining alcove, kitchen and two bedrooms were proportioned like thousands of others in the high-rental section of New York's East Side north of 57th Street. Few, however, were furnished with the extravagant amount of cash spent on the nine-foot velvet Empire couch, the carved mahogany console, lined inside with mirrors, which housed his liquor supply, and the massive desk which Merlotti had imported from Italy.

If any other criminal activities were carried on in the building, Frank Merlotti did not know of them. He was acquainted with none of his neighbors and certainly not with their business affairs, nor they with his. He had long made it a practice never even to nod a greeting to his next-door neighbor or to discuss the weather with a stranger in the elevator. He was a New York apartment dweller who minded his own business, paid his rent on time and conducted his affairs with quiet decorum.

He shared the apartment with his partner, Big Joe Biani,

although almost all the callers and sometimes he himself considered the apartment all his. Biani, who lived with his family in Virginia, used the second bedroom only when he was in New York. Merlotti's wife and three small children basked in the Florida sunshine of Miami. He loved them dearly, denying them little that money could buy. Whenever he could find three or more days clear of business he would fly down for a quick visit. A proud and confident man, who had had to fight his way to the top, he conducted himself as one of those big men in the rackets whom the newspapers and television reporters alluded to as the untouchables of crime. He had not been in police custody for more than twenty years, long enough for the law to have forgotten about him.

In the old days, Frank Merlotti had been a jack-of-all-trades, running errands for a *capo don* of the Mafia on the Lower East Side, a tough old Sicilian who could hardly speak and certainly could not write English. But he had known how to handle men, how to put the arm on someone and to get what he wanted. To Frank Merlotti he had been like a kindly old uncle, teaching him, protecting him and trusting him until almost the very end when he had become senile and had raged in paranoia at everyone near him, dying finally of advanced old age in a tremendous four-poster feather bed. By then Frank Merlotti had made himself competent at planning and executing one or two extortion rackets, handling hijacked shipments of whiskey, selling counterfeit OPA stamps, until he had found his niche in narcotics and had given up almost all other activities. In narcotics, he soon found he could make more money more easily than from all of his past schemes combined.

Frank Merlotti himself did not actually see heroin from one year to the next, although he understood purity strength, current market prices and, above all, the needs of his customers. He sold only to men whom he knew and trusted, and sold in such a way that he, and certainly his partner, Biani, were protected at all times. Big Joe, with his overseas connections, was the true proprietor of the business: He invested his money in France or Canada, arranged deliveries, decided upon the cutting and the purity. Merlotti served, in effect, as the sales manager. The difference was that he did not invest his own money. While he did not reap the profits Biani reaped, neither did he risk the loss. Merlotti took a standard cut: one thousand dollars for each and every kilo of heroin he sold. And he sold only to a select clientele, in kilo or higher lots, usually in the privacy of his own apartment. As in all businesses, there were problems, but heroin had always been a seller's market, a salesman's delight, and Merlotti ran a smooth, efficient operation.

A few minutes before three o'clock, he lit a cigar and waited for the sound of the buzzer announcing his first customer of the afternoon.

At that moment, the customer was impatiently driving a 340-horsepower Cadillac at an average speed of fifteen miles per hour in the mid-afternoon traffic of East 63rd Street. His five o'clock shadow always came two hours early. His sallow complexion made it impossible for him ever to look as well-groomed as his car; his shirt showed the wrinkles if not the dirt of a second day's wear. But his mind was as sharp as ever. He was sober. His own peculiar and personal code precluded him from drinking while on the job. He drove past the front entrance of the apartment house, taking note of the normalcy of the scene. He noticed the usual glum expression on the face of the doorman whom he had recognized long ago as a fellow secret drinker. Rounding the corner, he stopped for yet another traffic light, and then, rounding the next corner, he came finally to the entrance of the underground garage in the rear of the building. The big automobile glided in silently, and Angelo Minetti backed it into the stall marked 7-K. He locked the four doors of the car, and, looking around first to be sure no one else was in the garage, he unlocked the car's trunk. He left it open, but unnoticeably so, just a fraction of an inch off the latch. Then he strolled to the bank of elevators on the north side of the building. He stopped briefly at the board of bell buttons to signal his arrival: two long and two short blasts. Back down came the all clear: two short rings.

Angie Minetti was a rough piece of goods. Short, stocky, muscular and terribly strong, a street fighter good with his fists or an iron pipe or a switchblade, his scars and lumps served as badges of his experience. A member of an East Bronx organization, Angie had his own list of heroin customers, almost all of them in Harlem or Spanish Harlem. To the Negro and Puerto

Rican distributors, Angie was a big Mafia man commanding their respect, their fear and their envy. Within his own organization and among his peers, Angie was just a "soldier," a "button man," who could be trusted to live by the code of the organization and was capable, but was nothing special.

"You look like a slob," Merlotti sneered at him in the apartment. "Why in hell can't you put on clean clothes when you come up here? I told you not to come around looking like a bum."

"Agh, * * * that, no one sees me come up here anyway, you're gettin' too finicky in your old age, Frank." Angie flopped into an oversized armchair and waved his hand at the liquor cabinet. "Boy, did I have a rough night . . . why don't you pour me a drink and I'll tell you about this stacked dame?" The little gangster hardly waited for Merlotti to approach the supply of Scotch before he launched into the details of his latest sexual adventure. Merlotti listened with vicarious enjoyment while seeing to it that his guest's glass was never empty. This was the prelude to business, part of the routine. Both understood the necessity of their spending at least a half hour in each other's company while the merchandise was being delivered.

They swapped stories and gossiped guardedly about what was going on in their milieu, until Merlotti sensed the propitious moment to broach the delicate matter of money. Drawing from his pocket a slip of paper, a page torn from a small spiral notebook, he solemnly read his handwritten notation—"Angie—4/16—2—35,000"—and then waved the slip of paper at his guest. "Well, Angie, how much you come up with today?"

"I got all what I owe you for the last batch, Frank, thirty-five thou." Lumbering out of the chair, the East Bronx dealer tugged his shirttails from his trousers, loosened his belt and then stripped a bulky leather money belt from his waist. From the belt he took $35,000 in old bills of various denominations, which he piled in a heap upon a table as he counted off his debt. Merlotti grimaced at the slovenly habits of the hoodlum who refused to learn even basic manners in handling large sums of money, but he began recounting the cash.

"I got to ask you to give me today's three kees on consignment," Minetti said as Merlotti finished computing. "This guy who's my best customer lost his bundle again last week, so he's going to pay me for both weeks when he sells this batch. But he's good for it, I know that."

Merlotti frowned. "How long you gonna carry this stupid bastard? You know he can go broke for good or he can get busted and then you'll be in trouble. I got to get mine from you, no matter what happens to your man."

"Listen, Frank, you know I don't con you. This is no small-time bum, he's got the biggest operation in Harlem today, I swear, and he is slick as oil, got thirty or forty junkies pushing for him and he's got a regular shyster and a bail bondsman in on the operation, so just as soon as one of the junkies is picked up, he's sprung. No one has to talk to the cops 'cause inside of an hour the lawyer's there with the bail.

"I don't mind telling you because this guy is loyal, too," Angie continued. "He don't shop around, he buys all his stuff from me 'cause I started him out and now he's flying high. You wouldn't believe it, but you know what he buys from me every week? A kilo a week. Believe me, he's loaded."

"So, where's his money, if he's so loaded?" asked Merlotti.

"You know those guys, big car, lots of dames, and this one just loves the craps table," Angie sneered. "He can drop everything he got in his pocket in one night and that's all his loot for the week. So, I carry him for a week and he pays me off right away the next week before he blows it again. He loves to gamble —can't help it, like he's got a habit." Minetti stopped for a significant pause and then asked, "You get the picture?"

A proposition was in the offing. Merlotti leaned back in his chair and waited for it. To ask a man his customer's name or to be too inquisitive would have been a breach of etiquette. In the scheme of things, Merlotti had his own place: He was a wholesale distributor, and he did not sell to Negro or Puerto Rican dealers who were only once removed from the dangerous street-level sales, nor did he muscle in on his own customer's domain. This was the tacit code; this was the organization of organized crime. However, nothing in the code precluded a mutually beneficial deal at the expense of someone outside the organization.

A thin smile creased Merlotti's lips. "Go on," he said.

"I don't want to get in a game with him or nothing like that,"

Angie Minetti said, "but I can steer him and you set up the game with Tony and some of his boys. I don't have to explain the rest to you, eh?"

Merlotti, who had a financial partnership with three other men in backing a floating dice game, remarked that he could accommodate Minetti's customer. The possibility of the customer's winning never entered the discussion. A man who plays dice or cards for the love and excitement of the game will always lose to the cold professional, even without sleight of hand.

Angie Minetti asked for a 10 percent cut on all of his customer's losses at craps. He settled for 5 percent. At the same time, Merlotti agreed to give him three kilos of heroin on consignment, to be paid for after he had disposed of them.

Upon Merlotti's pledge that no one would try to muscle in on Angie's heroin arrangement, the Bronx mobster revealed the identity of his customer. "Nobody knows this guy's real name, except his brother who works with him, but he's called Georgia Jack. Maybe you heard of him? He puts out good junk, they say, about 10 percent, in twenty-dollar bags, and he's got all the old-timers, the smart big habits, buying from him. He's a big black son of a bitch, six four and 250 pounds, and he's mean, I can tell you. He'd as soon cut you or kill you if you cross him. Spent fifteen or twenty years in the joint for shooting a cop, no less, and he served his time, no parole or nothing. You'll get the picture, Frank, when you see this guy. And, remember, he thinks I'm a friend of his and he's got respect for me so there's no funny stuff between us, just strictly aboveboard, I give him a fair shake on the junk and he pays me regular, except, of course, when he get's taken in a craps game."

While Angelo Minetti talked and laughed and drank in the comfort of Merlotti's apartment, his order for three kilos of heroin was delivered with ease and safety. Simplest plans are best. Tony Martino, having received the go-ahead from Merlotti, drove his automobile into the garage of the building, parked it in the slot alongside Minetti's Cadillac and, within fifteen seconds, transferred the three kilos of heroin from beneath the front seat of his car to the trunk of Minetti's automobile. Once he slammed the trunk of the Cadillac down upon its latch, the trunk was locked and Tony Martino was safe. He signaled the safe delivery by buzzing Merlotti's apartment and left the scene.

Minetti drove to his own stash, a rented tenement apartment near his home in the East Bronx, without opening the trunk until he was ready to carry the merchandise to the apartment. A specially built telescoping pipe allowed him to slide the stove away from the wall, and there, behind the plaster and lath, he maintained his cache in a hole big enough to accommodate at least ten kilos of narcotics, unknown to the police and safe from the happenstance of burglary.

Even before Angie reached his hideaway, Merlotti was arranging for the delivery of heroin with another associate of his organization. He preferred, when he could, to bunch all of his week's business into two or three days so that he could spend the remainder of each week seeing his family in Florida or just going on a bender without any business concerns hovering over him.

"We're checked in at the Edison Hotel, him and his partner in one room and Jimmy Sicardo and me in another on the same floor, so you can make the delivery tonight, like you wanted," Nick Golino of Philadelphia explained, leading up softly to the hitch in the previous arrangements he had made with Merlotti.

"How much does the guy want this time?" Merlotti asked.

"That's just it, Frank, the guy promised to buy three kees but when we got here he phoned his customer out West, and now he only wants a half a kilo."

Merlotti cursed. "Didn't you tell him we don't sell less than a kilo? You're a fool for setting this whole thing up for just a half a kee, 'cause that's the sort of penny-ante stuff which can get you in trouble."

"Nah, this is an okay guy, it's just that he's getting set up again because he's hot on the West Coast or somethin', and I just know he's goin' to be buying three or five kilos regular, but he wants to be careful. I like his style. No foolin' around, all business and takin' no chances, so I trust him 'cause I know it will work out."

Merlotti finally agreed to deliver that same night. "You tell him that this is the last half kilo he's getting; if he wants to do business, he's got to take a whole kee or more. We'll deliver around nine o'clock. Stay with both of them all day, take in a movie or something, and then, while Jimmy sticks with them, you get the key to their room and bring it here. But make sure Jimmy stays with them all the time. I don't want them to see anything. You understand?

"Around nine o'clock you all get back to the hotel and stand at the side-street entrance, and when you see The Nose leave, then you know it's okay to go back up to the room. The stuff will be in the second drawer of the bureau. Get it?"

"Yeah," said Golino. "Don't worry about a thing. I don't see how anything could go wrong."

# 18

# West Side Hotel

The two merchants, Nick Golino and Angie Minetti, went forth from their wholesaler's apartment each sublimely confident in his own ability and venture. Although they had never met, they matched one another in their singleness of purpose, their nerves of steel, their caution about the dangers involved. The fact that an Armenian Frenchman named Léon Levonian was a new and bountiful source of supply concerned these merchants no more than did the ultimate effect of the heroin upon the addicts all over the country who might be using the stuff. They were businessmen who bought a product wholesale, marked it up and sold it at a profit. In their arrangements with Merlotti, they had taken all the safety insurance available to them. They trusted their supplier and their proven methods of operation. They had no need to sneak about, to use back alleyways or behave like common criminals.

Angie Minetti drove off in his handsome Cadillac. In the trunk were three kilos of junk, about six and a half pounds of white powder, for which he would pay $52,500 and would sell for $60,000 or more before the week was out. If he had been stopped, the heroin in his car would have been valued at their street prices and the headlines would have screamed, "Quarter of a million dollars' worth of heroin seized," but that was one of the risks of the business. Nick Golino strode down the street to the corner of Second Avenue in search of a taxicab, his head held up high, his shoulders back, his gray suit neatly pressed, his shoes spotlessly shined, with not a speck of the heroin he had purchased on his person. How could either man suspect that as he left the apartment he was in the line of sight of four agents of the Bureau of Narcotics, posted in unmarked cars, one on the side street, the other on the avenue?

Angie Minetti, who was taking the far greater risk, was lucky. None of the four agents recognized him. And so, passing his greatest danger unaware, he traveled to his East Bronx stash in complete safety, alone and undetected.

It was for Nick Golino that the four agents were posted and waiting. Nor did they have a bit of trouble spotting him. His police-file photograph had been studied carefully before the agents had picked him up at the Hotel Edison and followed him to Merlotti's apartment. Golino, of course, thought he was controlling the situation, as any experienced narcotics seller would, by insisting that his customers Telano and Gold come in to New York to pick up their purchases and then carry the stuff themselves back to Philadelphia. Delivery in an empty room seemed foolproof to Golino, who was more worried about a heist or hijacking job than about police interference.

Telano, who wanted to see a dentist in New York, had come ahead and booked the rooms for the four men the day before and then, apparently through no fault of his own, could not reach one of his customers on the West Coast to find out how much junk he wanted to buy. And so the deal was put off one day. Golino took it upon himself to show his new customer a good time in New York. There was, after all, a good chance that Telano would order three or five kilos. Dinner for four at a top restaurant had set Golino back $125. Another century note went fast in a well-known nightclub where the headwaiter greeted Golino by name for only a sawbuck tip. At the ensuing round of bar hopping late into the night, each of the men took turns digging into their pockets. Golino beamed when an entertainer, headwaiter or bar owner took the time to join his table for a round of drinks. This was status as well as good business.

Mixing business with social pleasures, Golino suggested that

Telano buy heroin in substantial lots. "You ought to take five kees at a whack so we don't have to carry the stuff around so much," he urged. "You can stash it in that motel of yours and get rid of it whenever you want since you got such a good place to keep the stuff."

"Why should I keep the stuff around?" Telano countered. "It's just as easy to line up the customers first, and then I can buy what I can use. Don't worry, it should be three or maybe five kees this time, and then once we get this thing set right, I can take three to five on a regular basis."

Golino's hopes were kept high until the following afternoon when he and Sicardo entered Telano's hotel room just as the heavyset racketeer was ending a call apparently to the West Coast. "You get your ✻ ✻ ✻ end straightened up out there this week because I got to know if you want to do business or not. No, don't phone me . . . I'll call you." He slammed down the receiver and turned to Golino. "The stupid bastard's run into some sort of trouble and he's reneged. Says he can only take a half a kee this week and no more."

Golino shook his head in consternation. "I don't think my connection will sell in less than kilo lots. Maybe you don't understand, he's a big operator and he don't deal under a kilo."

Telano was adamant, even to the point of rejecting Golino's most reasonable offer that he take a kilo, pay for only a half on delivery and for the remainder when he sold the first half. Golino tried various approaches, but finally, when he realized that he could sell either half a kilo of heroin or nothing at all, he agreed to talk to his connection about "this one exception" to the kilo rule.

Thus, leaving Sicardo with the two customers, he had gone on his mission alone to see Merlotti. At least, he had thought he was alone.

As Golino left the hotel elevator, a tall, blond man took up his trail in the lobby. Agent Leonard Shuster nodded to his partner, John Connelly, standing at the 47th Street entrance to the hotel, and both men joined in the surveillance. When Golino took a taxi, Shuster hopped into a cab behind him. Connelly followed in a radio car, reporting in to the Bureau as he trailed Golino to his souce of supply. A second government car, with two agents, was dispatched to cover the back entrance to the East Side apartment house.

When Golino returned to the Hotel Edison, he told Telano, "My connection, he didn't like it much but I talked him into a half a kilo, but you better come across with a better deal next time. You got the money with you, eh?"

"Yeah, I got it."

"Well, delivery's tonight," Golino said. "My connection's got to make certain arrangements, you understand, so I thought maybe we'd all take in a movie or something to pass the time."

"What ever you say, Nick."

Golino and Telano got along well together. Each recognized in the other the attributes of a successful and experienced trafficker. Words were not wasted, confidences were not exchanged. Among experienced rackets men, anyone inclined to talk too much about past business deals was not to be trusted with current secrets. Anyone who likes to talk in the narcotics business talks too much. Golino silently appreciated Telano's restraint in not inquiring into the delivery arrangements. He had no way of knowing, of course, that Telano's restraint was calculated to allay any possible suspicions. Without Golino knowing it, control of the situation had passed almost but not quite completely into his customer's hands.

Telano's dental appointment the day before had been spent, of course, at the Bureau's New York office where he, the regional supervisor, a group leader and six surveillance agents worked out the strategy for covering this second purchase of heroin from Golino and Sicardo. They spent hours devising alternative plans to cover all the contingencies possible. Agent Fulgoni described the characteristics, personalities and habits of the two narcotics traffickers he had come to know so well over the past few months. The other agents had to know what to expect of Golino and Sicardo, which one was liable to become violent, which one of them was suspicious of a close surveillance, whether to stick with a man at the risk of being uncovered or to drop a tail if Golino or Sicardo displayed any suspicions. To make this buy from the two of them, whom Fulgoni had cultivated so well and for so long, was relatively simple and basic for the experienced agent and his partner. To keep the buy under observation for future court evidence was not difficult. That was all fundamental *modus operandi* for trained narcotics agents. But to make the buy and keep it under surveillance in such a way that the suspects would lead the agents to their source or sources of supply—that was the tantalizing challenge of the job.

While the agents could not know how or when Golino might contact his supplier, it was apparent that the connection was somewhere in New York and that Golino would have to meet or telephone the man higher up to place the order and that either he or Sicardo would have to get the narcotics from someone somewhere. To control that situation, it was planned and programmed that agent Fulgoni, as Telano, would order a half kilo of heroin on the following day only at the last minute and in his own hotel room. This would oblige Golino, it was hoped, to see his connection in person in order to explain the change from the expected three-kilo sale to a half-kilo sale. If he telephoned, the agents would be out of luck, since Bureau policy prohibited telephonic wire taps; but if Golino went in person to see his connection, the Bureau's agents would not be far behind.

Nick Golino, suspecting nothing of what was going on beyond his ken, followed his own design in leading Sicardo and his two customers from the hotel to a Broadway movie house which was featuring a three-hour religious epic. They were followed by all four surveillance agents who had been assigned to the hotel lobby and by two other agents in separate radio cars. Neither Fulgoni nor his partner, Weiner, gave the slightest sign of recognition. Golino and Sicardo were absorbed in cussing out New York's inclement weather and irreducible street crowds. Only two agents, Connelly and Fred Robinson, followed them into the theater. The other two agents, on foot, took up positions outside, but just under the marquee, ready to move with any one of the four who came out of the theater. Agent Shuster reported the whereabouts of the four to the Bureau's office by car radio. Unless and until one or the other of the undercover agents, Fulgoni or Weiner, reported, the Bureau would know nothing further on the delivery scheduled for that night.

Golino waited until the intermission before he broached the

subject. Drawing Fulgoni aside, Golino asked, "You take the key to your room with you?" The agent nodded. "Okay, so here's the way we'll work it," Golino explained in a whisper. His voice could hardly be heard in the din of a thousand people smoking and talking in the lobby of the theater. "You give me the key and I'll pass it to my connection and he'll put the stuff in your room, in the second drawer of that bureau there, and then later, when I tell you it's up there, either you or Johnny can go up to the room with Sicardo and check it, while the other guy stays with me in the lobby. So, that way we won't get separated and nothing can get mixed up, and when the stuff checks out, why then you can pay me then and there."

"Sounds good to me," said Fulgoni.

"Don't forget, nobody's supposed to be in that room when the stuff is delivered 'cause my connection don't want to meet nobody or have anybody see him."

"That's all right, so long as I can check the stuff before I pay," commented Fulgoni.

"It's not my idea, you understand," Golino explained. "I don't mind if you meet the guy or anything, it's just his way of working."

Fulgoni then explained that he himself did not have the key to the room, his partner carried it. So, he called Weiner over and in asking for the key, explained the delivery plan to his partner. Weiner promptly turned the key over to Golino.

"You guys go see the end of the movie, I got to phone this guy and take over the key. I'll meet you at the bar on the corner, Jimmy knows which one." When the Philadelphia mobster walked towards the pay telephone, Fulgoni asked Sicardo if he thought he could set up any girls for the night after the business of the evening was completed.

While Sicardo's attention was fully engaged, Weiner commented, "See you in a minute, I gotta go to the john."

On the invariable queue at the men's urinals during a fifteen-minute intermission in the three-hour epic, agent Weiner found no trouble at all in whispering the details of the delivery plan to the man standing in front of him, agent John Connelly.

Connelly telephoned the office, and agents Hal Cooper and Arthur Tysen were immediately dispatched to the Hotel Edison where they placed Fulgoni's room, 1217, under observation. Their job was to wait for the delivery man.

Ted Harnett and Ken Taub, the two agents waiting outside the movie theater, needed no instructions when they observed Golino coming out. Taub trailed the suspect. Harnett hit the nearest phone. The word was relayed from 90 Church Street by radio to the Bureau car positioned outside the East 63rd Street apartment building. It had all been anticipated.

When Golino reached the East Side building, there was a man waiting at the elevator before him. Another man walked in behind him. All three entered the self-service elevator together, each of them, like typical New Yorkers, respecting the privacy of strangers obliged to share a small space. Golino pushed the button for the seventh floor. The man who had followed him into the elevator, agent John Riley, rang the eighth floor. The first fellow in the elevator, agent Danny Monahan, just leaned back against the wall.

At the seventh floor, the door opened and Golino got out. Monahan walked out behind him. Riley remained behind. Golino turned left and walked toward the north end of the building, and then suddenly he stopped and looked back. Monahan, without a pause, turned right and walked slowly toward the south end of the building. What he would have done if Golino had chosen to follow him, he did not know. But from behind his back, the agent could sense that Golino was moving in the opposite direction, his suspicions apparently quelled. Monahan continued down the corridor as slowly as he dared until he heard Golino speaking to someone. Then he whipped around, but too late to glimpse an open door. Golino had disappeared into an apartment in the north bank of the building.

Agent Monahan tiptoed to the north end of the building, putting his ear to each of the doors of the five apartments in that wing, but no sound of voices penetrated the soundproof doors. So, the agent noted all five apartment numbers and made his retreat before he could be discovered there.

Golino remained in the apartment no more than ten minutes. When he returned to the street, the watchful agents waited patiently while the Philadelphia kingpin spent another fifteen minutes trying to hail a taxicab. Then they followed him back to

Broadway. The feature apparently was entertaining enough for Golino to buy himself another ticket to see what remained of the second half of the film.

At about the same time, agents Cooper and Tysen scouted the layout of the twelfth-floor corridor outside Fulgoni's hotel room. They chose a stairway landing at the end of the corridor at a right angle to the bank of elevators. With the door propped open and the light bulb unscrewed, the two agents posted themselves in complete darkness with a clear view of the lighted hallway leading to Room 1217. And then they waited. The whirling sound of the elevator cables in operation hummed clearly in the silence. The click of the elevator stopping on that floor and then the noise of the doors opening and shutting were unmistakable, but the thick hallway carpeting muffled all sounds of footsteps. Not until a person appeared in the west corridor, which they had under observation, could the agents see who or how many persons were there on the twelfth floor with them. And so they waited, silent, standing, whispering to one another only when necessary, tensing for action each time the elevator stopped on the twelfth floor.

From the movie theater, the four conspirators, working at cross-purposes, had two drinks at a bar and then dined well at a steak specialty restaurant about a block from the hotel. The conversation was general and convivial. Golino, as host, kept the wineglasses full. Outside the steak house, two surveillance agents ate hot dogs at a sidewalk stand. There was always the possibility of a switch in plans, with the delivery of the heroin being made at any place other than the expected hotel room. Four other agents went without dinner, covering the entrances to the Edison Hotel and the bank of elevators leading to Room 1217.

For three hours, agents Cooper and Tysen waited on the darkened stairway landing for the right man to walk down the twelfth-floor corridor. They sensed action almost as soon as they saw him. He was a big man, over six feet, a two-hundred-pounder, about thirty-three or thirty-five years old, with a prominent nose, wearing a gray topcoat and gray hat. He walked rapidly down the hall, dangling a tagged key in his hand and glancing at the room numbers. At Fulgoni's room, he paused, inserted the key and went in, closing the door behind him. Agent

Cooper noted the time, and with a nod to his partner, he moved out into the corridor. Agent Tysen remained there, keeping the room under observation.

When the courier returned to the elevator on the twelfth floor he found agent Cooper, as innocent-looking as any hotel guest, waiting for a down elevator. How could he know that the narcotics agent had pushed the elevator signal only at the moment he rounded the corner from the corridor to the bank of elevators? When the elevator arrived, Cooper became engaged in lighting a cigarette so that the courier could board the cubicle before he did. They stared at each other in the small space until the courier, in a broad accent of a native New Yorker, demanded, "Don't I know you from someplace?"

"I don't think so," replied the agent, putting a lilt in his tone, "unless you come from Boston."

The courier shrugged and cut off further conversation. But Cooper, considering the odds, could not resist a try. "I thought maybe you looked familiar, too, but I dunno. Would you care to join me in a drink?"

"No, I got a date tonight," the suspect said as they reached the lobby. He strode out of the elevator without looking back and was on his way. Agent Cooper followed only a few steps to a cigarette stand and there he gave the nod to agent Shuster.

Through the lobby and out the 47th Street doorway, the courier was followed by Shuster. On the sidewalk outside the hotel entrance, the agent noted the presence of all the principals in the escapade. Golino was standing, smoking, and listening to agent Fulgoni; Sicardo was conversing with agent Weiner a few steps away; and nearby was agent John Connelly, taking it all in. The courier walked by within a few feet of Golino without a flicker of recognition from either man. Shuster stalked past Fulgoni without a sign, and agent Connelly, sizing up the situation in a moment, followed up 47th Street, focusing on the man ahead of Shuster. The suspect paced off half a block, slipped between two cars and climbed into the driver's seat of a Plymouth sedan parked at the curb. Agent Shuster noticed another man in the passenger seat of the Plymouth. He was looking about nervously, and so the agent changed his direction and crossed the street. Behind him agent Connelly walked slowly past the parked car and, with a glance, read and memorized the license plate. The next day the motor vehicle bureau would tell him the name of the registered owner of the sedan, and most probably it would be that of the courier or at least of someone connected with the heroin. Narcotics traffickers seldom went to the trouble and risk of stealing a car just to deliver drugs.

By the time the Plymouth pulled out into traffic, agents Shuster and Connelly were in their radio car and not far behind. The trail led back to the apartment house on East 63rd Street. There the Plymouth pulled up to the curb. The six-foot courier in gray hat and topcoat got out, and while he went into the garage under the building, the passenger in the Plymouth shifted over to the driver's seat. The agents, not daring to approach too closely, observed the scene with binoculars from half a block away, waiting and expecting the man in the Plymouth to leave the car and enter the building. But a few minutes later, a late-model Ford sedan roared out of the garage, turned the corner and disappeared down Second Avenue. The Plymouth took off after it. The agents sped after them.

But the men in the two cars ahead apparently had a preconceived plan, either because they had become suspicious or merely as a normal maneuver, for they acted in concert. They ran deliberately through two red traffic lights. The agents drove through one but stopped for the second, and the two cars ahead raced on through traffic, made a turn and were lost. The agents had no way of knowing if they had been spotted, but they realized that if they had followed the two cars through both stop signals and around a corner, they would have run the risk of tipping the whole of Fulgoni's undercover work.

At the Hotel Edison, Golino had waited only a moment until the courier was past him and then announced, "Everything's okay now; it's in the room."

Weiner, as Johnny Gold, requested a second key to the room from the front desk and went up with Sicardo to check on the delivery. Sicardo chose to remain in the hallway rather than enter the room containing evidence of a felony. In the second drawer of the bureau, Weiner found the heroin. He field tested the white drug with a chemical, and when it turned a deep purple in color, he knew he had genuine heroin.

The four men rendezvoused in the men's room near the hotel bar, and there Mike Telano counted out and paid Golino ten thousand dollars in United States government money, the serial number of each bill having been duly registered at the Bureau's office. The conspirators parted the best of friends.

Later that night, the agents on the case met at 90 Church Street. There, over hot coffee, Fulgoni and Weiner, Shuster and Connelly, Riley and Monahan, Harnett and Taub, and Cooper and Tysen all swapped details of their day's work and rejoiced. The investigation now was in full swing, and expanding. Everything seemed to be going their way. The agents had a near perfect case now, with two sales, on Golino and Sicardo. They had located Golino's connection in the East 63rd Street apartment building and they had a line on the organization's courier, which might lead them anywhere.

# 19

# Harlem

Angie Minetti was not a bit craftier or more experienced than Nick Golino, only luckier. His little florist shop off East Tremont Avenue in the Bronx, a front for several of his nefarious activities, just had never been tumbled to. The local precinct detectives, as well as the federal agents working the area, had Angie tagged as a button man, associated with one particular Mafia organization in the neighborhood, but they could not move against him. Rumors, suspicions and indications had it that Angie was in narcotics, but so many other illicit activities were open to the hoodlum florist that the police could not find a lever with which to pry Angie Minetti out into the open. The daily flow of customers in and out of his florist shop made surveillance useless. Spot raids, unofficial visits, unexpected questioning had over the years uncovered neither narcotics, numbers, stolen goods or illicit weapons, only flowers and funeral wreaths. Angie met all police visits with a smile and an irritating bravado. His business flourished, he insisted, because he had so many friends who loved flowers, and then there were the confirmations, the weddings and the funerals that required his flowers.

The little back room in the shop was his business office, and Angie kept a bottle of whiskey and some glasses in his desk drawer so that he could entertain his friends and good customers. There was no law against that. What he did in the back room was nobody's business but his own. Angie knew his rights.

Until someone flipped and squealed, Angie was safe. His security rested in the organization—call it a mob, Mafia, Cosa Nostra, family or what you will—because the organization stood behind him with considerable status and power in the neighborhood, ready and able to enforce its own code of ethics, which was as well known as the statutes of criminal law. The keystone of that code was loyalty to those within the "family" and silence to outsiders, and upon that keystone rested the safety of Angie Minetti and all those like him.

Angie's relationship with the organization was unique. While he was under the control of the boss of the organization, he was not in his employ. As a button man or soldier, he took orders from the boss, when necessary; he was obliged never to engage in an activity deemed at cross-purposes with that of the organization; yet he was an independent entrepreneur. Years before he had worked for this same boss as a driver, a courier and a strong-arm man. But then he had set himself up in the narcotics business with his boss's blessings. The head of the organization now acted as a financier of a variety of projects which interested him, and Angie was one of several he had staked with a loan. Like a banker, the boss had been advised of the nature of the business investment, the source of supply and the method of operation, although not the identity of the customers, and upon approval, he had made the loan, telling Angie, "You got the money and you are responsible for it, so you better make no mistakes, but if the thing blows, remember, you still owe me sixty thousand dollars two months from now."

Angie personally played it loose. By nature he was not a calculating or worrying man. His methods of operation had evolved over the years, drawn from his experience and his instincts as an alley cat in a jungle of city streets. He knew how, when and where to buy heroin, just as he understood how to handle the selling end. He knew how to instill just enough fear in those with whom he dealt to insure his own safety without incurring dangerous animosity. He knew when to deal straight and when to cut a corner. He was, in short, street smart.

His operation was simple. To the three kilos of heroin which he bought from Merlotti, he added one kilo of mannite, a children's laxative popular in Italy, which blended with the fluffy white heroin in appearance and texture. The strength and purity of the heroin, to be sure, was reduced by one-quarter, from approximately 77 percent to about 58 percent, but where he once had three he now had four kilos of heroin to sell. And in that adulteration lay the economics of the business. What made the narcotics racket so profitable was not that Angie Minetti bought his heroin wholesale at $17,500 a kilo and sold it to Harlem distributors at $20,000, but rather that he bought three kilos of heroin for $52,500, added nine dollars' worth of white, crystalline powder to it, and sold it for at least eighty thousand dollars.

There were no hard and fast rules governing the quality, quantity and price of illicit drugs, only what the market would bear. Angie, like a good businessman, tried to sell his steady customers the best product at the lowest practical price. Georgia Jack always got heroin with a purity higher than 50 percent at about twenty thousand dollars a kilo, which was one or two thousand under the price a newcomer would pay if he could buy heroin at all from someone like Angie. Most of Angie's customers were smaller operators than Georgia Jack, buying in quarter-kilo lots, one or two at a time, and paying six thousand dollars a quarter or higher. And if Angie were short of cash at any given time, for one reason or another, he could supplement his profits merely by increasing the proportion of mannite or milk sugar in his product. He handled the money himself, taking payment or promise of payment in the privacy of the back room of his florist shop. Deliveries were made by a young paisano whom Angie had properly trained, disciplined and checked out as his runner. For that chosen youth, an Italian, most often in his early twenties, to be a runner for a man like Angie Minetti was considered a privileged opportunity to work in a syndicate operation, to be near the big guys of the underworld, and to advance yourself from there, as Angie did, by dint of hard work, loyalty, and keeping your eyes open for that lucky break.

Angie arranged all the details of the deliveries so that his runner and the customer had no more contact than was absolutely necessary. When Georgia Jack phoned in to place his order, he was invited to the florist shop. He knew to bring his money with him. Then, in the back room, he would be told the time and place of delivery, which was different on each occasion. There were thousands of dark, deserted city streets to choose from, hundreds of neutral bars and grills outside of Harlem where a Negro and an Italian could meet without arousing suspicion. The timing had to be precise. Jack would arrive first, wait in his parked car at a prescribed time for fifteen minutes. The courier would drive by and then stop, pass the package and drive on. Or Jack would wait at a bar until the runner walked by him, showing no sign of recognition, and the delivery would be made in the men's room. Angie did not want the two of them together with the heroin. If one were picked up, it was his tough luck and the other was not implicated. If for any reason the customer was not at the rendezvous at the prearranged time, the courier returned to the stash with the heroin; if the runner was late, the customer took off and phoned in for another delivery rendezvous.

Georgia Jack guarded the identity of Angie Minetti and his courier zealously: Angie was the key to his lock on his own organization. Only after six months of operation did Jack tell his own partner how he picked up his weekly supply of junk, how much he paid, and from whom he received it. His partner was his younger brother, Clee, or, to be more precise, his half brother; both had been raised in a fashion by their mother and neither knew a father, other than that there had been two different men five years apart. Since his mother's death, Jack trusted no one, with the possible exception of his brother Clee, and at times even their relationship was tinged with mutual suspicion.

An unabashed product of his time and environment, Jack lived by the law of the jungle, self-preservation and survival of the fittest. In the ghettos of Cleveland, Chicago and New York, he had learned to use his fists, brass knuckles, bicycle chains, switchblades and finally a gun. A thief at eleven years of age, a strong-arm extortionist of other kids at fourteen, a stick-up and robbery man at seventeen, he had been in and out of various institutions which failed to "correct" him. His first felony conviction for armed robbery when he was twenty-two cost him three years, but in the "joint" he had hardened and matured, and when next he was interrupted during a robbery, he tried to shoot his way out to freedom and in the process wounded a policeman. The penalty for that was fourteen years in Sing Sing with no probation and no parole, but when he emerged that time he was a free man again, forty-three years old and as knowledgeable in the ways of the underworld as any experienced ex-con, only stronger, more menacing, more dangerous. He was a huge man, big and burly, 245 pounds, hard and hardened, older and wiser, eager to get what he could have for the taking. He staked himself and his brother Clee with a caper in Miami, returned to Harlem with his new name, Georgia Jack, which was unknown to the police, and dived into the most lucrative operation of his career.

Six good months in narcotics and he was a rich man. His wife and three grown children were reclaimed and established in a new house in Queens under their legal name, far from the scene. In Harlem, he kept two mistresses living together in one pad. He drove a new lavender-hued Cadillac. He wore a different suit every day. He bought silk underwear. He had a stake in a bar on 138th Street where a table in the rear was reserved for him and the bartenders greeted him with the respect due a proprietor. He had girls, whiskey and the awe of bookies and gamblers, all because of money. He had all the money he wanted and everything that money could buy in Harlem, and it came flowing in every day. Of all the men trafficking in illicit narcotics—the Turks, the Lebanese, the Armenians, the Corsicans, the American mafiosi —this Negro, ex-convict who had spent seventeen years of his life in prison, was making the most money and the greatest profits day by day. He took greater risks than the others, of course, but it was his key position which accounted for his huge profits. He was the distributor who supplied the pushers who sold to the junkies, and, moreover, he controlled the major cutting of the heroin from its high purity state to the retail product at street level. He produced, in effect, the finished product, and to him went the biggest profits.

Once, twenty or thirty years before, this seemingly enviable position had been held predominantly by Jewish racketeers, and then, about twenty years ago, it had become the domain of the Italians and Sicilians, up until the famous Apalachin meeting of 1957.

The withdrawal of the Mafia organizations from this level of narcotics distribution left a vacuum soon filled by the more adept of the Negro and, to a somewhat lesser extent, the Puerto Rican hoodlums, who were quite willing to assume the risks involved. Just as every junkie dreams of becoming a pusher, so does almost every pusher aspire to become a distributor, handling ounces, quarter-kilos and more. That is where the "real money" is. That is also where the attrition is fearsome. Pushers and distributors, along with the junkies who operate at the street level, are periodically getting arrested, conned, heisted, knifed and occasionally killed in the jungle warfare over the white powder more valuable than gold.

In this jungle, Georgia Jack thrived as he never had before. After his first six months in the business, by which time he had perfected his own particular operation, his name became legend throughout Harlem and even beyond the borders of the black ghetto. He succeeded where many others failed largely because he put out a better product than his competitors. The purity of heroin sold by Georgia Jack, it became known, was often twice that of anyone else's. It was *dynamite*. The junkies with money in hand flocked to Georgia Jack's pushers, eager to score big. The word spread, and more and more junkies, like women rushing to the bargain-basement sales, sought out the pushers working for the man called Georgia Jack.

Varying from time to time, his work force ranged from twenty to forty street peddlers, most of them concentrated in the area between 114th and 120th streets and Lennox and Eighth avenues. Each one of them had been carefully chosen, interviewed, tested and trained as well as any executive of a large, enterprising corporation.

Georgia Jack's specialty was not the usual five-dollar cap but a twenty-five-dollar bag, reputed to contain an eighth of an ounce of heroin. It was merchandised to appeal not to troublesome kids, neophytes or hard-luck losers, but rather to the old-timers, the hard-core addicts who knew their way around both in stealing or swindling enough "bread" to pay the price and in knowing how and when to buy junk without tipping the deal to the police. Junkies with big habits bought Georgia Jack's stuff, and that's the way he wanted it. Lest there be any doubt about his merchandise, Georgia Jack labeled each twenty-five-dollar bag with three staples across the top of the fold and three more staples at 45-degree angles to the first three. Those staples served as a brand name to all his consumers and he let it be known that any competitor who mislabeled his own product to resemble that of Georgia Jack's did so at his own mortal risk. There is, after all, a code of conduct in every walk of society.

Not only the addicts but the street peddlers and pushers too sought out Georgia Jack; he was, in effect, the man on the scene who had built a better mouse trap, and they wanted to work for him. Georgia Jack was a great connection. Of course, he was not to be found as readily as the man with the mouse trap. He remained as best he could in the background, out of sight, away from the street transactions. Out in front, he had his two lieutenants, his brother Clee and his old cellmate from the state prison, a tall, skinny, rat-faced killer with a thick, ugly scar beneath his chin running from ear to ear, attesting to anyone foolish enough to try to tangle with him that he had already survived having his throat cut. Legally and according to his police and prison records, he was born Orville Henderson. On the street he was known only as Skeetch. Clee, a "partner," took a cut of the profits, the size of which depended upon his half-brother's disposition at the end of each week. Skeetch, a sort of personnel manager of the sales force, worked for a straight salary: five hundred dollars a week. Both of them recruited the pushers, explaining the arrangements under which all the peddlers worked. Not until both Clee and Skeetch agreed upon and approved a new worker would he or she be brought before the boss.

The pushers were chosen for their street savvy, their experience in dealing with junkies, their reliability and their control over their own habits. They were addicts themselves, as most pushers are, for it is believed that it takes a junkie to know how to deal with another junkie. Jack preferred women as his pushers, hard, tough, degenerate women, who nevertheless were more likely than male junkies to work honestly for the pay and protection the Georgia Jack organization offered them. When they came upon the boss man in person, he appeared as awesome as his reputation had led them to expect.

He strutted like a champion in Harlem, six feet high with

big football shoulders, flashy clothes, and a mean slant to his eyes. His voice, thick and hoarse, carried in every word the menace of potential violence. He would explain to each new pusher, no matter how much experience he or she had previously, that the recruit had to meet each and every day of the week either with Clee or with Skeetch. The time and place would be different each time, arranged the day before. At each meeting, the pusher would turn over the money collected the previous day, twenty dollars to the organization for every bag sold, and five dollars for the pusher. For each twenty dollars turned in, the pusher would take out another bag to sell at twenty-five dollars. And he or she was expected to sell no less than twenty bags a day, turning in a minimum of four hundred dollars. Any pusher who could not sell twenty bags of Georgia Jack's stuff daily was no damn good and would be kicked out. Twenty bags a day was a minimum. Jack expected each one to sell thirty or forty bags. Some of his girls sold fifty or sixty bags in a day's time.

Jack would go over with each one the various means of avoiding police detection while selling on the street. There were hundreds of ways. But the important point each time was to handle junk as little as possible. Put the stuff somewhere, take the money and then tell the junkie where to go to pick up the bag himself.

Urging his pushers to hustle all the time, Georgia Jack would warn them against carrying a load of heroin at any one time. The practice to be followed, as most experienced pushers knew, was to carry only one bag at a time so that if he or she were picked up, the charge would be a misdemeanor. The dividing line for narcotics between a felony and a misdemeanor under New York State law is precisely one-eighth of an ounce. Therefore, smart pushers carry no more than an eighth at any time.

Each recruit was also instructed on what to do if and when he or she was picked up by the police or the feds. Georgia Jack gave each and every one of his pushers the name and telephone number of an attorney and a bail bondsman. Both were working on retainers for Georgia Jack. All the pusher had to do was to get in touch with one or the other and keep his mouth shut. The bondsman would put up bail immediately for any of Jack's pushers and the lawyer would handle the case—all free to the pusher.

Jack would take care of those bills for his own people. What he expected in return, he explained, was loyalty, playing the game straight, no cheating on the merchandise, and, above all, no talking to the police or to anyone outside the organization about the business.

The only way a person could get hurt, Georgia Jack would explain, would be by flipping to the police. Then that person would find himself in the gutter with his throat slit. One way or another, no matter who got picked up by the police, an informer would get his. Someone would be around to take care of him.

Georgia Jack varied the speech from occasion to occasion but he covered the same points each time. His pushers got the message. They had no reason to doubt that he could and would do what he threatened. He dominated his organization by his potential for sheer brute force. At the same time, he was not stupid. He rewarded his pushers with frequent bonuses for good work. He gave gifts at holidays. And they were always the same: five free bags of heroin to sell or to shoot up oneself. It made for a very happy, satisfied family of pushers.

To be sure, the organization had its share of troubles: a pusher would turn into a "pig" and shoot up junk that ought to have been sold, another was mugged and robbed of a whole day's supply, two others just took off and disappeared. But by and large, considering the nature of the work and the employees, the organization was run as efficiently as a successful corporation. Sales increased; the police and federal agents were baffled by the number of twenty-five-dollar packets of high-quality heroin secured by the six wire staples which they found on junkies and which they could not trace to the man called Georgia Jack.

Despite the busy activities of twenty to forty pushers out on the street, the heart of the operation was completely hidden to the outside world. Only Jack, Clee, Skeetch, and Jack's favorite girl friend, Mary Lou Lincoln, were in on the preparation and stashing of the heroin itself. However dangerous, selling is the easy part of the narcotics business; it is the buying of the essential supplies which is crucial.

Jack controlled the pipeline to Angie Minetti, and that he would not share with anyone, but he could not handle the whole inventory himself when he reached the kilo-a-week level of business. Clee and Skeetch were needed to distribute to the pushers and collect the money on a daily basis, and to help in the cutting, mixing and final processing. He discovered he needed his girl friend in the business, too.

Burglaries are so common in New York that in a district like Harlem it was only good sense for Jack to ply his girl friend with furs, jewelry trinkets and some cash just to stay at home, keep her door locked, and her hands out of the organization's supplies. He had been burgled just once and that had been enough. He had lost some ten thousand dollars' worth of heroin, and he had wasted no time in moving his stash from an empty apartment on 150th Street to his girl friend's pad in the New Delano Village Development on West 142nd Street.

For a time Jack had insisted that Clee and Skeetch wear bandanas over their faces so that Mary Lou could not recognize them. But before long that idea was abandoned as plain silly. The four of them got to know one another rather well as they worked in such close proximity week after week.

They would meet by prearrangement at Mary Lou Lincoln's apartment every week, or rather every six or seven or eight days, depending upon when a new kilo of heroin was needed and bought. They worked in remarkable harmony together, these four conspirators, big, burly Georgia Jack who had served a full fourteen-year prison term; his brother Clee, a petty crook, who had been in and out of jail all of his adult life; Skeetch, a three-time loser who had killed more men than he could remember and was somehow free on parole from cumulative sentences which, if he had served them, would have kept him in prison until the year 2004; and Mary Lou, who was as sharp as any of the others. She was thirty-two, tall and shapely, with a pretty face, light-brown skin and bleached blond hair carefully coiffured. Unlike the others, she had never been inside a jail cell, not even inside a police station. With her attractive looks she had always found it easy to get a job. She had worked as a beautician and then as a bar girl or tavern hostess, traveling from city to city as she changed jobs whenever trouble appeared. Each job was a means for Mary Lou to find a man who could support her. More often than not, her breadwinner was a crook of one sort or other. It was a way of life. But not until she had come upon Georgia Jack had she been importuned into actually taking part in an illegal act. Jack had a way of getting what he wanted. He had told her she would be his stash, and she, aware of the violence in the man, just did not know how to say no. Besides, she reasoned, she was learning the ropes of a new business.

With the front door double-locked and bolted against any unwanted immediate entry, the Georgia Jack laboratory was set up in Mary Lou's back bedroom. A solid-colored table oilcloth was spread in the center of Mary Lou's king-sized bed, and the three men went to work for most of the day, while Mary Lou watched, fetched beer and sandwiches, talked, but did not leave the apartment. From a hiding place in the bottom of the bedroom closet, the men brought to the bed the ingredients which they had accumulated during the week. Clee and Skeetch had the responsibility of buying mannite and quinine from different drugstores so as not to arouse suspicions by any single large purchase. They were common items and cheap enough, about twelve dollars an ounce for quinine and twenty-five cents an ounce for mannite, but the men needed to buy a substantial amount each week to cut a kilo of heroin.

When they were set for the cutting, they had in the center of the bed one kilo of heroin, 245 ounce-blocks of mannite and thirty-five ounces of quinine. Then, working with a large common kitchen sifter, one man poured the ingredients into the sifter, and another meshed the wire screens of the sifter so that the heroin, mannite and quinine were thoroughly integrated as the mixture floated down onto the center of the oilcloth. The third man used a cardboard spatula to stack the white powder in the center of the oilcloth.

Once thoroughly mixed, the stuff was put through the sifter again to fluff it out so that the final product would be an extremely light and fluffy powder. The final mound of powder in the center of the bed looked to the three men like a mountain. By mixing one kilo of heroin, one kilo of quinine and seven kilos of cheap mannite, they now had twenty pounds of horse. A fortune in heroin.

The work was laborious, more tedious than back-breaking. Some of the time they wore handkerchiefs over their noses and mouths in order to reduce inhalation of the light powder. The masks were hot and cumbersome. When they were too lazy to wear the face masks, Jack insisted they stop for rest periods. No one wanted to become addicted by mistake. None of them used heroin personally or had any desire to do so. They knew better than that. No matter what the climate or temperature, Jack insisted also that the bedroom windows be kept shut. A breeze could scatter the fluffy gold across the room. "If you feel a tickle, get out from the bed," Jack always warned the conspirators, " 'cause if you sneeze on this stuff, it's gonna cost you ten thousand bucks."

Before final packaging, the quality of the product was tested quite simply. Clee brought a sample to a junkie who was quite happy to cook up the heroin and take a free fix when all he had to do in return was to report on the jolt received. Only once had the sample tested out below standards, and then Georgia Jack, knowing full well that his adulterants had been the same, had gone back to his supplier and insisted that Angie provide him with enough new heroin to bring his product back up to its proper strength.

Packaging was the most laborious part of the preparation. Both Jack and his brother measured out the eighth-ounce portions by dipping a half-teaspoon measuring spoon into the mound of heroin, leveling off the measure with a cardboard, and then dumping the portion into a small glassine bag. Skeetch took each bag from the brothers, folded the top twice, fastened it with six staples and passed it on to Mary Lou. She secured them in twenty-bag bundles with rubber bands, and stacked them in a large leather suitcase.

When they were through, Jack, Clee and Skeetch had at least 2,500 bags of heroin to sell. Usually they made a hundred extra or more to be sure that each bag contained less than an eighth of an ounce, the legal dividing line in New York between a misdemeanor and a felony. From the single kilo he had bought, Georgia Jack made nine kilos of heroin, which divided precisely into 315 ounces or 2,520 eighth-ounces. He figured, however, on selling 2,500 bags a week, at twenty-five dollars a bag, and so he could afford to be generous with free samples, gifts and bonuses.

By street standards, it was an excellent buy. The usual five-dollar cap sold by most pushers contained a mere five or six grains of adulterated heroin, the purity of which usually ranged from 3 to 5 percent. Georgia Jack sold an eighth of an ounce for twenty-five dollars, but an eighth of an ounce contains fifty-five grains, or eleven times as much heroin for five times the price of a five-dollar cap. And Jack's quality was better than ordinary, too, at 6.5 percent purity or higher.

The organization was well aware that some junkies bought the Jack bags and turned around and became pushers themselves, merely by repackaging the heroin and selling it for twice what they paid. But he did not want to deal with the dregs who could afford only five-dollar caps. He preferred being a big man on the street, letting the little guys get what they could so long as he got his.

And Georgia Jack's profits were surely there:

*EXPENSES:*

| | |
|---|---:|
| *One kilo of "pure" heroin weekly* ____ | $20,000.00 |
| *245 blocks of mannite weekly* | |
| *at $00.25 each* _____ | 61.25 |
| *35 ounces of quinine weekly* | |
| *at $12.00 each* _____ | 420.00 |
| *Weekly salary to Skeetch* _____ | 500.00 |
| TOTAL WEEKLY EXPENSES _____ | $20,981.25 |

*INCOME:*

| | |
|---|---:|
| *2,500 one-eighth-ounce packages per* | |
| *week at $25 each* _____ | $62,500.00 |
| *Less commission to street peddlers* ____ | 12,500.00 |
| *Less total weekly expenses* _ _____ | 20,981.25 |
| NET WEEKLY PROFIT _____ | $29,018.75 |

Like a businessman, this strong-arm ex-convict kept the books on income and outgo. To be sure, he did not keep them long. Each week he tallied the cost of his supplies, commissions, salaries as against the income from narcotics packets sold. The weekly profits varied according to market conditions, but more often than not Georgia Jack's take exceeded thirty thousand dollars a week. He found it was just as easy to make up 2,600 or 2,800 bags of junk from his nine kilos of heroin, mannite and quinine as it was to make an even 2,500. Mary Lou kept a log on the packages sold as they were taken out of her apartment so that Jack could know on any day whether or not to put more pressure upon his sales force. Clee and Skeetch were under instructions to ring her bell, identify themselves through the locked door, and then, upon being admitted, to take whatever quantity they needed from the suitcase in the closet. Mary Lou would mark the amount against each man's initial in a small spiral notebook. At the end of the week or whenever the closet supply dwindled down to the point where a new batch was needed, Jack would tally the amount of heroin sold with the amount of money handed over to him by his two lieutenants. Once the figures checked out, the accounts were destroyed. Jack recognized the irreducible risk of prison for selling illicit narcotics, but he had no intention of leaving himself open to any such charge as income tax evasion.

Georgia Jack's operation was undoubtedly one of the most successful and lucrative in all of Harlem and therefore in all of New York, but still, his method of cutting, packaging and distributing heroin was only one of many. His sales from a single kilo of heroin, two point two pounds, grossed sixty-two thousand dollars. But his kilo was no longer identical to that originally brought to the United States by Léon Levonian, for which the Armenian had paid the equivalent of $350 in Istanbul. The Biani organization had cut one-eighth out of Levonian's kilo and Angie Minetti had cut another quarter of the weight, substituting milk sugar. So, the kilo from which Georgia Jack had grossed $62,000 was only five-eighths of the original Levonian kilo. If Jack had had the other three-eighths of 88 percent heroin, it would have meant another $37,000 in sales. Therefore, Levonian's kilo, as sold in one-eighth-ounce packages by Georgia Jack, was worth in street sales to addicts $99,000. And if all those addicts had cut the Georgia Jack packets two or three times and resold them, as they well could have, then Levonian's $350 worth of Turkish opium had a potential sales value of from $200,000 to $250,000.

There are at least five large, well-organized Mafia families in the city of New York and others throughout the country known to the Federal Bureau of Narcotics to be dealing in heroin and other narcotics drugs. There are a great many more smaller syndicates and individual entrepreneurs. Each of them has its own variation of buying, cutting and reselling heroin. Yet the basic methods are the same and the economics of the business holds true for all of them. The Bureau of Narcotics estimates that between one and one and one-half *tons* of heroin is brought into this country each year; that the purity of the full-strength heroin averages between 80 and 85 percent; and that the final adulterated heroin bought by most addicts for five dollars is a cap containing about five grains of 5 percent heroin. Thus, the Bureau estimates that one so-called pure kilo of heroin, 80 percent or higher purity, as brought in from France, produces at least sixteen kilos of 5 percent heroin. With 437 grains to the kilo, those sixteen kilos are divided into approximately 45,000 five-dollar caps, for which the poor harassed and scrambling American junkie pays $225,000.

If, as the Bureau of Narcotics estimates, the total importation of heroin to the United States is between one and one and a half tons—and many believe the actual figure to be higher—then the illicit traffic of heroin alone in these United States amounts to between 225 and 337 million dollars a year. That is big business indeed, bigger than even those figures intimate.

What makes the narcotics racket so attractive to the professional criminal is that in narcotics the money is almost all clear profit. The cost of material is minimal; the men hired to smuggle, transport and distribute the goods are few, and so labor is relatively cheap. Essentially, the product is so small in size and so precious in quality that the net profit to the individual entrepreneur is higher than in any other underworld activity. Only illegal gambling—the numbers, off-track betting, cards and craps—has an overall take greater than that of narcotics in the United States. But illicit gambling is so highly organized, with such high operational expenses, including payoffs, protection money and bribes, that it leaves little room for a single adventurer to make his fortune.

Narcotics has long been the king of the rackets for the professionals: It was the easiest money to be taken. To men who chose crime as their career, narcotics was simply a good racket. They cared nothing about the effects of heroin upon those weak enough to succumb to it. That it destroyed the moral fiber, the inner strength and eventually the physical health of its victims did not trouble the merchants. They could shrug off the forlorn misery of the addict world, because to them their customers were stupid jerks, junkies, unworthy of their concern, their trust or even their interest. Narcotics was a business and they were the merchants.

Only the law stood in their way. The only pause in the head-long race for profits in narcotics was occasioned by the law's stiff penalties for dealing in narcotics. And to this, the professionals again shrugged and exclaimed, "If you want to play the game, you got to be willing to pay the price."

# 20

# The Stash

Those outstanding, memorable moments in life, when all the past anxiety, toil and deprivation that went into an effort seem quite worthwhile for the accomplishment at hand, come not when success is crowned but rather at some point before that, when the light dawns and the road appears clear and easy all the way down to the rainbow at the end. Willie Sutton, the extraordinary bank robber, is said to have described the sublime moments of his career as "standing there at night in a big empty bank with the door of the vault open and you are there all alone."

For Léon Levonian, the exhilarating sense of accomplishment dawned upon him the first night after he had sent Pierre Trigano back to France to arrange details for the second shipment of merchandise. It was then, alone in his apartment, that he realized he was already well on his way towards becoming one of the biggest international smugglers of heroin in the business. He had established his position with the top men of the business in Montreal, New York and Mexico City. In Canada, he was known as "François," the American agent for the Benucci syndicate of Marseilles which supplied twenty to thirty kilos of French heroin each month into the major pipeline of the American Mafia, and he was wined and dined and womened on each of his

short business trips to Montreal. In New York, only Big Joe
Biani himself knew him by his true name; Merlotti and Tony the
Nose called him François. And in Mexico City, the other pipeline into New York, one of the most famous of all Corsican
narcotics traffickers, a man in the business for more than twenty
years, had entertained Levonian in his own home as though he
were a true cousin rather than an Armenian outsider. He had
showered Levonian with gifts, and now in the privacy of his
apartment, Léon enjoyed the fine Cuban cigars and the expensive brandy he had brought back from Mexico City.

Levonian recognized the ingredients of his own success to
date, and, further, he could see many more opportunities to expand his money-making ventures in the future. He had charm,
wit and good humor, for he was fundamentally an extrovert who
genuinely liked people. And the men with whom he did business
liked him. He exuded a sincerity in his dealings which seemed to
say, "I have no need or desire to cheat you; I know the code
and I am a man of my word, and so long as you do not try to
cheat me, I will not cheat you." And with his quick acquisition of
the expertise of the business, Léon Levonian had prospered.

With ten kilos of his original shipment in his hallway
closet, presold to Biani and his organization, he had already
discussed selling part of his next shipment of heroin for "queer
money" at three times the normal price in Montreal. With his
contacts in Beirut who would buy counterfeit American bills at
fifty cents on the dollar, he contemplated turning a quick profit.
Counterfeit money was a "hot" item in the freewheeling money
market, if only he could solve the logistics of smuggling the
"queer money" into the Near East. Then there was a Bolivian he
had met in New York who promised to arrange a good price on
cocaine, which Léon figured could be traded profitably in Beirut,
where "sugar" was short and horse was plentiful. Léon Levonian
envisioned himself as an international businessman in the import
and export of all contraband items. There were even certain
legitimate enterprises in which he could invest his profits—a
mink farm in Canada, an automobile plant in Mexico—and, all
in all, many avenues yet to be explored. Meanwhile, while his
friend, Trigano, was away in France, Levonian thought he could
afford the risk of moving his New York mistress into the apart-

ment. She trusted Léon implicitly. She thought he was a French importer in the produce business and she believed also he was on the verge of proposing marriage. Of course, being persuaded by his charm, she was mistaken on both counts.

The rewards of ingenuity, diligence, the taking of the calculated risk and plain hard work are not confined to the entrepreneurs of the underworld, not by any means. The wondrous thrill felt by Willie Sutton inside a closed bank building was not unlike the emotional charge of the federal narcotics agents who had followed the trail set by undercover agent Fulgoni and discovered the stash of a major narcotics organization. To find such a stash or plant is the dream and goal of every narcotics agent. Such success is a rarity in the business, for a stash is like a vault in a bank; it is where the actual merchandise of the business is stored; in narcotics, it is the source of a river from which all the water downstream flows.

The agents did not come by their discovery with any ease. They had traced the automobile in which the heroin had been delivered to agent Fulgoni's room in the Hotel Edison, only to find the Plymouth was registered to one Enrico Martino of Valley Stream who, unlike the suspect courier followed, was age sixty-seven, with no record with the Bureau of Narcotics or the New York City police department. But the FBI produced from its fabulous criminal identification files the information that Enrico Martino had served three separate jail terms for operating stills and selling illicit whiskey back in the 1930's. Surveillance of his home on the third day disclosed that the tall, husky Italian with the big nose, who was recognized as the courier, was residing on the same block. Subsequent investigation revealed that the courier was one Tony Martino, son of Enrico, who also had an FBI record: five years imprisonment as an army deserter during the Korean War. Round the clock surveillance followed.

The routine of both men, their goings and comings, their habits, the hours they put in at work, in the house, elsewhere— all were observed and noted. The investigation continued for more than a week. Neither the suspects, their relatives nor their neighbors could be approached directly lest the word get back to the suspects. Only by indirection could the teams of surveillance agents, operating out of parked automobiles and posts along the residential street in Valley Stream, draw their information, their inferences and their suspicions. But on the tenth night of the stakeout in Valley Stream, the patience and perseverance of the federal agents were rewarded. They observed the suspect, Tony Martino, enter his father's home. Moments afterwards they could see the light go on in the attic, and five minutes later the light went out again. Tony emerged from the house, carrying a package under his arm that he did not have going into the house. The agents trailed Tony to a Howard Johnson's restaurant not far away, and there they observed him pass the oblong package to one Louie Pacinello, a well-known trafficker in the East Bronx. Then the agents knew that they had indeed located in the home of Tony's father the stash for the narcotics being sold to agent Fulgoni. Beyond even that gratification, the agents had the pleasure of trailing Pacinello and the package back to his own stash in Teaneck, New Jersey, knowing they would so testify in court some day soon. This was their first free look.

During the next three weeks, the agents observed and recorded two more deliveries to Pacinello. They noted that Pacinello stored the heroin he bought behind the back seat of the car.

When the time came to arrest the East Bronx trafficker, his new Chrysler sedan would be seized, and not only would the government confiscate the car for illegal usage, but the solenoid trap arrangement for the back seat would bear further evidence against Pacinello in court.

The agents assigned to Tony Martino were delighted with the results of their surveillance. Each time he left his father's home with a package under his arm, he led the Bureau of Narcotics to another trafficker in drugs. Once they knew his routine, the agents put Tony Martino to bed each night and woke up with him in the morning. During those three weeks they knew where he was at every moment and had a fairly good idea of what he was doing. They knew that his wife rarely left his home except to shop and to walk the baby. They knew he met his mistress, a young Italian bookkeeper hoping to get married, once or twice a week, and they surmised that the girl knew nothing of Tony's wife or his underworld connections.

The agents followed Tony Martino with discretion, preferring to allow him to give them the slip rather than have him discover his tail. But each time they succeeded in following him to a delivery, he was dropped at the scene, and the man picking up the goods was trailed by two, three or even four Bureau cars in radio communication with each other. Each delivery was another free look, evidence of a felonious sale of heroin for which the Bureau of Narcotics did not have to pay out any money to make the buy. Each of Tony Martino's deliveries opened a new case for the federal agents. Some of his customers were arrested, following the second sale, in such a way that they themselves could not trace their downfall back to its source. Others were assigned to undercover agents with the hope that they would lead the Bureau to other syndicates, other operations, and the men behind and above them. Meanwhile, the agents assigned to Tony Martino continued their daily surveillance, arriving at his home a full hour before he got up at eight in the morning and remaining outside his home a full hour after he turned out the lights for the night. When Tony stayed up until the early hours of the morning, the agents would curl up and spend the night in the cars, it being hardly worthwhile for the surveillance men to travel home for less than four hours' sleep.

The federal agents did not begrudge Tony Martino the long hours of work they put in, the nights spent away from their own families, the discomforts of living in an automobile and ducking out of sight each time someone walked by. It was part of the job. Other surveillance assignments had been far less rewarding. In fact, the Martino case was so productive, the agents delighted in keeping their unsuspecting subject under their microscope. They knew that at the end this young stash man and courier, with all his hopes of the future, would be spending a good many years behind prison bars. The intangible rewards of all police work rest, to a great extent, in the personal and private satisfaction of the policeman who is giving the comeuppance to the man who breaks society's rules. Narcotics agents individually, as well as the Federal Bureau of Narcotics, maintain a different attitude toward the amateur and professional lawbreaker. They often feel pity and sympathy for the drug addicts and their pathological weaknesses. But they have no pity whatsoever for the professionals like Martino and his father, Merlotti and Golino, and the others who break the law soberly, sanely and expertly, with a disregard for the harm they do, just so that they can enrich themselves with money, power and privilege.

By following Martino, the agents were making case after case. It was so easy, and yet a narcotics courier could not be permitted to continue his illegal deliveries indefinitely. The surveillance of Martino was only one part of the overall case which was reviewed almost daily in Washington, New York and Philadelphia. Martino had led the agents to his organization's customers, but thus far not to his suppliers. The heroin obviously came from the attic; the attic was obviously the stash. But how big was that stash? Why had the agents never observed Martino bringing packages into his father's home? Was the stash in the attic so big that it did not have to be replenished more than once a month or more than once every three months? Or did Martino have some method of getting the drugs into the house and into the attic which could not be observed by surveillance teams? These questions were pondered and debated vigorously in the conferences, reports and telephone conversations of the top officers and agents of the Bureau of Narcotics. Queries were sent to agents stationed in Paris, Marseilles and Beirut. Was there any source they had heard of supplying Joseph (Big Joe) Biani in New York? Agent Morton Pelas, a graduate of Northwestern University who had majored in anthropology, reported on six possible sources of heroin to the Biani organization, but he had nothing definite. The most promising new lead offered by agent Pelas from his informer sources was that lately a Frenchman had been seen about the bars of Montreal with the syndicate leaders there and it was *thought* that he was the new supplier from France. No one knew much about him; sometimes he would be around for two or three days and then he would not be seen for weeks. He was known as François. That's all, just François, and he probably lived somewhere in the United States or perhaps in Marseilles or Paris, but not in Canada.

"That's a hell of a lead, a Frenchman named François who could be anywhere in this country or in France," commented the Deputy Commissioner of Narcotics.

During these weeks, agent Fulgoni in Philadelphia was actively involved in resisting the sales pressure of Golino and Sicardo. For the most part during this time he avoided them as much as he could without arousing their suspicions. He told them tall tales of why he wanted to stay out of Philadelphia at that time, why he was not ready to make any more buys. He suspected the state police might have been informed he was in the area; he was having trouble with some of his customers on the West Coast; he was not feeling too well; he had dropped a bundle at the race track.

Golino pressed him to make his first *real* buy, as he had promised, five kilos of junk guaranteed to be of the highest purity, uncut, beautiful new stuff from a new supplier. Their meetings in out-of-the-way bars in nearby Atlantic City almost followed a pattern, they were so similar.

"You just give me the word, Mike, and we can set this up in a day or two," Golino would tell him. "I've got five kees set aside especially for you in New York, and my partners there are expecting you to take it this week, like I promised them. You know, I had to promise them you'd take a five kee order so I could get you those half kilos at the wholesale price. They were doing you a favor, you know that, selling you small samples, 'cause, like I told you, this organization they don't sell less than a kilo a throw."

Agent Fulgoni, in the role of Mike Telano, responded with the same answer each time. "Yeah, I know all that, but I don't want to be a stash for you. I want to buy what I can sell right away. What do I want three or four kilos of hot junk sitting around in my motel for? Any fuzz walks in on me, I'm a pigeon with egg on my face."

Sicardo, with his usual bravado, derided the possibility of the police being smart enough to tumble to their operation. But Fulgoni sensed he was convincing Golino of his sincerity, and also winning the experienced racketeer's respect. Only the punks in crime profess no fear of the police. Top racketeers take care to avoid any possible contact with the police. In fact, Fulgoni knew that men like Golino preferred to do business with cautious men who feared the police, who knew how to lay low and keep their mouths shut. These were the men who stayed out of trouble and did not bring the police to the door of the men selling junk. Golino was such a businessman. But he did want to know, and he asked, as patiently as any salesman handling a big contract, just when did Telano propose to make his buy.

"Just as soon as I set it up right, Nick, when I have my own customers set and I can unload the stuff after I cut it."

Nick Golino understood and Mike Telano promised his next buy would indeed be for five kilos. They bargained over price once again. To neglect that point could in itself arouse suspicions, just as it would if Fulgoni increased the order to anything over five kilos. He allowed Golino to win that argument over price. The five kilos would cost twenty thousand dollars each, but there would be a reduction of price on the next order. Golino pointed out, quite reasonably, that the five kilos were Telano's first *real* buy from the organization and would have to go at the regular price. Fulgoni did not point out what he knew. It would be the third and final buy, and upon delivery nothing would be paid; instead, all the salesmen would be arrested.

By the time the Bureau of Narcotics gave agent Fulgoni the go-ahead for the third and final buy, Nick Golino, one of the top and most experienced racketeers, was anxious to sell. Jimmy Sicardo was overanxious. He rubbed his hands with glee and talked at length of a partnership of trust between the four men and the future great profits to be made by all of them. Certainly, neither he nor Golino seemed to have the slightest suspicion of the truth of their situation.

The buy was finally arranged at a dinner meeting in the quiet atmosphere of a pine-paneled tavern, which specialized in barbecued steaks, on the outskirts of Atlantic City. Certain suspicions did rise to the surface when Fulgoni informed Golino he was ready to buy.

"That's great, Mike," Golino said. "I told you you can take the stuff on consignment, but my partners in New York say you should show some good faith money out front, at least some kind of down payment on delivery."

Fulgoni looked at his partner, then back at Golino and said nothing. Golino added: "I trust you for the money, Mike, but these guys are all business, you know, and it is the first time we are dealing in this kind of stuff. Five kees is a lot of stuff."

"How much you want?" asked Fulgoni.

"Whatever you say," Golino replied. "Just enough to show good faith."

Fulgoni feigned contemplation and came up with an offer. "If we make it a week from tonight," he said, "I can have forty grand ready. Payment on delivery and the rest I can give you in either one or two weeks. Okay?"

"Yeah, they'll go for that," Golino said. "You'll have the money there when they come with the stuff."

When the dinner had reached the coffee and dessert course, Fulgoni asked for details on the delivery. "Don't worry about a thing, Mike, I got it all arranged with the boys in New York. They'll bring the stuff right down to you at the motel."

Fulgoni professed dissatisfaction with the lack of details. "Look, Nick, I'm going to be sitting there in the motel with forty thousand dollars and I won't know what's happening. Somethin' could go wrong. Your boys might get hit or the police might latch on to them. I want to be in on the details, just to make sure everything is going to jell."

Golino leaned forward and said, in barely more than a whisper, "The boys in New York are going to make this delivery and they will take full responsibility for getting the junk to you in the motel. Jimmy here will be with them. You just stay in your motel room and wait. They'll bring the stuff down with insurance. I think they'll come down in three cars, one with the stuff in it and two for protection. Maybe they'll even make a dry run.

"And let me warn you, Mike," Golino added, "play this one straight, absolutely straight. This is your first big buy. And if anything at all goes wrong, you're going to be the first guy hit."

Fulgoni nodded. He knew now what to expect, what to plan for.

# 21

# A Small Motel

Cabin 12 of the King Cole Motel on the Black Horse Pike midway between Philadelphia and Atlantic City was no more than an ordinary room 20 by 15 feet, accommodating a double bed, a single bed, two bureaus, three chairs and one night table. Painted an institutional cream color, with nary a picture on the walls, it was not much more than a dump. But it was centrally located in the row of attached wooden buildings which formed a ∪ around a central courtyard, and it was for its location that the two agents of the Bureau of Narcotics had chosen Cabin 12 for the night's rendezvous.

Mike Fulgoni paced the overheated room like a caged black bear, unable to contain his anxiety over having nothing at the moment to do. His tie hung askew from his open and wilted shirt collar, his suit jacket flopped behind him as he marched from one end of the room to the other. Only his service revolver was tight and secure, holstered on his hip. In contrast, Alan Weiner stood immobile, smartly attired in a sports jacket, at the front window beside the door, looking out into the courtyard. It was more than an hour past eight o'clock. The telephone remained silent. They had not heard from Sicardo since noon that day when he had confirmed the meeting for between eight and midnight. There was just nothing more Fulgoni could think of to do. Having devoted almost a year's time to this case, topped by a full week of preparation for this night, all they could do now was wait. Fulgoni hated to wait.

"See anything?"

"No, I'll tell you soon as something turns up," Weiner replied softly.

"Remember, you get out there soon as you see a car show up, 'cause he just might be coming in a different car."

"Okay, I know."

"Get him to bring the stuff in here no matter what," Fulgoni said. "Shouldn't be any trouble in that, but if so, you just tell him I'm not coming out into any car with that much money. Tell him I want to see the stuff before I pay for it. That'll bring him in."

"Don't worry, Mike, there's no reason he shouldn't walk right in here with the stuff."

"There's always something that can go wrong and when you least expect it," Fulgoni reminded his younger partner. "When you get in here, just keep talking and tell me right out if there's anybody else in the car and how many. If you got to bring them in too, okay, if not, let them stay out there. Just play it by ear."

"I've got it straight, Mike."

The police radio equipment, tuned to a special channel for this operation and concealed in the night table between the two beds, interrupted. "There's a black Buick sedan, one or two years old, coming up the Pike, very slow, maybe twenty-five to thirty miles an hour. This might be something, Mike."

Mike lumbered over to the radio which was tuned to monitor any conversation in the room. "Got you," he shouted. "How far away is it?"

"About a mile down the road, now, and as best we can see, it's got two men in the front seat."

Fulgoni sat on the edge of a bed, his ear to the radio, while his partner continued to peer out into the night, unable to distinguish one car from another flashing by the motel. The progress of the Buick sedan was reported on the radio as it approached the motel. It paused as it reached the motel but it did not pull into the courtyard. Sicardo must not be in that car, Fulgoni concluded. The Buick cruised by, but then moments later came the report the car had made a U-turn on the highway. It came back at no more than twenty-five miles an hour, stopped, and then backed into a side road opposite the motel, so that it faced the motel courtyard. The two men slid down in the front seat. They could see out of the front windshield, but unless someone knew they were there, the car would appear to be empty.

What the two men in the Buick did not know was that they had chosen to park not more than ten yards from a trailer loaded with state police and an arsenal capable of overpowering a bus-load of strong-arm men. The center piece was a .50 caliber machine gun, mounted on a tripod with its muzzle positioned behind a curtained window of the trailer, ready to be thrust forward and out in command of the motel courtyard. The trailer was inconspicuous among other such vehicles in a trailer camp on the roadside opposite the motel. Its primary function was that of a radio communications center coordinating the activities of more than fifty state troopers and detectives participating in the expected arrest of the narcotics syndicate supplying Nick Golino.

"What do you think, Mike," asked Lieutenant John Bromley from the trailer radio, "should I take these two guys out now or do you want to wait on Sicardo?" Lieutenant Bromely was the commanding officer of the district's state police, a close friend of the federal agent with whom he had worked on many cases over the years. Fulgoni, as senior agent in a small office of the Federal Bureau of Narcotics, frequently called upon Bromley to provide cover and protection on special cases. Such inter-bureau cooperation is common throughout the country, depending as much upon individual personal friendships as upon official policy of agencies on the federal, state or city levels.

Lieutenant Bromley and Fulgoni, in discussing the Buick sedan, concluded that it was in fact Sicardo's lead car, the "protection" he had promised he would have. But whether or not there might be further protection on the way could not be known. The two detectives assigned to watch Sicardo reported that the club manager had not left his home since four-thirty that afternoon. Apparently he was not going to the club that night.

"Let's just hold tight a while and see what develops," Fulgoni decided.

Mike Fulgoni, John Bromley and other key law-enforcement men involved had planned for this night all during the week. Sometimes ten, twenty or more men would confer at night after their regular working hours to plan one phase or another. They met either in the federal post office building in downtown Philadelphia or in the basement playroom of Mike's development home in Pennsauken, a suburb of Camden, New Jersey, just across the Delaware River from Philadelphia. Planning a mass arrest of criminals who must be rounded up at the same time in different places is routine in the sense that a pilot covers the same check list each time he takes his plane off the ground. Yet, each arrest is different from every other, depending upon the idiosyncrasies of the suspects and the circumstances involved. Beyond the legal technicalities of making arrests which would stand up in court, including arrest and search warrants for each of the suspects, the officers concentrated on anticipating and devising countermeasures for what Sicardo and Golino might do on the night of delivery. For each possibility, they devised a plan of action, and although the contingencies stretched as wide as a man's imagination, Fulgoni and Bromley were determined that they would not be surprised.

In New York, the district supervisor of the Bureau took personal command of the roundup of Martino, his father, Merlotti and whoever else might be involved in that part of the operation. Teams of men were out at each location but were under orders to wait, to do nothing until the signal came in from the Philadelphia office that Golino, Sicardo and the others had been arrested. Then, before the underworld grapevine could spread the word, they would swoop. The key spot in the New York area was the suspected stash in Martino's father's attic, and the district supervisor intended to be on that scene himself.

In planning the surveillance for that night, it was decided that it would be too risky to attempt to follow whoever made the delivery from New York to Philadelphia. Instead, Mike Fulgoni and Lieutenant Bromley arranged for stationary surveillance. Along the New Jersey Turnpike, the most likely route, on that Monday afternoon and into the night, unmarked radio police cars were parked along the roadside at ten- to twelve-mile intervals. The passing traffic was checked against a list of car descriptions and license plate numbers of various known couriers. There was an outside chance, it was thought, that the delivery of the drugs to Philadelphia might be spotted. The surveillance teams assigned to Martino were under orders to trail him from his home if possible, but to drop the tail rather than risk frightening Martino from making delivery.

On the Black Horse Pike, Lieutenant Bromley had assigned fourteen unmarked radio cars to park inconspicuously at intervals all the way from Philadelphia to Atlantic City, so that the troopers could report on the progress of Sicardo's car, without trying to follow it, no matter from which direction he approached the motel. Two Bureau radio cars, each containing two agents, cruised back and forth on the Pike for a distance of five miles in either direction from the motel. There was an outside chance Sicardo might be spotted making his pick-up of the drugs from another car on the roadside near the motel.

At the motel itself, Fulgoni and Lieutenant Bromley had arranged an overwhelming show of force. No one can foretell how a man will react when cornered. Some of the mildest of narcotics traffickers have been known to go berserk when faced with arrest and, in panic, try to shoot their way out of trouble. Over the years, three agents of the Bureau of Narcotics, including one district supervisor, have lost their lives by misjudging the mentality of the suspect they were in the process of arresting. In appraising this case, agent Fulgoni doubted that Jimmy Sicardo would try to fight his way out of a corner, but he warned that Nick Golino might prove highly dangerous. As for the protection men, if they came, Fulgoni could guess that they would be ready for trouble, prepared to shoot it out against a rival gang, and the shooting could begin before the lawmen could properly convince the delivery men of their true identity. And so, that Monday night, in addition to the heavy machine gun in the trailer, Lieutenant Bromley had eight state troopers posted with rifles at either end of the motel and across the road. Fulgoni had two agents in each of the cabins on either side of his room. One man in each room was armed with a Thompson submachine gun. The strategy (not unlike that of United States foreign policy) was to display enough armed strength at the critical moment so that no matter how many men Sicardo might have with him, they would be dissuaded from chancing a gun battle against overwhelming odds.

Fulgoni explained the preparations the day before to Jimmy Gibbons, the owner of the motel. "I got a big H deal on for tomorrow night and I need four rooms 'cause I got to move my men in for protection," Fulgoni told him. The fat Negro watched in awe the small army moving into the motel. "I'm carrying two hundred grand for this deal, Gibbie, and I got to guard against a heist," Fulgoni confided.

Gibbie offered his help. He liked how big-time hoods worked. "Look," he said in his office, "I got a good shotgun here and I can cover you from the window."

"You stay the hell away from that window and keep your fat belly out of sight," Fulgoni warned him. "I don't want them to see you at all with a gun 'cause you liable to mess things up." As an afterthought, Fulgoni had Weiner give Gibbie a small balance scale, with instructions to guard it in his office until they needed it to weigh the junk that would be delivered. The scale would give the overexcited hotel owner something to do and, at the same time, would provide Weiner with an excuse to leave the cabin after Sicardo arrived.

A state trooper in mufti, whom Gibbie took to be a fellow hoodlum, lounged in the motel office that night in order to keep an eye on the hotel manager and any customers who might drop in. The motel was open for business but quiet that night. At nine-thirty, no one was stirring outside. The night was dark, cloudy and cold. The front courtyard was rather eerie, lighted only by two stanchion lamps outside the front office and an oversized red neon sign announcing the name of the place. It was at this time that Fulgoni decided that it might be better to take the protection car out of action before Sicardo arrived with the drugs. Lieutenant Bromley agreed.

Leaving one detective behind to monitor the radio in the trailer, Lieutenant Bromley, with three detectives behind him, crept stealthily from the trailer to the parked Buick. He advanced step by step in a squatter's crouch, carrying in his right hand the deadliest of all hand weapons, a .45 automatic. At the driver's door of the car, he paused in a deep squatting position, his head down almost to the level of his knees so that he could not be seen from the window of the car. Not a sound came from within the automobile. Then slowly he pressed the door button in, ready to dive out of the way if anyone inside opened fire. The door was not locked. Lieutenant Bromley braced himself, drew a deep breath and flung the door open. At the same time, as the interior lamp of the car went on, the lieutenant thrust his gun directly into the face of the closest man, shouting, "Put your hands over your heads! Right now! Quick, or I'll blast you."

The violent thrust lodged the barrel of the automatic inside the man's mouth and sent him sprawling against his partner. They were terrified. The man with the gun barrel in his mouth gagged and the other cried out, "Don't shoot . . . for God's sake, don't shoot!"

The two men scrambled out of the car, holding their arms stretched full-length over their heads, docilely obeying orders and pleading, to no avail, to be permitted to explain their presence there. But only after they had assumed the classic frisk position, hands against the side of their car, feet spread apart, body bent slightly over so that their weight was leaning against the car, and they were found to be unarmed, only then were they allowed to explain.

They were reporters from the Philadelphia *Ledger*. They identified themselves. They showed their press cards, and they explained how they had surmised a big police operation was under way from the frequent night meetings in the federal building, and had followed the police cars out to the motel, returning at night on the assumption that whatever the action was going to be, it would be after dark, and they wanted to be in on it.

The anticlimax was reported to Fulgoni and only afterwards, in retrospect, did the humor of the situation strike him. At the time, with their nerves on edge, both Fulgoni and the police lieutenant were furious at the prospect that two news reporters might have destroyed a year's investigation work. The reporters, closely questioned, swore that they had told no one of what they were up to, not even their city editor. "Now, what should we do with these two guys?" asked Bromley.

"Move their car back down that road, out of the way, and

keep someone with them until this thing comes to a head," Fulgoni advised, adding, "Just make sure they stay put and if they try any shenanigans, we'll lock 'em up for the night."

The law men settled back in their positions at the motel, somewhat emotionally drained from the false encounter, and waited. At midnight, after considering the pros and cons, Fulgoni suggested that Weiner telephone Sicardo to find out when they could expect delivery.

"Can't make it tonight," said Sicardo, "there's a twenty-four-hour delay, so we'll make delivery tomorrow night."

Weiner covered the mouthpiece of the telephone with his hand and repeated the message. "Get mad and pump him," Fulgoni advised. The unwritten social structure of the situation, as rigid as that of an army's chain of command, demanded that Weiner, as the junior partner, carry on the conversation with Sicardo, his equal, while Fulgoni spoke only to Golino.

"I can't tell you anything now," Sicardo insisted. "Call me tomorrow around seven and I'll give you the definite time then."

There was nothing the law men could do then but ponder the situation and wait. They maintained their watch until a half hour past midnight, just in case Golino and Sicardo had bluffed on the delay in order to observe what was going on at the motel. But nothing suspicious transpired. The New York agents were advised of the postponement. And the two newspaper reporters were given a thorough tongue-lashing for their intrusion and, after being threatened with twenty-four hours' imprisonment to insure their silence, they were invited back to the motel to observe the action the next night, upon their solemn pledge of silence over the following twenty-four hours.

The next day was a pure sweat. There was no way of reading the minds of their adversaries. At four-thirty in the afternoon, Sicardo was observed going into Golino's home in a suburb of Atlantic City. He had not emerged by seven o'clock when Weiner telephoned him at the club and at his home, leaving a message at each place that Johnny Gold had called. Almost one hundred narcotics agents and police were back at their stations again, along the roads leading to the motel and at the homes and haunts of the various suspects in New York, New Jersey and Pennsylvania. At seven-thirty, Sicardo telephoned the motel. "I'll

see you tonight about eleven-thirty," he told Weiner, and hung
up.

Again the agents and detectives searched for a lead or protection automobile. Two Bureau cars cruised the Pike near the
motel but all other vehicles were stationary.

At 10:30 P.M., then 11 and then 11:30, the two detectives
outside Golino's home reported that they had not observed Sicardo leaving the place. At the motel, no one was sure. In New
York, the agents were beginning to have their doubts. At midnight, Sicardo telephoned. "I'm goin' be an hour or so late, but
I'll be there."

"Okay, we're waiting," Weiner responded, quite truthfully.

At ten minutes to one in the morning, Sicardo left the house
alone, got into his Chrysler and drove down the block. He
stopped there and checked for a tail. But no one was following
him. The police knew where he was going.

He was free of surveillance for about fifteen or twenty minutes. At the Black Horse Pike outside of Atlantic City, he was
spotted and reported: driving most cautiously at speeds between
twenty-five and thirty-five miles per hour, apparently on the
lookout for anyone who might be following him. Each time he
passed an unmarked police car parked at a service station or a
diner along the Pike, he was reported.

Pinpointing Sicardo's car from the radioed reports, agents
Irving Feldman and Dan Harris of the Philadelphia office of the
Bureau picked up the surveillance several miles from the motel.
They swung out on the Pike about two miles ahead of Sicardo's
car, and with binoculars trained on his headlights as they maintained the same speed, the two agents trailed Sicardo from ahead
rather than behind. At that distance with binoculars they could
see his car's headlights without fear that he could see the tail-
lights of their own vehicle. All the while the agents were on the
lookout for any other car which might be waiting to meet Sicardo. The strategy was designed to forewarn Fulgoni and
Weiner of any possible plan of Golino's to arrange for a holdup
coincident with the delivery. One of the tricks of the trade is for
the seller to arrange with a third party to hold up the customer
waiting with money for the delivery and then to share the pro-
ceeds later. But all went well on this night. Sicardo met no one.

He pulled into the motel courtyard at two-ten in the morning, and Weiner came out to motion to him to park directly in front of Cabin 12.

Opening the passenger door on the right side, Weiner poked his head in to see that no one else was in the car. "It's about time you got here," he said in greeting. "We've been cooling our heels for two whole days now. Where's the stuff?"

Sicardo reached under the front seat and took out a small canvas zippered bag and swung it at Weiner. "I got it all right, right here."

"Okay, let's get out of the cold," said Weiner, walking ahead to the cabin. Sicardo paused first and looked around, observing only the stillness of late night. The only cabin lights aglow came from the cabin ahead.

"Come on in, Jimmy," Weiner urged. "We've been waiting for you."

# 22

# Round-Up

Sicardo came into the cabin with distrust in his eyes. He stood as if on the balls of his feet, ready to flee, casting about as if he expected something unusual in the cabin. Perhaps it was merely his being alone with two crooks he knew as Telano and Gold. Whatever the reason, he did not accept Fulgoni's invitation to remove his hat and coat. "It's late," he said. "Gimme the dough and let me get out of here."

"What's the matter with you, Jimmy? You keep us waiting for two days and now you want to scamper," Fulgoni mocked him. "Let's see the junk first."

Sicardo handed over the bag and Fulgoni turned his back to the little man and dumped the contents onto the bed. Two brown paper bags wired at the top tumbled onto the bed. Fulgoni struggled with the wires and then turned the task over to his sidekick. Then, turning to Sicardo, he asked what had occasioned the twenty-four-hour delay.

"Aw, there was a mix-up in New York and the five kilos that was supposed to be for you were sold to someone else so they had to go and get five other kilos."

"This is good stuff, ain't it?" Fulgoni demanded with only half-feigned suspicion.

"Oh yeah, this stuff is absolutely pure 'cause they told Nick they had to go get another shipment from some Frenchman," Sicardo explained. "Nick said it was better stuff than you got before, so you're lucky."

Weiner unwrapped the two paper bags and displayed to his partner the ten half-kilo packages of white powder that had been inside. He laid the ten plastic bags in two rows on the bed and counted and re-counted them.

"Where's Nick now?" Fulgoni asked. "I thought maybe he'd come with you."

"Oh, he's out of town," Sicardo lied. "Come on, the stuff's all there, let's have the money." He was becoming more and more anxious, as if he were trying to read Fulgoni's intentions.

"We got to weigh this stuff first, while you're here, so we know how much we got."

"Come on, Mike, it's all there," Sicardo whined. "I want to get to bed tonight."

"No, we'd better make sure first it's all there," said Fulgoni with a nod to Weiner. "Go get the scale from the office, Johnny." That was their prearranged signal for the bust. The younger agent turned on his heel and strode out of the cabin.

Alone with Sicardo, Fulgoni attempted to pump him for more information, but the little club manager seemed to have lost his usual bravado and penchant for talk. He disclaimed any further knowledge of the Frenchman who supplied the drugs. He shrugged off Fulgoni's questions about the supposed protection car without actually admitting that he had no protection behind him. Fulgoni sensed the little man's nervousness which he thought was most likely due to his being alone with a man so much bigger, tougher and more dangerous than himself. In any event, Sicardo himself did not appear to present any danger. He stood in the middle of the room, his hands in plain view, the pockets of his coat flat and apparently empty of any weapon. Fulgoni savored this moment of truth which was at hand.

Meanwhile, Weiner reconnoitered the area outside as he walked to the motel office. He took the white balance scale from Gibbons and gave the nod to the detective there; on his return to his cabin, he rapped twice on the doors of Cabin 11 and Cabin 14 (there being for superstitious reasons no Cabin 13). Four men, two with submachine guns, followed him back to Cabin 12, where he knocked ever so gently on the door.

At the sound, Fulgoni drew his gun and pointed it at Sicardo's flat stomach. "Put your hands up high, Jimmy," he announced with a broad smile of pleasure. "I'm a federal agent and you're under arrest."

Sicardo simply did not believe him. Neither did he put up his hands. He sort of waved one arm as though to shoo away the revolver. "Aw, Mike, this is a heist and I know it," Sicardo exclaimed. "I can tell you, you're making a big mistake and you'll never get away with it."

Fulgoni called out for Weiner to come in, and the five men poised outside came rushing into the room. Sicardo looked over the arsenal of weapons and submitted to being handcuffed, and still he did not believe. Only when Fulgoni uncovered the concealed radio equipment and gave the signal to Lieutenant Bromley for Golino to be placed under arrest at his home and for the New York agents to be notified to move, only then did Sicardo explode with a torrent of choice expletives culled from a lifetime's associations. He cursed and snarled, he ranted and raved, but he put up no physical struggle against the inevitable. To be flummoxed by a crook was one thing, but to be taken in so thoroughly by a federal narcotics agent was a blow to his pride as a professional. He faced a long prison term. That he realized immediately. But even worse was the danger of retribution from a man like Golino: Jimmy Sicardo remembered that it had been he who had introduced and vouched for Mike Telano.

When Gibbons was brought into the cabin, he shook his befuddled head in disbelief at Sicardo in handcuffs, bags of heroin on the bed, submachine guns held poised, and the man he knew to be from the Mafia standing there smiling at him and being introduced as an agent of the Federal Bureau of Narcotics. "No, no, say it ain't so, Mike . . . you ain't no cop . . . you can't be a cop . . . no, you just can't be . . ." Gibbie was still muttering to himself when he was hustled away in a squad car.

Shortly after two-thirty in the morning, detective John Taller jabbed the doorbell of Golino's home and kept his finger there. His partner, Peter Holmes, stood at his side, his hand in his pocket upon his service .38. The underworld lord of Philadelphia came to the door in bare feet and pajamas.

"Nicolas Golino, I'm a police officer and I have here a warrant for your arrest."

In the federal courthouse, Golino saw Sicardo only moments before their arraignment when they were brought together in an interrogation room in the early hours of the morning. A silent, cold stare of hate and condemnation was enough to launch a quivering Sicardo into a plea for mercy. "It ain't my fault, Nick, I swear it, I'm in this as bad as you. . . . How was I to know he was a cop? . . . I had no idea. . . ." Sicardo's pleas flowed like a torrent as though he were bleeding from the mouth, and when finally he ceased and stood there like a disobedient dog awaiting word from his master, Golino, without raising his voice, told his erstwhile partner in narcotics, "You are just a stupid son of a bitch . . ." and he went on from there.

Short of murder, espionage and other crimes punishable by death, no defendants in the United States may be held in jail without bond prior to trial. But when the scope of this narcotics conspiracy was outlined at the arraignment to United States Commissioner Felix Budd, he granted the government's request for bail high enough to hold these defendants at least until others in the conspiracy were arrested.

Bail was set at $125,000 for Golino, $100,000 for Sicardo, and $75,000 each for the others rounded up in the Philadelphia area: John Sudora, who had first sold heroin to Fulgoni; Gibbons; John Marion and Mrs. Marion Medley, the friends of Gibbons who had sold Fulgoni and Weiner marijuana at the motel. A bench warrant for immediate arrest was issued for Frank Malti, who had escaped the dragnet and was not apprehended until federal agents uncovered his hideaway apartment several weeks afterwards.

Mike Fulgoni did not wait for the arraignments. As preplanned, soon after Nick Golino, the top man in the Philadelphia phase of the conspiracy, was taken into custody, Mike set off at turnpike speed for Merlotti's apartment in New York City. It was three o'clock in the morning and the roads were as clear as the agent's mind. Fatigue might come later as a delayed reaction to the long hours he had put in, but at the moment Mike Fulgoni felt only elation and boundless energy. He wanted to be where the action was. As the suspected nerve center of the New York operation, Merlotti's apartment was expected to yield whatever evidence the Bureau could hope to find on the sources of supply and other points of distribution used by the mob, and it was thought that Fulgoni might recognize some names found in the apartment. As he drove to New York, he still had hope that he would arrive in time to witness Merlotti's arrest. Before he had left Philadelphia he had checked with his office and learned that the roundup in New York was being held off until Merlotti returned home from what seemed to be a night out on the town. According to the radioed reports, Tony Martino and his father were tucked in and asleep in their respective homes; no matter what they heard, they could not get much beyond their doors without barging into the federal agents posted outside. But Merlotti still was somewhere on the loose and the Bureau wanted him in custody before any word of the arrests could reach him.

For six hours in the cold of a winter night, five federal agents waited for Frank Merlotti to come home. Two were posted outside the front entrance of the apartment building, one enjoyed the warmth of the garage, and two watched the back entrance to the building. At 4:40 A.M., Merlotti approached the rear entrance to the apartment house, walking alone down the block from Third Avenue. As he slipped his key into the lock, agent Danny Monahan, a thin scarecrow of a man, staggered out of a vestibule of a building across the street as if drunk, and in a besotted voice, as he came reeling towards Merlotti, he cried out, "Hey, wait a minute, I forgot my key and I'm locked out . . . let me in."

Merlotti obliged and held the door open. Monahan stumbled right up to him and caught him completely unawares. "I'm a federal agent and you're under arrest," Monahan announced, and only then did Merlotti notice the snub-nosed .38 in the agent's hand.

The fat, middle-aged gangster protested all the way as Monahan marched him around the block to the front entrance of the building. There the agents produced their search warrant for the apartment. "Aw, you got nothing on me and you won't find a thing in the apartment," he insisted, after reading over the warrant with care. Four agents escorted him up the elevator and to the apartment. At the door, Monahan thought to ask, "Is there anyone in the apartment?"

"I don't know, I've been gone all night."

He may or may not have known, for the agents never did find that out, but in one of the twin beds of the guest bedroom a very surprised man awoke, instantly alert to the situation, to find himself embarrassingly unclothed and trapped. With a shrug of his shoulders, he identified himself in a well-modulated, unaccented voice as Joe Biani of Alexandria, Virginia.

"I place you Joseph Biani under arrest," announced agent Mort Pelas, who recognized Biani's name immediately from his work on overseas sources of heroin.

"What's the charge?" Biani demanded. "I only came here visiting."

"You're listed as one of the tenants of this apartment from which large quantities of heroin have been sold," Pelas shot back, "and the charge is conspiracy to sell narcotics."

With Biani and Merlotti sitting glumly on the living-room couch observing in silence, three of the four agents began a most thorough search of the apartment, not quite inch by inch, but close to it.

Tony Martino answered the ringing of his doorbell at five minutes to five and was immediately placed under arrest. His wife began to wail in long, gasping sobs which grew louder and louder as she watched the officers search through her home. It was as if, one officer said afterwards, she had known this night would come in one form or another, without truly realizing the precise nature of her husband's illegal activities. Tony Martino, refusing to answer questions put to him, insisted that there were no narcotics in his home. He denied with vehemence that he had anything whatever to do with narcotics. "We know, we know," the New York supervisor told him, "you have nothing to do with narcotics. You don't know Frank Merlotti or Big Joe Biani or . . ." and he reeled off a list of names which caused the young Martino to blanch and fall silent until the final thrust. "All right, then we'll go over to your father's house and see what's there."

Martino screamed in protest. "You leave him out of this, he's an old man, and he's got nothing at all to do with this."

Enrico Martino observed only one man on the stoop when he looked out of the peephole in his door at five-fifteen in the morning. The man was impudently leaning on his doorbell. When he unlatched the door, five agents rushed in, one of then handing him the search warrant as the others climbed up to his second-floor apartment in the two-family home. Over the old man's protestations, the federal agents went through his home swiftly, then demanded the key to the padlocked door leading to the attic. "There's nothin' upstairs, we don't use it ever," the former bootlegger insisted. "I don't even know where the key is."

Nothing the agents could say, and none of their threats, influenced Enrico. "Go 'head, bust the lock, bust the door down, but you'll pay for it, 'cause there's nothing upstairs."

Agent Harnett found a key ring in the old man's trousers which had been dumped on a chair in the bedroom, and Martino said nothing as he watched the agent unlock the door and lead another agent up to the attic.

In the center of the room, the agents came upon a large wooden trunk, painted black, of the type often used by Italian immigrants. Another key on the ring opened the trunk.

Inside the trunk was a brown leather suitcase, also locked, and inside the suitcase, like a Chinese puzzle, the agents found eighteen brown paper bags, tied on top with wire, and inside the paper bags were waxed-paper bags sealed with staples, and inside the waxed-paper bags was heroin. They had found the stash. Each of the bags contained approximately half a kilo of heroin, packaged and ready for delivery. Moreover, the bags and the way they were folded over on top and stapled matched the bags of heroin which had been sold to agent Fulgoni on three separate occasions. The eighteen half-kilo bags (which were later found, in the Bureau laboratory, to contain nineteen pounds, two ounces and 112.5 grains of heroin) would be used in court to provide the tangible evidence needed to assure a conviction of the Martinos and, most probably, of everyone whom the Bureau could connect with them. Of that the agents were sure.

Enrico saw the truth also when the heroin and the paraphernalia of the trade (bottles of acid, milk sugar, a scale and weights, and supplies of waxed-paper bags) was brought down to the living room. He announced that everything there belonged to him and that his wife and son knew nothing about this business.

The agents quickly stripped him of that line of defense, reciting the number of nights the attic had been watched and his son followed on his delivery rounds. The old man then refused to say anything more.

Tony Martino tried to absolve both his father and mother when questioned at 90 Church Street later that morning. The agents put the pressure on Tony, considering him the weakest link in the syndicate and the man most likely to flip, and to this end they had taken his mother into custody although they had no intention of pressing charges against her. "I assume full responsibility," Tony repeated over and over. "They had nothin' to do with it."

The interrogation officer threatened the young Martino with at least twenty years in prison. He outlined the strong evidence the Bureau had gathered against him and his father. He threatened twenty years in prison for his father. "Your father will die there, you know." Martino refused to cooperate. "Your mother will go to prison too and I can't say for how long." Martino pleaded for his parents, not for himself.

"The only way you can help your parents and yourself now," the federal agent told him, "is to make a clean breast of the whole thing. We want to know all about Biani, his position in the organization, and where any more drugs might be hidden and how they were smuggled into the country." The agent made quite a long speech.

Tony shifted uneasily in his chair and finally, in his broad New York accent, exclaimed, "I know all that but you're not fooling around with boys now. Biani is a big man. If I opened my mouth, I'd be dead in twenty-four hours."

To the offer of police protection, he just shook his head. "I'm just a slob in this outfit," he pleaded. "That's all I'm going to say. I admit you got me, what more can I say? You treated me all right and I gave you some answers. Now I want to see my lawyer." He knew his rights and to all further questions he merely repeated, "I have nothing to say, I want to see my lawyer."

No one in the entire conspiracy had anything to say to the authorities, nor were any drugs found outside of the stash in Enrico Martino's attic. But in Merlotti's living-room desk, the agents found the next most valuable cache: written records of the business. The center drawer was crammed with pads, loose slips of paper and three address books. The notations were, to be sure, mostly in makeshift codes. Initials, nicknames and first names were used for identification next to figures which apparently indicated quantities of heroin sold, money paid and amounts owed. The address books contained listings of many known narcotics violators from all parts of the country, as well as unfamiliar names, all of which would be investigated for many months to come, providing the Bureau with a treasure trove of potential new cases.

Agent Pelas went through the address books on the spot. His primary job in the Bureau was that of coordinator: He read each and every agent's report from around the world which came into the New York Bureau office, searching for conspiracies or dovetailing evidence of a single operation spread beyond the borders of the Bureau's sixteen regional districts. In one book, Pelas' trained eyes lit upon the name "François." It stood there alone with a telephone number, and he remembered the reports of the Frenchman doing business in Canada.

That telephone number alone probably never would have led the Bureau of Narcotics to the right man. But Merlotti's mistake was making a notation of the correct telephone number upon a slip of paper found in the same drawer. While the slip of paper held the correct telephone number, it had only the letter *F* before it. But it differed from François' number only in that the final two digits were raised by one. It was an opportunity not to be missed, and Pelas, who had been pursuing the slimmest of hearsay reports on the mysterious François for months, was quite excited. The two telephone numbers were relayed to 90 Church Street, and there an agent put in an emergency request to the telephone company for immediate information on the names and addresses of the persons to whom the numbers were listed. While waiting, Pelas discussed with his fellow agents just what course of action they could best follow when the information reached them. Mike Fulgoni arrived at the apartment in time to join in the planning of a raid upon what could well be the European source of heroin to the Biani-Merlotti organization, the Montreal syndicate and unknown others. The problem was not only to flush out François but to do it in such a manner that he could be arrested with his incriminating evidence on him. Otherwise, the agents might have an arrest but not a conviction.

When the names and addresses corresponding to the telephone numbers reached Pelas, Fulgoni and the others, the choice was simple. One name was that of Martha Abramowitz; the other was Pierre Trigano. Nevertheless, two agents were sent to the address of the woman listed, with instructions to stand by there on the remote possibility that Mr. Trigano was an innocent citizen with, under the circumstances, a suspicious name. Six agents drove out to Kew Gardens to call on Pierre Trigano with the hope he was François. En route, Mort Pelas and his friend Mike Fulgoni embellished their scheme to unveil François. They even acted out the parts.

It was almost seven o'clock when Mike Fulgoni knocked on the door. He felt quite light-headed after the long, long night, almost gay, with a sense of confidence that even this foolish trick would work. After a few seconds he rapped again, harder, on the door, disdaining the doorbell in plain view. So what if he raised all the neighbors? he thought. That would get him inside the apartment, if the joker was really François. He pounded the door so that it shuddered.

"Who is there?" came the voice from the other side of the door. The stilted accent was definitely French.

The burly agent leaned his two-hundred-plus pounds against the door, and in the loudest whisper he could muster, he croaked, "Open up, I got a message for you, François."

Dead silence. Fulgoni stood back from the door. He sensed intuitively that the door would open soon and he would see François.

It did open, but only two inches and secured by a chain. "What is it?" the man demanded. Through the opening, Fulgoni saw a fat, swarthy face, thick lips and heavy eyelids. He then noticed the Chinese-red dressing gown, silk pajamas and bare feet.

What Léon Levonian saw was a heavyset, tough-looking Italian with a twenty-three-hour growth of black beard on his face, bloodshot eyes, heavy jowls, a wrinkled overcoat and old snap-brim hat. The caller looked as though he either had just tumbled out of bed or had been up all night.

"Are you François?"

"What do you want?"

"I ain't got all day," the agent rasped in irritation. "If you're this guy François, I got a message for you, so let me in."

"I don't know you, so why should I let you into my house?" Levonian whispered through the chained door.

"Oh, what the hell, don't let me in," exclaimed Fulgoni, looking around the hall as if to check if anyone might be listening.

"Big Joe sent me to tell you your place here is hot. Merlotti's been busted, you know, picked up by the feds, and some of the other guys've got it too, so Big Joe told me to get you out of here. He says he thinks the feds are coming out here."

"You say they are all arrested?" Levonian asked slowly. Fulgoni repeated the message in basic English, sensing that this man François understood what he was saying but perhaps did not believe him. He did not open the door. In a way, Fulgoni admired his caution; but the agent still had more to say. "I got a place down the road where I can put you up, if you want to come, but you better make up your mind, 'cause I don't want to hang around too long."

"And where is Joe?"

"I don't know. He phoned me and I don't know if the police got him or not or where he is, but he told me to tell you to get out of here and to take the junk out of here 'cause the feds will be comin' round. I got the feeling the boys were busted not too long ago and Joe was thinking about the junk you got here, you understand?"

"Yes, I understand, and I thank you for the message," Levonian said cautiously. "But I think I better go myself. Thank you."

Fulgoni gave him a fictitious address and Levonian promised he would look him up there, and then Fulgoni retreated down the stairs, leaving behind the warning that François did not have much time.

The agent left the building by the front entrance and then doubled back to the rear yard where Pelas and two other agents were waiting. Fulgoni recounted the face-to-face meeting, concluding that he had indeed spoken to François; but whether or not the Frenchman had believed him, he did not know. And so the agents waited.

Later, they found out that François had indeed believed him. He had telephoned Merlotti's apartment and had hung up the phone when an agent there answered the first ring with the unmistakable tone of voice of a policeman.

In the cold outside the three-story building, the suspense lasted no more than fifteen minutes. They were long minutes, each one of them. When the man called François emerged from the back door, he had on his right arm a young blond woman as tall as himself, stumbling to keep up with him, and in his left hand he carried a tan leather suitcase.

Léon Levonian, with the girl just behind him, had reached the alleyway leading to the street when he was greeted by three big men, each of them displaying a gun and smiling dangerously.

"*Bonjour,* François!" Mort Pelas sang out, face to face with him. Mike Fulgoni stood a few feet to his right and agent Al Pizzuti was planted several feet to the left of Pelas. "*Qu'est-ce que vous avez dans votre valise?*"

Levonian stared for a moment at the three grinning men, then at their guns. The girl whimpered. Then, with unexpected speed for so fat a man, Levonian swung the suitcase at Pelas, lowered his head and charged the smallest of the agents, bolting in the direction away from Fulgoni. But agent Pizzuti was quick. He took one step back, extended a rigid leg in the path of the fleeing man and sent him sprawling. Léon Levonian looked up from the pavement just as one of the men announced they were all federal agents, and then, with a glance at his suitcase, he knew that he had lost.

# Epilogue

The Honorable Judge of the United States Court for the Eastern District of New York adjusted his spectacles, gazed down from the raised bench of justice upon the attorney for the defense and said, "Is there anything that the defendant wishes to say before the court imposes sentence?"

The agile defense attorney, a veteran in narcotics cases, interpreted the judge's question for Levonian and then informed the court, "He says no."

"Is he willing to explain to the court this half million dollars and particularly the sixty-nine thousand dollars that was sent over into his numbered Swiss account? Ask him that."

Léon Levonian did not respond; he could not answer that question satisfactorily then or during his three-week trial. And so he had been convicted on a two-count indictment: possession of illicit narcotics and having "knowingly, willfully and unlawfully conspired with Pierre Trigano and others . . . to import heroin hydrochloride into the United States, and to receive, conceal, sell and facilitate the transportation, concealment and sale of said narcotic drug . . ."

It was only after his arrest that the Bureau of Narcotics amassed the evidence of the conspiracy, tracing his activities back to Istanbul and forward to his Swiss bank-account deposits in the United States. Three separate numbered accounts had been located through the deposit slips, and for the first time in history, Swiss banks in Geneva had opened and revealed for use in a United States court its coded, numbered accounts. It came as a shock to Levonian, confronted on the witness stand with the evidence, and also surprised the underworld at large, who had not understood that Swiss numbered accounts were inviolate and secret only in civil and financial disputes. Where a "heinous crime" was linked directly to the money deposited, Swiss banks, like all others, followed a policy of full disclosure upon the proper governmental demands. Narcotics smuggling was considered a heinous crime, and the Justice Department, in this case, made its official demands.

Those bank accounts, it can be said, served as the government's star witnesses against the French defendant, as the judge pointed out in sentencing the defendant. "This was a long trial and I listened very attentively to the evidence, and I know the jury did, and they found him guilty of this conspiracy to import narcotics into the United States," the judge said.

"On the basis of the evidence which they heard, they apparently believed that he was a big operator and that he and his pal Trigano delivered from the United States to numbered Swiss accounts, something over a half a million dollars. And it was done through a bank in New York and through Perera & Co. in New York. And, as you know, they were going in there almost every day for certain periods of time, always with cash, twenty thousand dollars, ten thousand dollars, nine thousand dollars, eight thousand dollars. False names and false addresses were given.

"And, of the five hundred thousand dollars, the Government was able to establish that sixty-nine thousand dollars of it was sent to a bank account, a numbered bank account in the name of this defendant's brother, and that when that bank account was opened, the brother gave this defendant a power of attorney, and this defendant signed the power of attorney. I observed him during the trial when he was confronted with a photostatic copy of that power of attorney and he was a very surprised man on the stand. I seem to recall him saying [to the prosecutor], 'Where did you get this?' or 'How did you get this?'

"Now, throughout this trial, this defendant kept insisting

about his legal money businesses that he was in, but supported it by not one shred of evidence.

"You may recall that I asked him to explain where this money came from, this cash, and why it went into his account. And I heard some fancy double-talk in French, which I happen to understand. And then it was translated, and I asked him again, and again, and again, because it wasn't clear and he didn't answer the question.

"I think the jury felt, as I felt, that he was a liar, and that he lied on the stand."

The judge went on to review the evidence in the case and he read aloud a report from the Sûreté on Levonian's known activities in Marseilles, and then he lashed out:

"This is one of the worst crimes on the books. Narcotics operators, whether they are big operators or small punks, are probably the worst enemies of the United States. He [pointing to Levonian] was undermining the physical stamina and the morale of our young generation. He stopped at nothing in order to make illegal profits in staggering amounts, and he must know that by their unlawful operations, they [narcotics operators] are sapping the strength of America in its younger strata . . . I cannot think of anyone who is a greater enemy of America than the trafficker in narcotics.

"Now, the Congress of the United States has recognized—and they are the representatives of the people—the seriousness of this crime and have reflected it in the appropriate statute that fixes the penalty.

"This defendant was indicted under a statute which makes a sentence mandatory, if the defendant is found guilty. And the period of incarceration under this mandatory section varies from the minimum of five years to a maximum of twenty years for the first offense, and that means the first time that the man is caught and convicted.

"Now, there is a reason, I must assume, for this spread of from five to twenty years. If he is a small punk, he probably comes at the lower end, or one end of the spectrum, and if he is a big operator, he comes possibly at the other end of the spectrum, and then those in between the small punks and the big operators may come somewhere in between.

"The jury was satisfied beyond a reasonable doubt in a trial in which this defendant had every protection of the laws that the United States gives to anybody. This man deserves a severe sentence under the mandate of the Congress of the United States."

The judge paused, and each man in the silent courtroom had a moment of awesome privacy, alone with his thoughts, until the judgment on Léon Levonian was announced.

On the count in the indictment covering possession of narcotics with intent to sell, Léon Levonian received the minimum sentence: five years imprisonment.

On the final count in the indictment covering the conspiracy to import, receive, conceal and sell heroin, the judge intoned his sentence with the severity of the penalty imposed: "On the conspiracy count, the sentence of the Court is that you be committed to the custody of the Attorney General or his duly authorized representative who shall designate the place of your confinement for twenty years."

The judge paused to allow for the gasps of reaction in the courtroom, and then he added: "And a fine of twenty thousand dollars is imposed on you. That is the maximum fine. These two sentences to run concurrently."

The duly authorized representative of the Attorney General assigned Léon Levonian, of Marseilles, France, to the federal penitentiary at Leavenworth, Kansas, where he now resides.

Pierre Trigano, indicted as a co-conspirator of his friend Levonian, is today a fugitive from American justice. Understandably, he never returned to the United States. He was, of course, hounded by the Marseilles police and brought up on charges of trafficking in narcotics, but the *juge d'instruction*, a sort of combination magistrate and prosecutor, dismissed the case before trial for lack of evidence.

The police kept a close watch on Trigano's activities, and when he built a rather sumptuous villa in the small fishing village of Cassis, a Corsican-dominated suburb of Marseilles, the police turned the case over to the French equivalent of the Internal Revenue Service and the latter brought charges against Trigano similar to those which sent Frank Costello to jail in the United States. The French revenue service proved that the Trigano family was living, far beyond its means, on about twenty-five thousand dollars a year over a four-year period when Pierre Trigano was ostensibly unemployed. Trigano was fined 140,000 new francs, or $28,000 for back taxes, and when he was pursued by the revenue service the following year, he solved his problem in the French manner. He divorced his beautiful wife and put the villa and bank accounts in her name. She in turn blithely informed the authorities, when pressed, that she was being supported in her present style of living by her lover. The French police could hardly invade her privacy, even though they suspected with certainty that her lover was her ex-husband Trigano.

The perseverance of the French Sûreté, for which it is duly famous, did cramp Trigano's style in the narcotics trade. With the police on his tail, no longer could he be trusted to carry narcotics by his Corsican colleagues. Shut out from one business, he turned to another, and in 1967 he was caught trying to smuggle liquor over the French-Italian border. He was sentenced to six months in prison.

Dominique Benucci evaded the French police all his life. But one Bastille Day not long ago, while watching the fireworks display over the Old Port, Benucci was shot in the head at close range and killed by a former colleague, who was later adjudged insane and put into an institution. The shooting was the result of an affair of the heart rather than narcotics, the police believe.

The French master chemist Paoli, in the scramble to take over Benucci's lucrative business, foolishly branched out to selling and distribution, and the greater his success, the more paths there were leading to his door, until finally the Marseilles police found the way to his laboratory.

A political change in government and an overall shake-up of the upper echelons of the Lebanese Sûreté brought about the end of Abou Salim Mallouke's career as a policeman. He was allowed to resign. He then turned his efforts full-time to smuggling, teaming up with several of the major smugglers of Beirut. He proved as elusive as ever, until one night he was caught flashing signals from a house on the waterfront to a ship in the bay. He was indicted in a conspiracy to smuggle into Lebanon several million American cigarettes. He bailed himself out of jail, fled the country and disappeared. The last word on this wily character was that he was being held for ransom by a Syrian band of thieves, who suspected him of informing upon them and so causing them to lose a contraband shipment of seven tons of marijuana. Some believe Abou Salim is now dead; others are convinced he is merely laying low or retired in some out-of-the-way paradise. No one knows.

Ahmet Baykal, by far the most successful of all Turkish smugglers, was finally sent to prison because he made the simplest of mistakes, one which has sent more narcotics traffickers to jail than any other: He trusted a previously reliable courier. In Geneva, Baykal engaged a Greek named Constantine to drive his car to Istanbul, pick up a load of morphine base and deliver it to Marseilles. Constantine, a sort of free-lance journalist whose papers and press passes enabled him to travel across Europe without suspicion, was also a smuggler, and Baykal had every reason to trust him. What Baykal did not know, however, was that Constantine had been recently expelled from Belgium for certain extralegal activities and was frantic to return to his sweetheart in Brussels. So, Constantine offered the Belgium police a deal: entrée into Belgium in exchange for an international dope smuggler. The Belgian Interpol man notified the U.S. Bureau of Narcotics agent in Paris, who interviewed Constantine and then notified his superior, the Bureau Chief in Rome, who notified the United States agent in Istanbul, who, in turn, was ready for Constantine when he drove into Istanbul. On that night that Baykal and his men returned to Constantine his automobile, in which they had secreted forty kilos of morphine base, they were arrested on the spot by the narcotics squad of the Istanbul police, accompanied by the American narcotics agent stationed in Turkey.

In the federal district courts of the United States, Nick Golino, Jimmy Sicardo and their New York partners were prosecuted, as the expression goes, to the fullest extent of the law. Golino and Sicardo received separate trials for their activities in the Philadelphia-Camden area and in New York City. As a result, with concurrent and consecutive running sentences, Nicolas Golino, one of the top ten racketeers of Philadelphia, was sent to a federal penitentiary for a period of forty years. Sicardo was sentenced to forty-three years. Tony Martino, their courier and plant man, was given seventeen years imprisonment. His father, Enrico, undoubtedly because of his advanced age, was given five years. Merlotti drew twenty years, and Biani, having guarded himself so well from evidence that could be used against him, escaped with ten years imprisonment.

Such harsh penalties for trafficking in narcotics, as provided by the Narcotics Control Act of 1956, were designed to dissuade professional criminals from engaging in the sale and distribution of so-called hard drugs, and to a greater extent than is realized by the general public, this design has succeeded. Over the past ten years, more and more men of the Mafia, who controlled narcotics distribution in the United States, have withdrawn from that particular field of endeavor. To some extent, to be sure, their roles have been taken over by single entrepreneurs, who, without the organization required, have been far less successful than the Mafia men before them. As a result, there has been less heroin reaching the United States than ever before. While this is difficult to measure accurately, there is no doubt that in the last ten years the price of wholesale heroin, such as sold to agent Mike Fulgoni, has doubled and more than doubled. For the addict, a cap or a bag still costs five to twenty dollars, but the amount of actual heroin or narcotic drug in that five-dollar cap or twenty-dollar bag has been cut in half. As a result, addicts nowadays inject a much diluted poison into their system, heroin often so weak it is called lemonade. Many addicts today are known to have more a "needle habit" than a true heroin addiction. While they themselves may be chagrined over such a state of affairs, it means that addicts today can be weaned, physically at least, from heroin more easily than before.

That addicts today are taking less heroin into their systems than before can be deemed real progress, although this can be discerned only subjectively by comparing the agonies of addicts ten or twenty years ago with the miseries of drug-enslaved men and women today. Possibly there are even fewer addicts today than years ago, and, considering the population increase since the Second World War, it is a fair estimate that the rate of addiction has not increased. Certainly this must be counted as a measure of progress on a problem that has defied complete solution.

Someday, perhaps, society may solve the problem of drug addiction by erasing the pain and suffering from our everyday existence, by eradicating poverty, slums, racial hatred, pure hate, greed, inner turmoil, physical and mental frustrations, and the need for men sometimes to escape. But short of that millennium, our society thus far has found only one weapon against the problem: passing and enforcing laws to keep drugs away from those who desire them, while, at the same time, providing addicts with whatever medical help and facilities we now have at our disposal.

Thus, to date, we must credit any amelioration of the heroin problem to the Federal Bureau of Narcotics and its three hundred agents who do daily battle against the suppliers of narcotic drugs. The Bureau has extended its influence worldwide by its work in foreign countries, and it has spread its expertise throughout the United States by teaching the intricacies of narcotics law enforcement in its training school in Washington, D.C., for local and state police officers. Without such efforts to stop the flow of narcotics, it is safe to assume that addiction to heroin would spread throughout the land, for in these troubled times there are proportions. Heroin has always been the addict's choice drug,

The widespread increase in the use of marijuana, LSD and the amphetamines in recent years, due in large part to the same underlying reasons for which men take heroin, should stand as a warning that heroin addiction can at any time spread to epidemic proportions. Heroin has always been the addict's choice drug, even when the weed and speedballs were available. Because heroin has not been readily available, because it is so expensive when available, and because of strict enforcement of heroin laws, those dropouts who fall back on drugs for psychological or other reasons have resorted to marijuana and pills rather than to seeking the greater euphoria of the addict's choice drug. Thus, the arrests of men like Nick Golino, Frank Merlotti and Léon Levonian do serve to check the contagion of heroin addiction and to contain within bounds a potential epidemic of young men and women dropping out into a fraudulent euphoria with the use of that white crystalline powder, heroin hydrochloride. For that, a nation has to be thankful.

# About the Author

ALVIN MOSCOW, a former general news reporter for The Associated Press, in New York, for eleven years, is the author of *Collision Course: The Andrea Doria and the Stockholm; Tiger on a Leash;* and *A City at Sea,* a juvenile. Mr. Moscow's research on *Merchants of Heroin* took him back and forth across this country, to Turkey, Syria, Lebanon, France, England and Mexico. Married and the father of three children, he now divides his time between Los Angeles and New York.

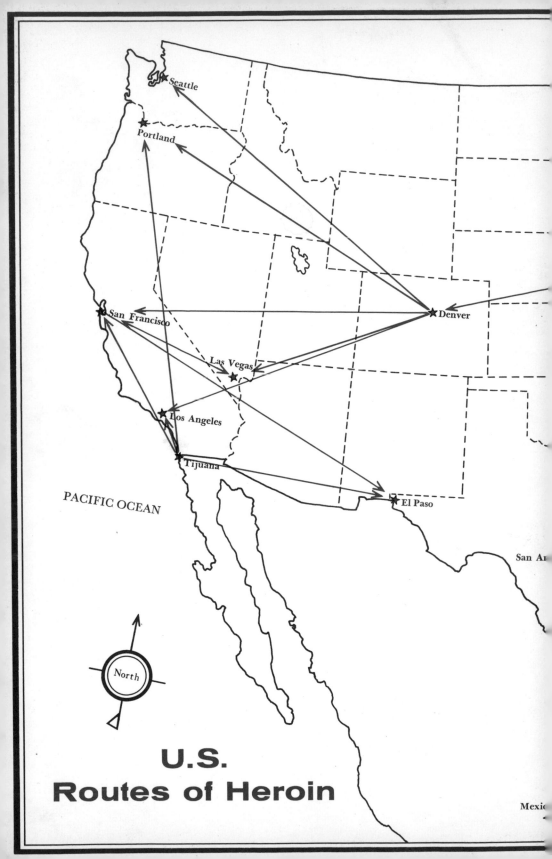

Seattle

Portland

San Francisco

Las Vegas

Los Angeles

Denver

Tijuana

El Paso

PACIFIC OCEAN

San An

North

## U.S.
## Routes of Heroin

Mexic